The Writings of
Henry D. Thoreau

Reform Papers

[Henry David Thoreau]

HENRY D. THOREAU

Reform Papers

EDITED BY WENDELL GLICK

PRINCETON, NEW JERSEY

PRINCETON UNIVERSITY PRESS

MCMLXXIII

The Center emblem means that one of a panel of textual
experts serving the Center has reviewed the text and
textual apparatus of the original volume by thorough and
scrupulous sampling, and has approved them for sound
and consistent editorial principles employed and
maximum accuracy attained. The accuracy of the text
has been guarded by careful and repeated proofreading
of printer's copy according to standards set by the Center.

Editorial expenses for this volume have been met in part
by grants from the National Endowment for the Humanities
administered through the Center for Editions of
American Authors of the Modern Language Association

Editorial Board

The Writings

Walden, J. Lyndon Shanley (1971)
The Maine Woods, Joseph J. Moldenhauer (1972)
Reform Papers, Wendell Glick (1973)
Cape Cod
Miscellanies
Excursions and Other Natural History Essays
A Week on the Concord and Merrimack Rivers
Translations
Poems
Correspondence
Notes on Fruits and Seeds
Journal

Contents

Textual Introductions, Notes, and
 Tables

Reform Papers

The Service

Qualities of the Recruit

Spes sibi quisque. Virgil
Each one his own hope.

THE brave man is the elder son of creation,
who has stept boyantly into his inheritance, while
the coward, who is the younger, waiteth patiently
till he decease. He rides as wide of this earth's
gravity as a star, and by yielding incessantly to all
the impulses of the soul, is constantly drawn upward and becomes a fixed star. His bravery deals not
so much in resolute action, as healthy and assured
rest; its palmy state is a staying at home and compelling alliance in all directions. So stands his life
to heaven, as some fair sunlit tree against the western
horizon, and by sunrise is planted on some eastern
hill, to glisten in the first rays of the dawn. The
brave man braves nothing, nor knows he of his
bravery. He is that sixth champion against Thebes,
whom, when the proud devices of the rest have been
recorded, the poet describes as "bearing a full orbed
shield of solid brass,"

"But there was no device upon its circle,
    For not to seem just but to be is his wish."

He does not present a gleaming edge to ward off
harm, for that will oftenest attract the lightning, but
rather is the all pervading ether, which the lightning
does not strike but purify. So is the profanity of his
companion as a flash across the face of his sky,
which lights up and reveals its serene depths. Earth
cannot shock the heavens, but its dull vapor and foul

smoke make a bright cloud spot in the ether, and anon the sun, like a cunning artificer, will cut and paint it, and set it for a jewel in the breast of the sky.

His greatness is not measurable. His is not such a greatness as when we would erect a stupendous piece of art, and send far and near for materials, intending to lay the foundations deeper, and rear the structure higher, than ever, for hence results only a remarkable bulkiness without grandeur, lacking those true and simple proportions which are independent of size. He was not builded by that unwise generation, that would fain have reached the heavens by piling one brick upon another, but by a far wiser, that builded inward and not outward, having found out a shorter way, through the observance of a higher art. The pyramids some artisan may measure with his line; but if he give you the dimensions of the Parthenon in feet and inches, the figures will not embrace it like a cord, but dangle from its entablature like an elastic drapery.

His eye is the focus in which all the rays, from whatever side, are collected; for, itself being within and central, the entire circumference is revealed to it. Just as we scan the whole concave of the heavens at a glance, but can compass only one side of the pebble at our feet. So does his discretion give prevalence to his valor. "Discretion is the wise man's soul," saith the poet. His prudence may safely go many strides beyond the utmost rashness of the coward; for, while he observes strictly the golden mean, he seems to run through all extremes with impunity. Like the sun, which, to the poor worldling, now appears in the zenith, now in the horizon, and again is faintly reflected from the moon's disk, and has the credit of describing an entire great circle, crossing the equinoctial and solstitial colures, without detriment to his steadfastness or mediocrity. The golden mean, in ethics as in physics, is the center of the system, and that about which all revolve; and, though to a distant and plodding planet it be the uttermost extreme, yet one day, when that planet's year is complete, it will be found to be central. They who are alarmed lest Virtue should so far demean herself, as to be extremely good, have not yet wholly embraced her, but described only a slight arc of a few seconds about her, and from so small and ill defined a curvature, you can calculate no center whatever, but their mean is no better than meanness, nor their medium than mediocrity.

The coward wants resolution, which the brave man can do without. He recognizes no faith but a creed, thinking this straw, by which he is moored, does him good service, because his sheet anchor does not drag. "The house roof fights with the rain; he who is under shelter does not know it." In his religion, the ligature, which should be muscle and sinew, is rather like that thread which the accomplices of Cylon held in their hands, when they went abroad from the temple of Minerva, the other end being attached to the statue of the goddess. But frequently, as in their case, the thread breaks, being stretched, and he is left without an asylum.

The divinity in man is the true vestal fire of the temple, which is never permitted to go out, but burns as steadily, and with as pure a flame, on the obscure provincial altar, as in Numa's temple at Rome. In the meanest are all the materials of manhood, only they are not rightly disposed. We say justly that the weak person is flat, for like all flat substances, he does not stand in the direction of his strength, that is, on his edge, but affords a convenient surface to put upon. He slides all the way through life. Most things are strong in one direction; a straw longitudinally; a board in the direction of its edge; a knee transversely to its grain; but the brave man is a perfect sphere, which cannot fall on its flat side, and is equally strong every way. The coward is wretchedly spheroidal at best, too much educated or drawn out on one side, and depressed on the other; or may be likened to a hollow sphere, whose disposition of matter is best when the greatest bulk is intended.

We shall not attain to be spherical by lying on one or the other side for an eternity, but only by resigning ourselves implicitly to the law of gravity in us, shall we find our axis coincident with the celestial axis, and by revolving incessantly through all circles, acquire a perfect sphericity. Mankind, like the earth, revolve mainly from west to east, and so are flattened at the poles. But does not philosophy give hint of a movement commencing to be rotary at the poles too, which in a millennium will have acquired increased rapidity, and help restore an equilibrium? And when at length every star in the nebulae and milky way, has looked down with mild radiance for a season, exerting its whole influence as the pole star, the demands of science will in some degree be satisfied.

The grand and majestic have always somewhat of the undulatoriness of the sphere. It is the secret of majesty in the rolling gait of the elephant, and of all grace in action and in art. Always the line of beauty is a curve. When with pomp a huge sphere is drawn along the streets, by the efforts of a hundred men, I seem to discover each striving to imitate its gait, and keep step with it,—if possible to swell to its own diameter. But onward it moves, and conquers the multitude with its majesty. What shame then, that our lives, which might so well be the source of planetary motion, and sanction the order of the spheres, should be full of abruptness and angulosity, so as not to roll nor move majestically.

The Romans "made Fortune sirname to Fortitude," for fortitude is that alchemy that turns all things to good fortune. The man of fortitude, whom the Latins called *fortis*, is no other than that lucky person whom *fors* favors, or *vir summae fortis*. If we will, every bark may "carry Caesar and Caesar's fortune." For an impenetrable shield, stand inside yourself; he was no artist, but an artisan, who first made shields of brass. For armor of proof, *meâ virtute me involvo*, I wrap myself in my virtue;

> "Tumble me down; and I will sit
> Upon my ruins, smiling yet."

If you let a single ray of light through the shutter, it will go on diffusing itself without limit till it enlighten the world, but the shadow that was never so wide at first, as rapidly contracts till it comes to naught. The shadow of the moon, when it passes nearest the sun, is lost in space ere it can reach our earth to eclipse it. Always the system shines with uninterrupted light, for as the sun is so much larger than any planet, no shadow can travel far into space. We may bask always in the light of the system, always may step back out of the shade. No man's shadow is as large as his body, if the rays make a right angle with the reflecting surface. Let our lives be passed under the equator, with the sun in the meridian.

There is no ill which may not be dissipated like the dark, if you let in a stronger light upon it. Overcome evil with good. Practise no such narrow economy as they, whose bravery amounts to no more light than a farthing candle, before which most objects cast a shadow wider than themselves.

Nature refuses to sympathize with our sorrow, she has not provided for, but by a thousand contrivances against it; she has bevelled the margins of the eyelids, that the tears may not overflow on the cheeks. It was a conceit of Plutarch, accounting for the preference given to signs observed on the left hand, that men may have thought "things terrestrial and mortal directly over against heavenly and divine things, and do conjecture that the things which to us are on the left hand, the gods send down from their right hand." If we are not blind, we shall see how a right hand is stretched over all, as well the unlucky as lucky, and that the ordering soul is only right handed, distributing with one palm all our fates.

What first suggested that necessity was grim, and made fate to be so fatal? The strongest is always the least violent. Necessity is my eastern cushion on which I recline. My eye revels in its prospect as in the summer haze. I ask no more but to be left alone with it. It is the bosom of time and the lap of eternity. To be necessary is to be needful, and necessity is only another name for inflexibility of good. How I welcome my grim fellow, and walk arm in arm with him. Let me too be such a Necessity as he. I love him, he is so flexile, and yields to me as the air to my body. I leap and dance in his midst, and play with his beard till he smiles. I greet thee my elder brother, who with thy touch ennoblest all things. Then is holiday when naught intervenes betwixt me and thee. Must it be so,—then is it good. The stars are thy interpreters to me.

Over Greece hangs the divine necessity ever a mellower heaven of itself, whose light gilds the Acropolis and a thousand fanes and groves.

What Music Shall We Have?

Each more melodious note I hear
Brings this reproach to me,
That I alone afford the ear,
Who would the music be.

THE brave man is the sole patron of music; he recognizes it for his mother tongue; a more mellifluous and articulate language than words, in comparison with which, speech is recent and temporary. It is his voice. His language must have the same majestic movement and cadence, that philosophy assigns to the heavenly bodies. The steady flux of his thought constitutes time in music. The universe falls in and keeps pace with it, which before proceeded singly and discordant. Hence are poetry and song. When Bravery first grew afraid and went to war, it took music along with it. The soul delighted still to hear the echo of her own voice. Especially the soldier insists on agreement and harmony always. To secure these he falls out. Indeed, it is that friendship there is in war that makes it chivalrous and heroic. It was the dim sentiment of a noble friendship for the purest soul the world has seen, that gave to Europe a crusading era. War is but the compelling of peace. If the soldier marches to the sack of a town, he must be preceded by drum and trumpet, which shall identify his cause with the accordant universe. All things thus echo back his own spirit, and thus the hostile territory is preoccupied for him. He is no longer insulated, but infinitely related and familiar. The roll call musters for him all the forces of nature.

There is as much music in the world as virtue. In a world of peace and love music would be the

universal language, and men greet each other in the
fields in such accents, as a Beethoven now utters
at rare intervals from a distance. All things obey
music as they obey virtue. It is the herald of virtue.
It is God's voice. In it are the centripetal and centrifugal forces. The universe needed only to hear a
divine melody, that every star might fall into its
proper place, and assume its true sphericity. It en-
tails a surpassing affluence on the meanest thing;
riding sublime over the heads of sages, and soothing
the din of philosophy. When we listen to it we are so
wise that we need not to know. All sounds, and
more than all, silence, do fife and drum for us. The
least creaking doth whet all our senses, and emit a
tremulous light, like the aurora borealis, over things.
As polishing expresses the vein in marble, and the
grain in wood, so music brings out what of heroic
lurks anywhere. It is either a sedative or a tonic to
the soul. I read that "Plato thinks the gods never
gave men music, the science of melody and harmony,
for mere delectation or to tickle the ear; but that the
discordant parts of the circulations, and beauteous
fabric of the soul, and that of it that roves about the
body, and many times for want of tune and air,
breaks forth into many extravagances and excesses,
might be sweetly recalled and artfully wound up to
their former consent and agreement."

A sudden burst from a horn startles us, as if
one had rashly provoked a wild beast. We admire
his boldness, he dares wake the echoes which he cannot put to rest. The sound of a bugle in the stillness
of the night, sends forth its voice to the farthest stars,
and marshals them in new order and harmony. Instantly it finds a fit sounding board in the heavens.
The notes flash out on the horizon like heat lightning,

quickening the pulse of creation. The heavens say, Now is this my own earth.

To the sensitive soul the Universe has her own fixed measure and rhythm, which is its measure also and constitutes the regularity and health of its pulse. When the body marches to the measure of the soul then is true courage and invincible strength.

The coward would reduce this thrilling sphere music to a universal wail,—this melodious chant to a nasal cant. He thinks to conciliate all hostile influences by compelling his neighborhood into a partial concord with himself, but his music is no better than a jingle, which is akin to a jar,—jars regularly recurring. He blows a feeble blast of slender melody, because nature can have no more sympathy with such a soul, than it has of cheerful melody in itself. Hence hears he no accordant note in the universe, and is a coward, or consciously outcast and deserted man. But the brave man, without drum or trumpet, compels concord everywhere by the universality and tunefulness of his soul.

Let not the faithful sorrow that he has no ear for the more fickle and subtle harmonies of creation, if he be awake to the slower measure of virtue and truth. If his pulse does not beat in unison with the musician's quips and turns, it accords with the pulse beat of the ages.

A man's life should be a stately march to an unheard music, and when to his fellows it seems irregular and inharmonious, he will be stepping to a livelier measure, which only his nicer ear can detect. There will be no halt ever, but at most a marching on his post, or such a pause as is richer than any sound—when the deepened melody is no longer heard, but implicitly consented to with the whole life and being. He will take a false step never, even in the most arduous circumstances, for then the music will not fail to swell into corresponding volume and distinctness and rule the movement it accompanies.

Not How Many But Where the Enemy Are

> "What's brave, what's noble,
>   Let's do it after the high Roman fashion."
> Shakspeare

WHEN my eye falls on the stupendous masses of the clouds, tossed into such irregular greatness across the cope of my sky, I feel that their grandeur is thrown away on the meanness of my employment. In vain the sun through morning and noon rolls defiance to man, and, as he sinks behind his cloudy fortress in the west, challenges him to equal greatness in his career; but from his humbleness he looks up to the domes, and minarets, and gilded battlements of the eternal city, and is content to be a suburban dweller outside the walls. We look in vain over earth for a Roman greatness, to take up the gauntlet which the heavens throw down. Idomeneus would not have demurred at the freshness of the last morning that rose to us, as unfit occasion to display his valor in; and of some such evening as this, methinks, that Greek fleet came to anchor in the bay of Aulis. Would that it were to us the eve of a more than ten years' war, a tithe of whose exploits, and Achillean withdrawals, and godly interferences, would stock a library of Iliads. Better that we have some of that testy spirit of knight errantry, and if we are so blind as to think the world is not rich enough nowadays to afford a real foe to combat, with our trusty swords and double handed maces, hew and mangle some unreal phantom of the brain. In the pale and shivering fogs of the morning, gathering them up betimes, and withdrawing sluggishly to their daylight haunts, I see Falsehood sneaking from the full blaze of truth, and with good relish could do execution on their rearward ranks with the first brand that came to hand. We too are such puny creatures as to be put to flight by the sun, and suffer our ardor to grow cool in proportion as his increases; our own short lived chivalry sounds a retreat with the fumes and vapors of the night, and we turn to meet mankind with its meek face preaching peace, and such nonresistance as the chaff that rides before the whirlwind. Let not our Peace be proclaimed by the rust on our swords, or our inability to draw them from their scabbards, but let her at least have so much work on her hands, as to keep those swords bright and sharp. The very dogs that bay the moon from farmyards o' these nights, do evince more heroism than is tamely barked forth in all the civil exhortations and war sermons of the age. And that day and night, which should be set down indelibly in men's hearts, must be learned from the pages of an almanack. One cannot wonder at the owlish habits of the race, which does not distinguish when its day ends and night begins, for as night is the season of rest, it would be hard to say when its toil ended and its rest began. Not to it

—returns
Day, or the sweet approach of even or morn,
Or sight of vernal bloom, or summer's rose,
Or flocks, or herds, or human face divine;
But cloud instead, and ever-during dark
Surrounds—

And so the time lapses without epoch or era, and we know some half score of mornings and evenings by tradition only. Almost the night is grieved and leaves her tears on the forelock of day, that men will not rush to her embrace, and fulfil, at length, the pledge so forwardly given in the youth of time. Men are a circumstance to themselves, instead of causing the universe to stand around the mute witness of their manhood, and the stars to forget their sphere music and chant an elegiac strain, that heroism should have departed out of their ranks and gone over to humanity.

It is not enough that our life is an easy one; we must live on the stretch, retiring to our rest like soldiers on the eve of a battle, looking forward with ardor to the strenuous sortie of the morrow. "Sit not down in the popular seats and common level of virtues, but endeavor to make them heroical. Offer not only peace offerings but holocausts unto God." To the brave soldier the rust and leisure of peace are harder than the fatigues of war. As our bodies court physical encounters, and languish in the mild and even climate of the tropics, so our souls thrive best on unrest and discontent. The soul is a sterner master than any King Frederick, for a true bravery would subject our bodies to rougher usage than even a grenadier could withstand. We too are dwellers within the purlieus of the camp. When the sun breaks through the morning mist, I seem to hear the din of war louder than when his chariot thundered on the plains of Troy. The thin fields of vapor spread like gauze over the woods, form extended lawns whereon high tournament is held

before each van

Prick forth the aery knights, and couch their spears,
Till thickest legions close.

It behoves us to make life a steady progression, and not be defeated by its opportunities. The stream which first fell a drop from heaven, should be filtered by events till it burst out into springs of greater purity, and extract a diviner flavor from the accidents through which it passes. Shall man wear out sooner than the sun, and not rather dawn as freshly, and with such native dignity stalk down the hills of the east into the bustling vale of life, with as lofty and serene a countenance to roll onward through midday, to a yet fairer and more promising setting? In the crimson colors of the west I discern the budding hues of dawn. To my western brother it is rising pure and bright as it did to me, but only the evening exhibits in the still rear of day, the beauty which through morning and noon escaped me. Is not that which we call the gross atmosphere of evening the accumulated deed of the day, which absorbs the rays of beauty, and shows more richly than the naked promise of the dawn? Let us look to it, that by earnest toil in the heat of the noon, we get ready a rich western blaze against the evening.

Nor need we fear that the time will hang heavy when our toil is done, for our task is not such a piece of day labor, that a man must be thinking what he shall do next for a livelihood, but such, that as it began in endeavor, so will it end only when no more in heaven or on earth remains to be endeavored. Effort is the prerogative of virtue. Let not death be the sole task of life, the moment when we are rescued from death to life. And set to work,—if indeed that can be called a task which all things do but alleviate. Nor will we suffer our hands to lose one jot of their handiness by looking behind to a mean recompense, knowing that our endeavor cannot be thwarted, nor we be cheated of our earnings unless by not earning them.

It concerns us rather to be somewhat here present than to leave something behind us; for, if that were to be considered, it is never the deed men praise, but some marble or canvass which are only a staging to the real work. The hugest and most effective deed may have no sensible result at all on earth, but may paint itself in the heavens with new stars and constellations. When in rare moments our whole being strives with one consent, which we name a yearning, we may not hope that our work will stand in any artist's gallery on earth. The bravest deed, which for the most part is left quite out of history, which alone wants the staleness of a deed done, and the uncertainty of a deed doing, is the life of a great man. To perform exploits is to be temporarily bold, as becomes a courage that ebbs and flows, the soul quite vanquished by its own deed subsiding into indifference and cowardice, but the exploit of a brave life consists in its momentary completeness.

Every stroke of the chisel must enter our own flesh and bone, he is a mere idolater and apprentice to art who suffers it to grate dully on marble; for the true art is not merely a sublime consolation, and holiday labor, which the gods have given to sickly mortals, but such a masterpiece, as you may imagine a dweller on the table lands of central Asia might produce, with threescore and ten years for canvass, and the faculties of a man for tools,–a human life,–wherein you might hope to discover more than the freshness of Guido's Aurora, or the mild light of Titian's landscapes;–no bald imitation nor even rival of nature, but rather the restored original of which she is the reflection. For such a masterpiece as this, whole galleries of Greece and Italy are a mere mixing of colors and preparatory quarrying of marble.

Of such sort, then, be our crusade, which, while it inclines chiefly to the hearty good will and activity of war, rather than the insincerity and sloth of peace, will set an example to both of calmness and energy;— as unconcerned for victory as careless of defeat, not seeking to lengthen our term of service, nor to cut it short by a reprieve, but earnestly applying ourselves to the campaign before us. Nor let our warfare be a boorish and uncourteous one, but a higher courtesy attend its higher chivalry, though not to the slackening of its tougher duties and severer discipline; that so our camp may be a palaestra, wherein the dormant energies and affections of men may tug and wrestle, not to their discomfiture, but to their mutual exercise and development.

What were Godfrey and Gonzalo unless we breathed a life into them, and enacted their exploits as a prelude to our own? The past is the canvass on which our idea is painted,—the dim prospectus of our future field. We are dreaming of what we are to do. Methinks I hear the clarion sound, and clang of corselet and buckler, from many a silent hamlet of the soul. The signal gun has long since sounded and we are not yet on our posts. Let us make such haste as the morning, and such delay as the evening.

Paradise (To Be) Regained*

WE learn that Mr. Etzler is a native of Germany, and originally published his book in Pennsylvania, ten or twelve years ago; and now a second English edition, from the original American one, is demanded by his readers across the water, owing, we suppose, to the recent spread of Fourier's doctrines. It is one of the signs of the times. We confess that we have risen from reading this book with enlarged ideas, and grander conceptions of our duties in this world. It did expand us a little. It is worth attending to, if only that it entertains large questions. Consider what Mr. Etzler proposes:

"Fellow Men! I promise to show the means of creating a paradise within ten years, where everything desirable for human life may be had by every man in superabundance, without labor, and without pay; where the whole face of nature shall be changed into the most beautiful forms, and man may live in the most magnificent palaces, in all imaginable refinements of luxury, and in the most delightful gardens; where he may accomplish, without labor, in one year, more than hitherto could be done in thousands of years; may level mountains, sink valleys, create lakes, drain lakes and swamps, and intersect the land everywhere with beautiful canals, and roads for transporting heavy loads of many thousand tons, and for travelling one thousand miles in twenty-four hours; may cover the ocean with floating islands movable in any desired direction with immense power and celerity, in perfect security, and with all comforts and luxuries, bearing gardens and palaces, with thousands of families, and provided with rivulets of sweet water; may explore the interior of the globe, and travel from pole to pole in a fortnight; provide himself with means, unheard of yet,

* The Paradise within the Reach of all Men, without Labor, by Powers of Nature and Machinery. An Address to all intelligent Men. In two parts. By J. A. Etzler. Part First. Second English Edition. pp. 55. London, 1842.

for increasing his knowledge of the world, and so his intelligence; lead a life of continual happiness, of enjoyments yet unknown; free himself from almost all the evils that afflict mankind, except death, and even put death far beyond the common period of human life, and finally render it less afflicting. Mankind may thus live in and enjoy a new world, far superior to the present, and raise themselves far higher in the scale of being."

It would seem from this and various indications beside, that there is a transcendentalism in mechanics as well as in ethics. While the whole field of the one reformer lies beyond the boundaries of space, the other is pushing his schemes for the elevation of the race to its utmost limits. While one scours the heavens, the other sweeps the earth. One says he will reform himself, and then nature and circumstances will be right. Let us not obstruct ourselves, for that is the greatest friction. It is of little importance though a cloud obstruct the view of the astronomer compared with his own blindness. The other will reform nature and circumstances, and then man will be right. Talk no more vaguely, says he, of reforming the world—I will reform the globe itself. What matters it whether I remove this humor out of my flesh, or the pestilent humor from the fleshy part of the globe? Nay, is not the latter the more generous course? At present the globe goes with a shattered constitution in its orbit. Has it not asthma, and ague, and fever, and dropsy, and flatulence, and pleurisy, and is it not afflicted with vermin? Has it not its healthful laws counteracted, and its vital energy which will yet redeem it? No doubt the simple powers of nature properly directed by man would make it healthy and paradise; as the laws of man's own constitution but wait to be obeyed, to restore him to health and happiness. Our panaceas cure but few ails, our general hospitals are private and exclusive.

We must set up another Hygeian than is now wor-
shipped. Do not the quacks even direct small doses
for children, larger for adults, and larger still for
oxen and horses? Let us remember that we are to
prescribe for the globe itself.

This fair homestead has fallen to us, and how
little have we done to improve it, how little have we
cleared and hedged and ditched! We are too inclined
to go hence to a "better land," without lifting a finger,
as our farmers are moving to the Ohio soil; but would
it not be more heroic and faithful to till and redeem
this New-England soil of the world? The still youthful energies of the globe have only to be directed in
their proper channel. Every gazette brings accounts
of the untutored freaks of the wind—shipwrecks and
hurricanes which the mariner and planter accept as
special or general providences; but they touch our
consciences, they remind us of our sins. Another
deluge would disgrace mankind. We confess we never
had much respect for that antediluvian race. A
thorough-bred business man cannot enter heartily
upon the business of life without first looking into
his accounts. How many things are now at loose ends.
Who knows which way the wind will blow to-morrow? Let us not succumb to nature. We will marshal
the clouds and restrain the tempests; we will bottle
up pestilent exhalations, we will probe for earth-
quakes, grub them up; and give vent to the dangerous gases; we will disembowel the volcano, and
extract its poison, take its seed out. We will wash
water, and warm fire, and cool ice, and underprop
the earth. We will teach birds to fly, and fishes to
swim, and ruminants to chew the cud. It is time we
had looked into these things.

And it becomes the moralist, too, to inquire what
man might do to improve and beautify the system;

what to make the stars shine more brightly, the sun more cheery and joyous, the moon more placid and content. Could he not heighten the tints of flowers and the melody of birds? Does he perform his duty to the inferior races? Should he not be a god to them? What is the part of magnanimity to the whale and the beaver? Should we not fear to exchange places with them for a day, lest by their behavior they should shame us? Might we not treat with magnanimity the shark and the tiger, not descend to meet them on their own level, with spears of sharks' teeth and bucklers of tiger's skin? We slander the hyena; man is the fiercest and cruelest animal. Ah! he is of little faith; even the erring comets and meteors would thank him, and return his kindness in their kind.

How meanly and grossly do we deal with nature! Could we not have a less gross labor? What else do these fine inventions suggest,—magnetism, the daguerreotype, electricity? Can we not do more than cut and trim the forest,—can we not assist in its interior economy, in the circulation of the sap? Now we work superficially and violently. We do not suspect how much might be done to improve our relation with animated nature; what kindness and refined courtesy there might be.

There are certain pursuits which, if not wholly poetic and true, do at least suggest a nobler and finer relation to nature than we know. The keeping of bees, for instance, is a very slight interference. It is like directing the sunbeams. All nations, from the remotest antiquity, have thus fingered nature. There are Hymettus and Hybla, and how many bee-renowned spots beside? There is nothing gross in the idea of these little herds,—their hum like the faintest low of kine in the meads. A pleasant reviewer has lately reminded us that in some places they are led out to pasture where the flowers are most abundant. "Columella tells us," says he, "that the inhabitants of Arabia sent their hives into Attica to benefit by the later-blowing flowers." Annually are the hives, in immense pyramids, carried up the Nile in boats, and suffered to float slowly down the stream by night, resting by day, as the flowers put forth along the banks; and they determine the richness of any locality, and so the profitableness of delay, by the sinking of the boat in the water. We are told, by the same reviewer, of a man in Germany, whose bees yielded more honey than those of his neighbors, with no apparent advantage; but at length he informed them that he had turned his hives one degree more to the east, and so his bees, having two hours the start in the morning, got the first sip of honey. True, there is treachery and selfishness behind all this; but these things suggest to the poetic mind what might be done.

Many examples there are of a grosser interference, yet not without their apology. We saw last summer, on the side of a mountain, a dog employed to churn for a farmer's family, travelling upon a horizontal wheel, and though he had sore eyes, an alarming cough, and withal a demure aspect, yet their bread did get buttered for all that. Undoubtedly, in the most brilliant successes, the first rank is always sacrificed. Much useless travelling of horses, *in extenso*, has of late years been improved for man's behoof, only two forces being taken advantage of,— the gravity of the horse, which is the centripetal, and his centrifugal inclination to go a-head. Only these two elements in the calculation. And is not the creature's whole economy better economized thus? Are not all finite beings better pleased with motions relative than absolute? And what is the great globe itself but such a wheel,—a larger tread-mill,—so that our horse's freest steps over prairies are oftentimes balked and rendered of no avail by the earth's motion on its axis? But here he is the central agent and motive power; and, for variety of scenery, being provided with a window in front, do not the ever-varying activity and fluctuating energy of the creature himself work the effect of the most varied scenery on a country road? It must be confessed that horses at present work too exclusively for men, rarely men for horses; and the brute degenerates in man's society.

It will be seen that we contemplate a time when man's will shall be law to the physical world, and he shall no longer be deterred by such abstractions as time and space, height and depth, weight and hardness, but shall indeed be the lord of creation. "Well," says the faithless reader, " 'life is short, but art is long;' where is the power that will effect all these changes?" This it is the very object of Mr. Etzler's volume to show. At present, he would merely remind us that there are innumerable and immeasurable powers already existing in nature, unimproved on a large scale, or for generous and universal ends, amply sufficient for these purposes. He would only indicate their existence, as a surveyor makes known the existence of a water-power on any stream; but for their application he refers us to a sequel to this book, called the "Mechanical System." A few of the most obvious and familiar of these powers are, the Wind, the Tide, the Waves, the Sunshine. Let us consider their value.

First, there is the power of the Wind, constantly exerted over the globe. It appears from observation of a sailing-vessel, and from scientific tables, that the average power of the wind is equal to that of one horse for every one hundred square feet. "We know," says our author—

"that ships of the first class carry sails two hundred feet high; we may, therefore, equally, on land, oppose to the wind surfaces of the same height. Imagine a line of such surfaces one mile, or about 5,000 feet, long; they would then contain 1,000,000 square feet. Let these surfaces intersect the direction of the wind at right angles, by some contrivance, and receive, consequently, its full power at all times. Its average power being equal to one horse for every 100 square feet, the total power would be equal to 1,000,000 divided by 100, or 10,000 horses' power. Allowing the power of one horse to equal that of ten men, the power of 10,000 horses is equal to 100,000 men. But as men cannot work uninterruptedly, but want about half the time for sleep and repose, the same power would be equal to 200,000 men. . . . We are not limited to the height of 200 feet; we might extend, if required, the application of this power to the height of the clouds, by means of kites."

But we will have one such fence for every square mile of the globe's surface, for, as the wind usually strikes the earth at an angle of more than two degrees, which is evident from observing its effect on the high sea, it admits of even a closer approach. As the surface of the globe contains about 200,000,000 square miles, the whole power of the wind on these surfaces would equal 40,000,000,000,000 men's power, and "would perform 80,000 times as much work as all the men on earth could effect with their nerves."

If it should be objected that this computation includes the surface of the ocean and uninhabitable regions of the earth, where this power could not be applied for our purposes, Mr. Etzler is quick with his reply—"But, you will recollect," says he, "that I have promised to show the means for rendering the ocean as inhabitable as the most fruitful dry land; and I do not exclude even the polar regions."

The reader will observe that our author uses the fence only as a convenient formula for expressing the power of the wind, and does not consider it a necessary method of its application. We do not attach much value to this statement of the comparative power of the wind and horse, for no common ground is mentioned on which they can be compared. Undoubtedly, each is incomparably excellent in its way, and every general comparison made for such practical purposes as are contemplated, which gives a preference to the one, must be made with some unfairness to the other. The scientific tables are, for the most part, true only in a tabular sense. We suspect that a loaded wagon, with a light sail, ten feet square, would not have been blown so far by the end of the year, under equal circumstances, as a common racer or dray horse would have drawn it. And how many crazy structures on our globe's surface, of the same dimensions, would wait for dry-rot if the traces of one horse were hitched to them, even to their windward side? Plainly, this is not the principle of comparison. But even the steady and constant force of the horse may be rated as equal to his weight at least. Yet we should prefer to let the zephyrs and gales bear, with all their weight, upon our fences, than that Dobbin, with feet braced, should lean ominously against them for a season.

Nevertheless, here is an almost incalculable power at our disposal, yet how trifling the use we make of it. It only serves to turn a few mills, blow a few vessels across the ocean, and a few trivial ends besides. What a poor compliment do we pay to our indefatigable and energetic servant!

"If you ask, perhaps, why this power is not used, if the statement be true, I have to ask in return, why is the power of steam so lately come to application? so many millions of men boiled water every day for many thousand years; they must have frequently seen that boiling water, in tightly closed pots or kettles, would lift the cover or burst the vessel with great violence. The power of steam was, therefore, as commonly known down to the least kitchen or wash-woman, as the power of wind; but close observation and reflection were bestowed neither on the one nor the other."

Men having discovered the power of falling water, which after all is comparatively slight, how eagerly do they seek out and improve these *privileges*? Let a difference of but a few feet in level be discovered on some stream near a populous town, some slight occasion for gravity to act, and the whole economy of the neighborhood is changed at once. Men do indeed speculate about and with this power as if it were the only privilege. But meanwhile this aerial stream is falling from far greater heights with more constant flow, never shrunk by drought, offering mill-sites wherever the wind blows; a Niagara in the air, with no Canada side;—only the application is hard.

There are the powers too of the Tide and Waves, constantly ebbing and flowing, lapsing and relapsing, but they serve man in but few ways. They turn a few tide mills, and perform a few other insignificant and accidental services only. We all perceive the effect of the tide; how imperceptibly it creeps up into our harbors and rivers, and raises the heaviest navies as easily as the lightest ship. Everything that floats must yield to it. But man, slow to take nature's constant hint of assistance, makes slight and irregular use of this power, in careening ships and getting them afloat when aground.

The following is Mr. Etzler's calculation on this head: To form a conception of the power which the tide affords, let us imagine a surface of 100 miles square, or 10,000 square miles, where the tide rises and sinks, on an average, 10 feet; how many men would it require to empty a basin of 10,000 square miles area, and 10 feet deep, filled with sea-water, in 6¼ hours and fill it again in the same time? As one man can raise 8 cubic feet of sea-water per minute, and in 6¼ hours 3,000, it would take 1,200,000,000 men, or as they could work only half the time, 2,400,-000,000, to raise 3,000,000,000,000 cubic feet, or the whole quantity required in the given time.

This power may be applied in various ways. A large body, of the heaviest materials that will float, may first be raised by it, and being attached to the end of a balance reaching from the land, or from a stationary support, fastened to the bottom, when the tide falls, the whole weight will be brought to bear upon the end of the balance. Also when the tide rises it may be made to exert a nearly equal force in the opposite direction. It can be employed whenever a *point d'appui* can be obtained.

"However, the application of the tide being by establishments fixed on the ground, it is natural to begin with them near the shores in shallow water, and upon sands, which may be extended gradually further into the sea. The shores of the continent, islands, and sands, being generally surrounded by shallow water, not exceeding from 50 to 100 fathoms in depth, for 20, 50, or 100 miles and upward. The coasts of North America, with their extensive sand-banks, islands, and rocks, may easily afford, for this purpose, a ground about 3,000 miles long, and, on an average, 100 miles broad, or 300,000 square miles, which, with a power of 240,000 men per square mile, as stated, at 10 feet tide, will be equal to 72,000 millions of men, or for every mile of coast, a power of 24,000,000 men."

"Rafts, of any extent, fastened on the ground of the sea, along the shore, and stretching far into the sea, may be covered with fertile soil, bearing vegetables and trees, of every description, the finest gardens, equal to those the firm land may admit of, and buildings and machineries, which may operate, not only on the sea, where they are, but which also, by means of mechanical connections, may extend their operations for many miles into the continent. (Etzler's Mechanical System, page 24.) Thus this power may cultivate the artificial soil for many miles upon the surface of the sea, near the shores, and, for several miles, the dry land, along the shore, in the most superior manner imaginable; it may build cities along the shore, consisting of the most magnificent palaces, every one surrounded by gardens and the most delightful sceneries; it may level the hills and unevennesses, or raise eminences for enjoying open prospect into the country and upon the sea; it may cover the barren shore with fertile soil, and beautify the same in various ways; it may clear the sea of shallows, and make easy the approach to the land, not merely of vessels, but of large floating islands, which may come from, and go to distant parts of the world, islands that have every commodity and security for their inhabitants which the firm land affords."

"Thus may a power, derived from the gravity of the moon and the ocean, hitherto but the objects of idle curiosity to the studious man, be made eminently subservient for creating the most delightful abodes along the coasts, where men may enjoy at the same time all the advantages of sea and dry land; the coasts may hereafter be continuous paradisiacal skirts between land and sea, everywhere crowded with the densest population. The shores and the sea along them will be no more as raw nature presents them now, but everywhere of easy and charming access, not even molested by the roar of waves, shaped as it may suit the purposes of their inhabitants; the sea will be cleared of every obstruction to free passage every-where, and its productions in fishes, etc., will be gathered in large, appropriate receptacles, to present them to the inhabitants of the shores and of the sea."

Verily, the land would wear a busy aspect at the spring and neap tide, and these island ships—these *terræ infirmæ*—which realise the fables of antiquity, affect our imagination. We have often thought that the fittest locality for a human dwelling was on the edge of the land, that there the constant lesson and impression of the sea might sink deep into the life and character of the landsman, and perhaps impart a marine tint to his imagination. It is a noble word, that *mariner*—one who is conversant with the sea. There should be more of what it signifies in each of us. It is a worthy country to belong to—we look to see him not disgrace it. Perhaps we should be equally mariners and terreners, and even our Green Mountains need some of that sea-green to be mixed with them.

The computation of the power of the waves is less satisfactory. While only the average power of the wind, and the average height of the tide, were taken before now, the extreme height of the waves is used, for they are made to rise ten feet above the level of the sea, to which, adding ten more for depression, we have twenty feet, or the extreme height of a wave. Indeed, the power of the waves, which is produced by the wind blowing obliquely and at disadvantage upon the water, is made to be, not only three thousand times greater than that of the tide, but one hundred times greater than that of the wind itself, meeting its object at right angles. Moreover, this power is measured by the area of the vessel, and not by its length mainly, and it seems to be forgotten that the motion of the waves is chiefly undulatory, and exerts a power only within the limits of a vibration, else the very continents, with their extensive coasts, would soon be set adrift.

Finally, there is the power to be derived from

sunshine, by the principle on which Archimedes contrived his burning mirrors, a multiplication of mirrors reflecting the rays of the sun upon the same spot, till the requisite degree of heat is obtained. The principal application of this power will be to the boiling of water and production of steam.

"How to create rivulets of sweet and wholesome water, on floating islands, in the midst of the ocean, will be no riddle now. Sea-water changed into steam, will distil into sweet water, leaving the salt on the bottom. Thus the steam engines on floating islands, for their propulsion and other mechanical purposes, will serve, at the same time, for the distillery of sweet water, which, collected in basins, may be led through channels over the island, while, where required, it may be refrigerated by artificial means, and changed into cool water, surpassing, in salubrity, the best spring water, because nature hardly ever distils water so purely, and without admixture of less wholesome matter."

So much for these few and more obvious powers, already used to a trifling extent. But there are innumerable others in nature, not described nor discovered. These, however, will do for the present. This would be to make the sun and the moon equally our satellites. For, as the moon is the cause of the tides, and the sun the cause of the wind, which, in turn, is the cause of the waves, all the work of this planet would be performed by these far influences.

"But as these powers are very irregular and subject to interruptions; the next object is to show how they may be converted into powers that operate continually and uniformly for ever, until the machinery be worn out, or, in other words, into perpetual motions." . . . "Hitherto the power of the wind has been applied immediately upon the machinery for use, and we have had to wait the chances of the wind's blowing; while the operation was stopped as soon as the wind ceased to blow. But the manner, which I shall state hereafter, of applying this power, is to make it operate only for collecting or storing up power, and then to take out of this store, at any time, as much as may be wanted for final operation upon the machines. The power stored up is to react as required, and may do so long after the original power of the wind has ceased. And though the wind should cease for intervals of many months, we may have by the same power a uniform perpetual motion in a very simple way."

"The weight of a clock being wound up gives us an image of reaction. The sinking of this weight is the reaction of winding it up. It is not necessary to wait till it has run down before we wind up the weight, but it may be wound up at any time, partly or totally; and if done always before the weight reaches the bottom, the clock will be going perpetually. In a similar, though not in the same way, we may cause a reaction on a larger scale. We may raise, for instance, water by the immediate application of wind or steam to a pond upon some eminence, out of which, through an outlet, it may fall upon some wheel or other contrivance for setting machinery a going. Thus we may store up water in some eminent pond, and take out of this store, at any time, as much water through the outlet as we want to employ, by which means the original power may react for many days after it has ceased." . . . "Such reservoirs of moderate elevation or size need not be made artificially, but will be found made by nature very frequently, requiring but little aid for their completion. They require no regularity of form. Any valley with lower grounds in its vicinity, would answer the purpose. Small crevices may be filled up. Such places may be eligible for the beginning of enterprises of this kind."

The greater the height, of course the less water required. But suppose a level and dry country; then hill and valley, and "eminent pond," are to be constructed by main force; or if the springs are unusually low, then dirt and stones may be used, and the disadvantage arising from friction will be counterbalanced by their greater gravity. Nor shall a single rood of dry land be sunk in such artificial ponds as may be wasted, but their surfaces "may be covered with rafts decked with fertile earth, and all kinds of vegetables which may grow there as well as anywhere else."

And finally, by the use of thick envelopes retaining the heat, and other contrivances, "the power of steam caused by sunshine may react at will, and thus be rendered perpetual, no matter how often or how long the sunshine may be interrupted. (Etzler's Mechanical System)."

Here is power enough, one would think, to accomplish somewhat. These are the powers below. Oh ye millwrights, ye engineers, ye operatives and speculators of every class, never again complain of a want of power; it is the grossest form of infidelity. The question is not how we shall execute, but what. Let us not use in a niggardly manner what is thus generously offered.

Consider what revolutions are to be effected in agriculture. First, in the new country, a machine is to move along taking out trees and stones to any required depth, and piling them up in convenient heaps; then the same machine, "with a little alteration," is to plane the ground perfectly, till there shall be no hills nor valleys, making the requisite canals, ditches and roads, as it goes along. The same machine, "with some other little alterations," is then to sift the ground thoroughly, supply fertile soil from other places if wanted, and plant it; and finally, the same machine "with a little addition," is to reap and gather in the crop, thresh and grind it, or press it to oil, or prepare it any way for final use. For the description of these machines we are referred to "Etzler's Mechanical System, pages 11 to 27." We should be pleased to see that "Mechanical System," though we have not been able to ascertain whether it has been published, or only exists as yet in the design of the author. We have great faith in it. But we cannot stop for applications now.

"Any wilderness, even the most hideous and sterile, may be converted into the most fertile and delightful gardens. The most dismal swamps may be cleared of all their spontaneous growth, filled up and levelled, and intersected by canals, ditches and aqueducts, for draining them entirely. The soil, if required, may be meliorated, by covering or mixing it with rich soil taken from distant places, and the same be mouldered to fine dust, levelled, sifted from all roots, weeds and stones, and sowed and planted in the most beautiful order and symmetry, with fruit trees and vegetables of every kind that may stand the climate."

New facilities for transportation and locomotion are to be adopted:

"Large and commodious vehicles, for carrying many thousand tons, running over peculiarly adapted level roads, at the rate of forty miles per hour, or one thousand miles per day, may transport men and things, small houses, and whatever may serve for comfort and ease, by land. Floating islands, constructed of logs, or of wooden-stuff prepared in a similar manner, as is to be done with stone, and of live trees, which may be reared so as to interlace one another, and strengthen the whole, may be covered with gardens and palaces, and propelled by powerful engines, so as to run at an equal rate through seas and oceans. Thus, man may move, with the celerity of a bird's flight, in terrestrial paradises, from one climate to another, and see the world in all its variety, exchanging, with distant nations, the surplus of productions. The journey from one pole to another may be performed in a fortnight; the visit to a transmarine country in a week or two; or a journey round the world in one or two months by land and water. And why pass a dreary winter every year while there is yet room enough on the globe where nature is blessed with a perpetual summer, and with a far greater variety and luxuriance of vegetation? More than one-half the surface of the globe has no winter. Men will have it in their power to remove and pre-

vent all bad influences of climate, and to enjoy, perpetually, only that temperature which suits their constitution
and feeling best."

Who knows but by accumulating the power until
the end of the present century, using meanwhile only
the smallest allowance, reserving all that blows, all
that shines, all that ebbs and flows, all that dashes,
we may have got such a reserved accumulated power
as to run the earth off its track into a new orbit, some
summer, and so change the tedious vicissitude of the
seasons? Or, perchance, coming generations will not
abide the dissolution of the globe, but, availing themselves of future inventions in aerial locomotion, and
the navigation of space, the entire race may migrate
from the earth, to settle some vacant and more western planet, it may be still healthy, perchance un-
earthy, not composed of dirt and stones, whose pri-
mary strata only are strewn, and where no weeds are
sown. It took but little art, a simple application of
natural laws, a canoe, a paddle, and a sail of matting,
to people the isles of the Pacific, and a little more
will people the shining isles of space. Do we not see
in the firmament the lights carried along the shore
by night, as Columbus did? Let us not despair nor
mutiny.

"The dwellings also ought to be very different from
what is known, if the full benefit of our means is to be
enjoyed. They are to be of a structure for which we have
no name yet. They are to be neither palaces, nor temples,
nor cities, but a combination of all, superior to whatever
is known. Earth may be baked into bricks, or even vitrified
stone by heat,—we may bake large masses of any size and
form into stone and vitrified substance of the greatest
durability, lasting even thousands of years, out of clayey
earth, or of stones ground to dust, by the application of
burning mirrors. This is to be done in the open air, without other preparation than gathering the substance, grinding and mixing it with water and cement, moulding or

casting it, and bringing the focus of the burning mirrors of proper size upon the same. The character of the architecture is to be quite different from what it ever has been hitherto; large solid masses are to be baked or cast in one piece, ready shaped in any form that may be desired. The building may, therefore, consist of columns two hundred feet high and upwards, of proportionate thickness, and of one entire piece of vitrified substance; huge pieces are to be moulded so as to join and hook on to each other firmly, by proper joints and folds, and not to yield in any way without breaking."

"Foundries, of any description, are to be heated by burning mirrors, and will require no labor, except the making of the first moulds and the superintendence for gathering the metal and taking the finished articles away."

Alas, in the present state of science, we must take the finished articles away; but think not that man will always be a victim of circumstances.

The countryman who visited the city and found the streets cluttered with bricks and lumber, reported that it was not yet finished, and one who considers the endless repairs and reforming of our houses, might well wonder when they will be done. But why may not the dwellings of men on this earth be built once for all of some durable material, some Roman or Etruscan masonry which will stand, so that time shall only adorn and beautify them? Why may we not finish the outward world for posterity, and leave them leisure to attend to the inner? Surely, all the gross necessities and economies might be cared for in a few years. All might be built and baked and stored up, during this, the term-time of the world, against the vacant eternity, and the globe go provisioned and furnished like our public vessels, for its voyage through space, as through some Pacific ocean, while we would "tie up the rudder and sleep before the wind," as those who sail from Lima to Manilla.

But, to go back a few years in imagination, think

not that life in these crystal palaces is to bear any analogy to life in our present humble cottages. Far from it. Clothed, once for all, in some "flexible stuff," more durable than George Fox's suit of leather, composed of "fibres of vegetables," "glutinated" together by some "cohesive substances," and made into sheets, like paper, of any size or form, man will put far from him corroding care and the whole host of ills.

"The twenty-five halls in the inside of the square are to be each two hundred feet square and high; the forty corridors, each one hundred feet long and twenty wide; the eighty galleries, each from 1,000 to 1,250 feet long; about 7,000 private rooms, the whole surrounded and intersected by the grandest and most splendid colonnades imaginable; floors, ceilings, columns with their various beautiful and fanciful intervals, all shining, and reflecting to infinity all objects and persons, with splendid lustre of all beautiful colors, and fanciful shapes and pictures. All galleries, outside and within the halls, are to be provided with many thousand commodious and most elegant vehicles, in which persons may move up and down, like birds, in perfect security, and without exertion. Any member may procure himself all the common articles of his daily wants, by a short turn of some crank, without leaving his apartment; he may, at any time, bathe himself in cold or warm water, or in steam, or in some artificially prepared liquor for invigorating health. He may, at any time, give to the air in his apartment that temperature that suits his feeling best. He may cause, at any time, an agreeable scent of various kinds. He may, at any time, meliorate his breathing air,—that main vehicle of vital power. Thus, by a proper application of the physical knowledge of our days, man may be kept in a perpetual serenity of mind, and if there is no incurable disease or defect in his organism, in constant vigor of health, and his life be prolonged beyond any parallel which present times afford."

"One or two persons are sufficient to direct the kitchen business. They have nothing else to do but to superintend the cookery, and to watch the time of the victuals being done, and then to remove them, with the table and vessels, into the dining-hall, or to the respective private apartments, by a slight motion of the hand at some crank. Any extraordinary desire of any person may be satisfied by going to the place where the thing is to be had; and anything that requires a particular preparation in cooking or baking, may be done by the person who desires it."

This is one of those instances in which the individual genius is found to consent, as indeed it always does, at last, with the universal. These last sentences have a certain sad and sober truth, which reminds us of the scripture of all nations. All expression of truth does at length take the deep ethical form. Here is hint of a place the most eligible of any in space, and of a servitor, in comparison with whom, all other helps dwindle into insignificance. We hope to hear more of him anon, for even crystal palace would be deficient without his invaluable services.

And as for the environs of the establishment,

"There will be afforded the most enrapturing views to be fancied, out of the private apartments, from the galleries, from the roof, from its turrets and cupolas,—gardens as far as the eye can see, full of fruits and flowers, arranged in the most beautiful order, with walks, colonnades, aqueducts, canals, ponds, plains, amphitheatres, terraces, fountains, sculptural works, pavilions, gondolas, places for public amusement, etc., to delight the eye and fancy, the taste and smell." . . . "The walks and roads are to be paved with hard vitrified, large plates, so as to be always clean from all dirt in any weather or season. . . . The channels being of vitrified substance, and the water perfectly clear, and filtrated or distilled if required, may afford the most beautiful scenes imaginable, while a variety of fishes is seen clear down to the bottom playing about, and the canals may afford at the same time, the means of gliding smoothly along between various sceneries of art and nature, in beautiful gondolas, while their surface and borders may be covered with fine land and aquatic birds. The walks may be covered with porticos adorned with magnificent columns, statues and sculptural works; all of vitrified substance, and lasting for ever,

while the beauties of nature around heighten the magnificence and deliciousness."

"The night affords no less delight to fancy and feelings. An infinite variety of grand, beautiful and fanciful
objects and sceneries, radiating with crystalline brilliancy,
by the illumination of gas-light; the human figures themselves, arrayed in the most beautiful pomp fancy may
suggest, or the eye desire, shining even with brilliancy of
stuffs and diamonds, like stones of various colors, ele-
gantly shaped and arranged around the body; all reflected
a thousand-fold in huge mirrors and reflectors of various
forms; theatrical scenes of a grandeur and magnificence,
and enrapturing illusions, unknown yet, in which any
person may be either a spectator or actor; the speech and
the songs reverberating with increased sound, rendered
more sonorous and harmonious than by nature, by vault-
ings that are moveable into any shape at any time; the
sweetest and most impressive harmony of music, produced by song and instruments partly not known yet, may
thrill through the nerves and vary with other amusements
and delights."

"At night the roof, and the inside and outside of the
whole square, are illuminated by gas-light, which in the
mazes of many-colored crystal-like colonnades and vault-
ings, is reflected with a brilliancy that gives to the whole
a lustre of precious stones, as far as the eye can see,—
such are the future abodes of men." . . . "Such is the
life reserved to true intelligence, but withheld from ignorance, prejudice, and stupid adherence to custom." . . .
"Such is the domestic life to be enjoyed by every human
individual that will partake of it. Love and affection may
there be fostered and enjoyed without any of the obstructions that oppose, diminish, and destroy them in the present state of men." . . . "It would be as ridiculous, then, to
dispute and quarrel about the means of life, as it would
be now about water to drink along mighty rivers, or about
the permission to breathe air in the atmosphere, or about
sticks in our extensive woods."

Thus is Paradise to be Regained, and that old and
stern decree at length reversed. Man shall no more
earn his living by the sweat of his brow. All labor
shall be reduced to "a short turn of some crank," and

"taking the finished article away." But there is a crank,—oh, how hard to be turned! Could there not be a crank upon a crank,—an infinitely small crank?—we would fain inquire. No,—alas! not. But there is a certain divine energy in every man, but sparingly employed as yet, which may be called the crank within,—the crank after all,—the prime mover in all machinery,—quite indispensable to all work. Would that we might get our hands on its handle! In fact no work can be shirked. It may be postponed indefinitely, but not infinitely. Nor can any really important work be made easier by co-operation or machinery. Not one particle of labor now threatening any man can be routed without being performed. It cannot be hunted out of the vicinity like jackals and hyenas. It will not run. You may begin by sawing the little sticks, or you may saw the great sticks first, but sooner or later you must saw them both.

We will not be imposed upon by this vast application of forces. We believe that most things will have to be accomplished still by the application called Industry. We are rather pleased after all to consider the small private, but both constant and accumulated force, which stands behind every spade in the field. This it is that makes the valleys shine, and the deserts really bloom. Sometimes, we confess, we are so degenerate as to reflect with pleasure on the days when men were yoked like cattle, and drew a crooked stick for a plough. After all, the great interests and methods were the same.

It is a rather serious objection to Mr. Etzler's schemes, that they require time, men, and money, three very superfluous and inconvenient things for an honest and well-disposed man to deal with. "The whole world," he tells us, "might therefore be really changed into a paradise, within less than ten years, commencing from the first year of an association for the purpose of constructing and applying the machinery." We are sensible of a startling incongruity when time and money are mentioned in this connection. The ten years which are proposed would be a tedious while to wait, if every man were at his post and did his duty, but quite too short a period, if we are to take time for it. But this fault is by no means peculiar to Mr. Etzler's schemes. There is far too much hurry and bustle, and too little patience and privacy, in all our methods, as if something were to be accomplished in centuries. The true reformer does not want time, nor money, nor co-operation, nor advice. What is time but the stuff delay is made of? And depend upon it, our virtue will not live on the interest of our money. He expects no income but our outgoes; so soon as we begin to count the cost the cost begins. And as for advice, the information floating in the atmosphere of society is as evanescent and unserviceable to him as gossamer for clubs of Hercules. There is absolutely no common sense; it is common nonsense. If we are to risk a cent or a drop of our blood, who then shall advise us? For ourselves, we are too young for experience. Who is old enough? We are older by faith than by experience. In the unbending of the arm to do the deed there is experience worth all the maxims in the world.

"It will now be plainly seen that the execution of the proposals is not proper for individuals. Whether it be proper for government at this time, before the subject has become popular, is a question to be decided; all that is to be done, is to step forth, after mature reflection, to confess loudly one's conviction, and to constitute societies. Man is powerful but in union with many. Nothing great, for the improvement of his own condition, or that of his fellow men, can ever be effected by individual enterprise."

Alas! this is the crying sin of the age, this want of faith in the prevalence of a man. Nothing can be effected but by one man. He who wants help wants everything. True, this is the condition of our weakness, but it can never be the means of our recovery. We must first succeed alone, that we may enjoy our success together. We trust that the social movements which we witness indicate an aspiration not to be thus cheaply satisfied. In this matter of reforming the world, we have little faith in corporations; not thus was it first formed.

But our author is wise enough to say, that the raw materials for the accomplishment of his purposes, are "iron, copper, wood, earth chiefly, and a union of men whose eyes and understanding are not shut up by preconceptions." Aye, this last may be what we want mainly,—a company of "odd fellows" indeed.

"Small shares of twenty dollars will be sufficient,"—in all, from "200,000 to 300,000,"—"to create the first establishment for a whole community of from 3000 to 4000 individuals"—at the end of five years we shall have a principal of 200 millions of dollars, and so paradise will be wholly regained at the end of the tenth year. But, alas, the ten years have already elapsed, and there are no signs of Eden yet, for want of the requisite funds to begin the enterprise in a hopeful manner. Yet it seems a safe investment. Perchance they could be hired at a low rate, the property being mortgaged for security, and, if necessary, it could be given up in any stage of the enterprise, without loss, with the fixtures.

Mr. Etzler considers this "Address as a touchstone, to try whether our nation is in any way accessible to these great truths, for raising the human creature to a superior state of existence, in accordance with the knowledge and the spirit of the most cultivated minds of the present time." He has prepared a constitution, short and concise, consisting of twenty-one articles, so that wherever an association may spring up, it may go into operation without delay; and the editor informs us that "Communications on the subject of this book may be addressed to C. F. Stollmeyer, No. 6, Upper Charles street, Northampton square, London."

But we see two main difficulties in the way. First, the successful application of the powers by machinery, (we have not yet seen the "Mechanical System,") and, secondly, which is infinitely harder, the application of man to the work by faith. This it is, we fear, which will prolong the ten years to ten thousand at least. It will take a power more than "80,000 times greater than all the men on earth could effect with their nerves," to persuade men to use that which is already offered them. Even a greater than this physical power must be brought to bear upon that moral power. Faith, indeed, is all the reform that is needed; it is itself a reform. Doubtless, we are as slow to conceive of Paradise as of Heaven, of a perfect natural as of a perfect spiritual world. We see how past ages have loitered and erred; "Is perhaps our generation free from irrationality and error? Have we perhaps reached now the summit of human wisdom, and need no more to look out for mental or physical improvement?" Undoubtedly, we are never so visionary as to be prepared for what the next hour may bring forth.

Μέλλει τὸ θεῖον δ'ἐστι τοιοῦτον φύσει.

The Divine is about to be, and such is its nature. In our wisest moments we are secreting a matter, which, like the lime of the shell fish, incrusts us quite over, and well for us, if, like it, we cast our shells from time to time, though they be pearl and of fairest tint. Let us consider under what disadvantages sci-

ence has hitherto labored before we pronounce thus
confidently on her progress.

"There was never any system in the productions of
human labor; but they came into existence and fashion
as chance directed men." "Only a few professional men
of learning occupy themselves with teaching natural
philosophy, chemistry, and the other branches of the
sciences of nature, to a very limited extent, for very
limited purposes, with very limited means." "The science
of mechanics is but in a state of infancy. It is true, improvements are made upon improvements, instigated by
patents of government; but they are made accidentally or
at hap-hazard. There is no general system of this science,
mathematical as it is, which developes its principles in
their full extent, and the outlines of the application to
which they lead. There is no idea of comparison between
what is explored and what is yet to be explored in this
science. The ancient Greeks placed mathematics at the
head of their education. But we are glad to have filled our
memory with notions, without troubling ourselves much
with reasoning about them."

Mr. Etzler is not one of the enlightened practical
men, the pioneers of the actual, who move with the
slow deliberate tread of science, conserving the world;
who execute the dreams of the last century, though
they have no dreams of their own; yet he deals in the
very raw but still solid material of all inventions. He
has more of the practical than usually belongs to so
bold a schemer, so resolute a dreamer. Yet his success is in theory, and not in practice, and he feeds
our faith rather than contents our understanding.
His book wants order, serenity, dignity, everything,—
but it does not fail to impart what only man can impart to man of much importance, his own faith. It is
true his dreams are not thrilling nor bright enough,
and he leaves off to dream where he who dreams just
before the dawn begins. His castles in the air fall to
the ground, because they are not built lofty enough;

they should be secured to heaven's roof. After all, the theories and speculations of men concern us more than their puny execution. It is with a certain coldness and languor that we loiter about the actual and so called practical. How little do the most wonderful inventions of modern times detain us. They insult nature. Every machine, or particular application, seems a slight outrage against universal laws. How many fine inventions are there which do not clutter the ground? We think that those only succeed which minister to our sensible and animal wants, which bake or brew, wash or warm, or the like. But are those of no account which are patented by fancy and imagination, and succeed so admirably in our dreams that they give the tone still to our waking thoughts? Already nature is serving all those uses which science slowly derives on a much higher and grander scale to him that will be served by her. When the sunshine falls on the path of the poet, he enjoys all those pure benefits and pleasures which the arts slowly and partially realize from age to age. The winds which fan his cheek waft him the sum of that profit and happiness which their lagging inventions supply.

The chief fault of this book is, that it aims to secure the greatest degree of gross comfort and pleasure merely. It paints a Mahometan's heaven, and stops short with singular abruptness when we think it is drawing near to the precincts of the Christian's,—and we trust we have not made here a distinction without a difference. Undoubtedly if we were to reform this outward life truly and thoroughly, we should find no duty of the inner omitted. It would be employment for our whole nature; and what we should do thereafter would be as vain a question as to ask the bird what it will do when its nest is built and its brood reared. But a moral reform must take place first, and then the necessity of the other will be superseded, and we shall sail and plough by its force alone. There is a speedier way than the Mechanical System can show to fill up marshes, to drown the roar of the waves, to tame hyenas, secure agreeable environs, diversify the land, and refresh it with "rivulets of sweet water," and that is by the power of rectitude and true behavior. It is only for a little while, only occasionally, methinks, that we want a garden. Surely a good man need not be at the labor to level a hill for the sake of a prospect, or raise fruits and flowers, and construct floating islands, for the sake of a paradise. He enjoys better prospects than lie behind any hill. Where an angel travels it will be paradise all the way, but where Satan travels it will be burning marl and cinders. What says Veeshnoo Sarma? "He whose mind is at ease is possessed of all riches. Is it not the same to one whose foot is enclosed in a shoe, as if the whole surface of the earth were covered with leather?"

He who is conversant with the supernal powers will not worship these inferior deities of the wind, the waves, tide, and sunshine. But we would not disparage the importance of such calculations as we have described. They are truths in physics, because they are true in ethics. The moral powers no one would presume to calculate. Suppose we could compare the moral with the physical, and say how many horsepower the force of love, for instance, blowing on every square foot of a man's soul, would equal. No doubt we are well aware of this force; figures would not increase our respect for it; the sunshine is equal to but one ray of its heat. The light of the sun is but the shadow of love. "The souls of men loving and fearing God," says Raleigh, "receive influence from that divine light itself, whereof the sun's clarity, and that of the stars, is by Plato called but a shadow.

Lumen est umbra Dei, Deus est Lumen Luminis.
Light is the shadow of God's brightness, who is the
light of light," and, we may add, the heat of heat. Love
is the wind, the tide, the waves, the sunshine. Its
power is incalculable; it is many horse power. It
never ceases, it never slacks; it can move the globe
without a resting-place; it can warm without fire; it
can feed without meat; it can clothe without garments; it can shelter without roof; it can make a paradise within which will dispense with a paradise without. But though the wisest men in all ages have labored to publish this force, and every human heart
is, sooner or later, more or less, made to feel it, yet
how little is actually applied to social ends. True, it is
the motive power of all successful social machinery;
but, as in physics, we have made the elements do
only a little drudgery for us, steam to take the place
of a few horses, wind of a few oars, water of a few
cranks and hand-mills; as the mechanical forces have
not yet been generously and largely applied to make
the physical world answer to the ideal, so the power
of love has been but meanly and sparingly applied,
as yet. It has patented only such machines as the
almshouses, the hospital, and the Bible Society, while
its infinite wind is still blowing, and blowing down
these very structures, too, from time to time. Still less
are we accumulating its power, and preparing to act
with greater energy at a future time. Shall we not
contribute our shares to this enterprise, then?

Herald of Freedom*

WE have occasionally, for several years, met with a number of this spirited journal, edited, as abolitionists need not be informed, by Nathaniel P. Rogers, once a counsellor at law in Plymouth, still further up the Merrimack, but now, in his riper years, come down the hills thus far, to be the Herald of Freedom to those parts. We have been refreshed not a little by the cheap cordial of his editorials, flowing like his own mountain-torrents, now clear and sparkling, now foaming and gritty, and always spiced with the essence of the fir and the Norway pine; but never dark nor muddy, nor threatening with smothered murmurs, like the rivers of the plain. The effect of one of his effusions reminds us of what the hydropathists say about the electricity in fresh spring-water, compared with that which has stood over night to suit weak nerves. We do not know of another notable and public instance of such pure, youthful, and hearty indignation at all wrong. The church itself must love it, if it have any heart, though he is said to have dealt rudely with its sanctity. His clean attachment to the right, however, sanctions the severest rebuke we have read.

We have neither room, nor inclination, to criticise this paper, or its cause, at length, but would speak of it in the free and uncalculating spirit of its author. Mr. Rogers seems to us to occupy an honorable and manly position in these days, and in this country, making the press a living and breathing organ to reach the hearts of men, and not merely "fine paper, and good type," with its civil pilot sitting aft, and

* Herald of Freedom; published weekly by the New Hampshire Anti-Slavery Society: Concord, N. H. Vol. X. No. 4.

magnanimously waiting for the news to arrive,—the vehicle of the earliest news, but the *latest intelligence*, —recording the indubitable and last results, the marriages and deaths, alone. The present editor is wide awake, and standing on the beak of his ship; not as a scientific explorer under government, but a yankee sealer, rather, who makes those unexplored continents his harbors in which to refit for more adventurous cruises. He is a fund of news and freshness in himself,—has the gift of speech, and the knack of writing, and if anything important takes place in the Granite State, we may be sure that we shall hear of it in good season. No other paper that we know keeps pace so well with one forward wave of the restless public thought and sentiment of New England, and asserts so faithfully and ingenuously the largest liberty in all things. There is, beside, more unpledged poetry in his prose, than in the verses of many an accepted rhymer; and we are occasionally advertised by a mellow hunter's note from his trumpet, that, unlike most reformers, his feet are still where they should be, on the turf, and that he looks out from a serener natural life into the turbid arena of politics. Nor is slavery always a sombre theme with him, but invested with the colors of his wit and fancy, and an evil to be abolished by other means than sorrow and bitterness of complaint. He will fight this fight with what cheer may be. But to speak of his composition. It is a genuine yankee style, without fiction,—real guessing and calculating to some purpose, and reminds us occasionally, as does all free, brave, and original writing, of its great master in these days, Thomas Carlyle. It has a life above grammar, and a meaning which need not be parsed to be understood. But like those same mountain-torrents, there is rather too much slope to his channel, and the rainbow sprays and evaporations go double-quick-time to heaven, while the body of his water falls headlong to the plain. We would have more pause and deliberation, occasionally, if only to bring his tide to a head,—more frequent expansions of the stream, still, bottomless mountain tarns, perchance inland seas, and at length the deep ocean itself.

We cannot do better than enrich our pages with a few extracts from such articles as we have at hand. Who can help sympathizing with his righteous impatience, when invited to hold his peace or endeavor to convince the understandings of the people by well ordered arguments?

"Bandy *compliments* and *arguments* with the somnambulist, on 'table rock,' when all the waters of Lake Superior are thundering in the great horse-shoe, and deafening the very war of the elements! Would you not shout to him with a clap of thunder through a speaking-trumpet, if you could command it,—if possible to reach his senses in his appaling extremity! Did Jonah *argufy* with the city of Nineveh,—'yet forty days,' cried the vagabond prophet, 'and Nineveh shall be overthrown!' That was his salutation. And did the 'Property and Standing' turn up their noses at him, and set the mob on to him? Did the clergy *discountenance* him, and call him extravagant, misguided, a divider of churches, a disturber of parishes? What would have become of that city, if they had done this? Did they 'approve his *principles*' but dislike his *'measures'* and his *'spirit' ! !*

"Slavery must be cried down, denounced down, ridiculed down, and pro-slavery with it, or rather before it. Slavery will go when pro-slavery starts. The sheep will follow when the bell-wether leads. Down, then, with the bloody system, out of the land with it, and out of the world with it,—into the Red Sea with it. Men *sha'nt* be enslaved in this country any longer. Women and children *sha'nt* be flogged here any longer. If you undertake to hinder us, the worst is your own." . . . "But this is all fanaticism. *Wait and see.*"

He thus raises the anti-slavery 'war-whoop' in New Hampshire, when an important convention is to be held, sending the summons

> "To none but the whole-hearted, fully-committed, cross-the-Rubicon spirits." . . . "From rich 'old Cheshire,' from Rockingham, with her horizon setting down away to the salt sea." . . . "From where the sun sets behind Kearsarge, even to where he rises gloriously over *Moses Norris's* own town of *Pittsfield*; and from Amoskeag to Ragged Mountains,–Coos–Upper Coos, home of the everlasting hills, send out your bold advocates of human rights,–wherever they lay, scattered by lonely lake, or Indian stream, or 'Grant,' or 'Location,'–from the trout-haunted brooks of the Amoriscoggin, and where the adventurous streamlet takes up its mountain march for the St. Lawrence.
>
> "Scattered and insulated men, wherever the light of philanthropy and liberty has beamed in upon your solitary spirits, come down to us like your streams and clouds;–and our own Grafton, all about among your dear hills, and your mountain-flanked valleys–whether you *home* along the swift Ammonoosuck, the cold Pemigewassett, or the ox-bowed Connecticut." . . .
>
> "We are slow, brethren, dishonorably slow, in a cause like ours. Our feet should be as 'hinds' feet.' 'Liberty lies bleeding.' The leaden-colored wing of slavery obscures the land with its baleful shadow. Let us come together, and inquire at the hand of the Lord, what is to be done."

And again; on occasion of the New England Convention, in the Second-Advent Tabernacle, in Boston, he desires to try one more blast, as it were, 'on Fabyan's White Mountain horn.'

> "Ho, then, people of the Bay State,–men, women, and children; children, women, and men, scattered friends of the *friendless*, wheresoever ye inhabit,–if habitations ye have, as such friends have not *always*,– along the sea-beat border of Old Essex and the Puritan Landing, and up beyond sight of the sea-cloud, among ʰthe inland hills, where the sun rises and sets upon the

dry land, in that vale of the Connecticut, too fair for human content, and too fertile for virtuous industry,— where deepens that haughtiest of earth's streams, on its seaward way, proud with the pride of old Massachusetts. Are there any friends of the friendless negro haunting such a valley as this? In God's name, I fear there are none, or few, for the very scene looks apathy and oblivion to the genius of humanity. I blow you the summons though. Come, if any of you are there.

"And gallant little Rhode Island; *transcendent* abolitionists of the tiny commonwealth. I need not call you. You are *called* the year round, and, instead of sleeping in your tents, stand harnessed, and with trumpets in your hands,—every one!

"Connecticut! yonder, the home of the Burleighs, the Monroes, and the Hudsons, and the native land of old George Benson! are you ready? 'All ready!'

"Maine here, off east, looking from my mountain post, like an everglade. Where is your Sam. Fessenden, who stood storm-proof 'gainst New Organization in '38? Has he too much name as a jurist and an orator, to be found at a New England Convention in '43? God forbid. Come one and all of you from 'Down East,' to Boston, on the 30th, and let the sails of your coasters whiten all the sea-road. Alas! there are scarce enough of you to man a fishing boat. Come up, mighty in your fewness.

"And green Vermont, what has become of your anti-slavery host,—thick as your mountain maples,—mastering your very politics,—not by balance of power, but by sturdy majority. Where are you now? Will you be at the *Advent* Meeting on the 30th of May? Has anti-slavery waxed too trying for your off-hand, how-are-ye, humanity? Have you heard the voice of Freedom of late? Next week will answer.

"Poor, cold, winter-ridden New-Hampshire,—winter-killed, I like to have said,—she will be there, bare-foot, and bare-legged, making tracks like her old bloody-footed volunteers at Trenton. She will be there, if she can work her passage. I guess her minstrelsy* will,— for birds can go independently of car, or tardy stage-coach." . . .

* The Hutchinsons.

"Let them come as Macaulay says they did to the siege of Rome, when they did not leave old men and women enough to *begin* the harvests. Oh how few we should be, if every soul of us were there. How few, and yet it is the entire muster-roll of Freedom for all the land. We should have to beat up for recruits to complete the army of Gideon, or the *platoon* at the Spartan straits. The foe are like the grasshoppers for *multitude*, as for *moral power*. Thick grass mows the easier, as the Goth said of the enervated millions of falling Rome. They can't stand too thick, nor too tall for the anti-slavery scythe. Only be there at the mowing."

In noticing the doings of another Convention, he thus congratulates himself on the liberty of speech which anti-slavery concedes to all,—even to the Folsoms and Lamsons:—

"Denied a chance to speak elsewhere, because they are not mad after the fashion, they all flock to the anti-slavery boards as a kind of Asylum. And so the poor old enterprise has to father all the oddity of the times. It is a glory to anti-slavery, that she can allow the poor friends the right of speech. I hope she will always keep herself able to afford it. Let the constables wait on the State House, and Jail, and the *Meeting Houses*. Let the door-keeper at the Anti-Slavery Hall be that tall, celestial-faced Woman, that carries the flag on the National Standard, and says, 'without *concealment*,' as well as 'without compromise.' Let every body in, who has sanity enough to see the beauty of brotherly kindness, and let them say their fantasies, and magnanimously bear with them, seeing unkind pro-slavery drives them in upon *us*. We shall have *saner* and *sensibler* meetings then, than all others in the land put together."

More recently, speaking of the use which some of the clergy have made of Webster's plea in the Girard case, as a seasonable aid to the church, he proceeds:

"Webster is a great man, and the clergy run under his wing. They had better employ him as counsel against the Comeouters. He would'nt trust the defence on the Girard will plea though, if they did. He would not risk his fame on it, as a religious argument. He would go and consult William Bassett, of Lynn, on the principles of the 'Comeouters,' to learn their strength; and he would get him a testament, and go into it as he does into the Constitution, and after a year's study of it he would hardly come off in the argument as he did from the conflict with Carolina Hayne. On looking into the case, he would advise the clergy not to go to trial,—to settle,—or, if they could'nt to 'leave it out' to a reference of 'orthodox deacons.' "

We will quote from the same sheet his indignant and touching satire on the funeral of those public officers who were killed by the explosion on board the Princeton, together with the President's slave; an accident which reminds us how closely slavery is linked with the government of this nation. The President coming to preside over a nation of *free* men, and the man who stands *next to him a slave*!

"I saw account," says he, "of the burial of those slaughtered politicians. The hearses passed along, of Upshur, Gilmer, Kennon, Maxcy, and Gardner,—but the dead slave, who fell in company with them on the deck of the Princeton, was not there. He was held their equal by the impartial gun-burst, but not allowed by the *bereaved* nation a share in the funeral." . . . "Out upon their funeral, and upon the paltry procession that went in its train. Why did'nt they enquire for the body of the *other man* who fell on that deck! And why has'nt the nation inquired, and its press? I saw account of the scene in a barbarian print, called the Boston Atlas, and it was dumb on the absence of that body, as if no such man had fallen. Why, I demand in the name of human nature, was that sixth man of the game brought down by that great shot, left unburied and above ground,—for there is no account yet that his body has been allowed the rites of sepulture." . . . "They did'nt bury him even as a slave. They did'nt assign him a jim-crow place in that solemn procession, that he might follow to wait upon his enslavers in the land of spirits. They have gone there without slaves or wait-

ers." . . . "The poor black man,—they enslaved and im-
bruted him all his life, and now he is dead, they have,
for aught appears, left him to decay and waste above
ground. Let the civilized world take note of the circumstance."

Such timely, pure, and unpremeditated expressions
of a public sentiment, such publicity of genuine indignation and humanity, as abound every where in
this journal, are the most generous gifts which a man
can make.

But since our voyage Rogers has died, and now
there is no one in New England to express the indignation or contempt which may still be felt at any
cant or inhumanity.

When, on a certain occasion, one said to him,
"Why do you go about as you do, agitating the community on the subject of abolition? Jesus Christ never
preached abolitionism:" he replied, "Sir, I have two
answers to your appeal to Jesus Christ. First, I deny
your proposition, that he never preached abolition.
That single precept of his—'Whatsoever ye would
that men should do to you, do ye even so to them'—
reduced to *practice*, would abolish slavery over the
whole earth in twenty-four hours. That is my first answer. I deny your proposition. Secondly, granting your
proposition to be true—and admitting what I deny—
that Jesus Christ did not preach the abolition of
slavery, then I say, *"he did'nt do his duty."*

His was not the wisdom of the head, but of the
heart. If perhaps he had all the faults, he had more
than the usual virtues of the radical. He loved his
native soil, her hills and streams, like a Burns or
Scott. As he rode to an antislavery convention, he
viewed the country with a poet's eye, and some of his
letters written back to his editorial substitute contain

as true and pleasing pictures of New England life and scenery as are anywhere to be found.

Whoever heard of Swamscot before? "Swamscot is all fishermen. Their business is all on the deep. Their village is ranged along the ocean margin, where their brave little fleets lay drawn up, and which are out at day-break on the mighty blue—where you may see them brooding at anchor—still and intent at their *profound* trade, as so many flies on the back of a wincing horse, and for whose wincings they care as little as the Swamscot Fishers heed the restless heavings of the sea around their barks. Every thing about savors of fish. Nets hang out on every enclosure. Flakes, for curing the fish are attached to almost every dwelling. Every body has a boat—and you'll see a huge pair of sea boots lying before almost every door. The air too savors strongly of the common finny vocation. Beautiful little beaches slope out from the dwellings into the Bay, all along the village—where the fishing boats lie keeled up, at low water, with their useless anchors hooked deep into the sand. A stranded bark is a sad sight—especially if it is above high water mark, where the next tide can't relieve it and set it afloat again. The Swamscot boats though, all look cheery, and as if sure of the next sea-flow. The people are said to be the freest in the region—owing perhaps to their bold and adventurous life. The Priests can't ride them *out into the deep*, as they can the shore folks."

His style and vein though often exaggerated and affected were more native to New England than those of any of her sons, and unfinished as his pieces were, yet their literary merit has been overlooked.

Wendell Phillips Before
Concord Lyceum

CONCORD, MASS. MARCH 12TH, 1845.
Mr. Editor:

We have now, for the third winter, had our spirits refreshed, and our faith in the destiny of the commonwealth strengthened, by the presence and the eloquence of Wendell Phillips; and we wish to tender to him our thanks and our sympathy. The admission of this gentleman into the Lyceum has been strenuously opposed by a respectable portion of our fellow citizens, who themselves, we trust, whose descendants, at least, we know, will be as faithful conservers of the true order, whenever that shall be the order of the day,—and in each instance, the people have voted that they *would hear him*, by coming themselves and bringing their friends to the lecture room, and being very silent that they *might* hear. We saw some men and women, who had long ago *come out, going in* once more through the free and hospitable portals of the Lyceum; and many of our neighbors confessed, that they had had a 'sound season' this once.

It was the speaker's aim to show what the state, and above all the church, had to do, and now, alas! have done, with Texas and slavery, and how much, on the other hand, the individual should have to do with church and state. These were fair themes, and not mistimed; and his words were addressed to 'fit audience, *and not* few.'

We must give Mr. Phillips the credit of being a clean, erect, and what was once called a consistent man. He at least is not responsible for slavery, nor for American Independence; for the hypocrisy and superstition of the church, nor the timidity and self-

ishness of the state; nor for the indifference and
willing ignorance of any. He stands so distinctly, so
firmly, and so effectively, alone, and one honest man
is so much more than a host, that we cannot but feel
that he does himself injustice when he reminds us
of 'the American Society, which he represents.' It is
rare that we have the pleasure of listening to so clear
and orthodox a speaker, who obviously has so few
cracks or flaws in his moral nature—who, having
words at his command in a remarkable degree, has
much more than words, if these should fail, in his
unquestionable earnestness and integrity—and, aside
from their admiration at his rhetoric, secures the
genuine respect of his audience. He unconsciously
tells his biography as he proceeds, and we see him
early and earnestly deliberating on these subjects,
and wisely and bravely, without counsel or consent
of any, occupying a ground at first, from which the
varying tides of public opinion cannot drive him.

No one could mistake the genuine modesty and
truth with which he affirmed, when speaking of the
framers of the Constitution,—'I am wiser than they,'
which with him has improved these sixty years' experience of its working; or the uncompromising consistency and frankness of the prayer which concluded,
not like the Thanksgiving proclamations, with—'God
save the Commonwealth of Massachusetts,' but God
dash it into a thousand pieces, till there shall not remain a fragment on which a man can stand, and dare
not tell his name—referring to the case of Frederick
_____. To our disgrace we know not what to call
him, unless Scotland will lend us the spoils of one
of her Douglasses, out of history or fiction, for a season, till we be hospitable and brave enough to hear
his proper name,—a fugitive slave in one more sense
than we; who has proved himself the possessor of a

fair intellect, and has won a colorless reputation in these parts; and who, we trust, will be as superior to degradation from the sympathies of Freedom, as from the antipathies of slavery. When, said Mr. Phillips, he communicated to a New-Bedford audience, the other day, his purpose of writing his life, and telling his name, and the name of his master, and the place he ran from, the murmur ran round the room, and was anxiously whispered by the sons of the Pilgrims, 'He had better not!' and it was echoed under the shadow of Concord monument, 'He had better not!'

We would fain express our appreciation of the freedom and steady wisdom, so rare in the reformer, with which he declared that he was not born to abolish slavery, but to do right. We have heard a few, a very few, good political speakers, who afforded us the pleasure of great intellectual power and acuteness, of soldier-like steadiness, and of a graceful and natural oratory; but in this man the audience might detect a sort of moral principle and integrity, which was more stable than their firmness, more discriminating than his own intellect, and more graceful than his rhetoric, which was not working for temporary or trivial ends. It is so rare and encouraging to listen to an orator, who is content with another alliance than with the popular party, or even with the sympathising school of the martyrs, who can afford sometimes to be his own auditor if the mob stay away, and hears himself without reproof, that we feel ourselves in danger of slandering all mankind by affirming, that here is one, who is at the same time an eloquent speaker and a righteous man.

Perhaps, on the whole, the most interesting fact elicited by these addresses, is the readiness of the people at large, of whatever sect or party, to entertain, with good will and hospitality, the most revolutionary and heretical opinions, when frankly and adequately, and in some sort cheerfully, expressed. Such clear and candid declaration of opinion served like an electuary to whet and clarify the intellect of all parties, and furnished each one with an additional argument for that right he asserted.

We consider Mr. Phillips one of the most conspicuous and efficient champions of a true church and state now in the field, and would say to him, and such as are like him—'God speed you.' If you know of any champion in the ranks of his opponents, who has the valor and courtesy even of Paynim chivalry, if not the Christian graces and refinement of this knight, you will do us a service by directing him to these fields forthwith, where the lists are now open, and he shall be hospitably entertained. For as yet the Red-cross knight has shown us only the gallant device upon his shield, and his admirable command of his steed, prancing and curvetting in the empty lists; but we wait to see who, in the actual breaking of lances, will come tumbling upon the plain.

Resistance to Civil Government

I HEARTILY accept the motto,—"That government is best which governs least;" and I should like to see it acted up to more rapidly and systematically. Carried out, it finally amounts to this, which also I believe,—"That government is best which governs not at all;" and when men are prepared for it, that will be the kind of government which they will have. Government is at best but an expedient; but most governments are usually, and all governments are sometimes, inexpedient. The objections which have been brought against a standing army, and they are many and weighty, and deserve to prevail, may also at last be brought against a standing government. The standing army is only an arm of the standing government. The government itself, which is only the mode which the people have chosen to execute their will, is equally liable to be abused and perverted before the people can act through it. Witness the present Mexican war, the work of comparatively a few individuals using the standing government as their tool; for, in the outset, the people would not have consented to this measure.

This American government,—what is it but a tradition, though a recent one, endeavoring to transmit itself unimpaired to posterity, but each instant losing some of its integrity? It has not the vitality and force of a single living man; for a single man can bend it to his will. It is a sort of wooden gun to the people themselves; and, if ever they should use it in earnest as a real one against each other, it will surely split. But it is not the less necessary for this; for the people must have some complicated machinery or other, and hear its din, to satisfy that idea of government which they have. Governments show thus how successfully men can be imposed on, even impose on themselves, for their own advantage. It is excellent, we must all allow; yet this government never of itself furthered any enterprise, but by the alacrity with which it got out of its way. *It* does not keep the country free. *It* does not settle the West. *It* does not educate. The character inherent in the American people has done all that has been accomplished; and it would have done somewhat more, if the government had not sometimes got in its way. For government is an expedient by which men would fain succeed in letting one another alone; and, as has been said, when it is most expedient, the governed are most let alone by it. Trade and commerce, if they were not made of India rubber, would never manage to bounce over the obstacles which legislators are continually putting in their way; and, if one were to judge these men wholly by the effects of their actions, and not partly by their intentions, they would deserve to be classed and punished with those mischievous persons who put obstructions on the railroads.

But, to speak practically and as a citizen, unlike those who call themselves no-government men, I ask for, not at once no government, but *at once* a better government. Let every man make known what kind of government would command his respect, and that will be one step toward obtaining it.

After all, the practical reason why, when the power is once in the hands of the people, a majority are permitted, and for a long period continue, to rule, is not because they are most likely to be in the right, nor because this seems fairest to the minority, but because they are physically the strongest. But a gov-

ernment in which the majority rule in all cases cannot be based on justice, even as far as men understand it. Can there not be a government in which
majorities do not virtually decide right and wrong,
but conscience?—in which majorities decide only
those questions to which the rule of expediency is applicable? Must the citizen ever for a moment, or in the
least degree, resign his conscience to the legislator?
Why has every man a conscience, then? I think that
we should be men first, and subjects afterward. It is
not desirable to cultivate a respect for the law, so
much as for the right. The only obligation which I have
a right to assume, is to do at any time what I think
right. It is truly enough said, that a corporation has
no conscience; but a corporation of conscientious men
is a corporation *with* a conscience. Law never made
men a whit more just; and, by means of their respect
for it, even the well-disposed are daily made the
agents of injustice. A common and natural result of
an undue respect for law is, that you may see a file
of soldiers, colonel, captain, corporal, privates, pow-
der-monkeys and all, marching in admirable order
over hill and dale to the wars, against their wills, aye,
against their common sense and consciences, which
makes it very steep marching indeed, and produces
a palpitation of the heart. They have no doubt that
it is a damnable business in which they are concerned;
they are all peaceably inclined. Now, what are they?
Men at all? or small moveable forts and magazines, at
the service of some unscrupulous man in power?
Visit the Navy Yard, and behold a marine, such a man
as an American government can make, or such as it
can make a man with its black arts, a mere shadow
and reminiscence of humanity, a man laid out alive
and standing, and already, as one may say, buried

under arms with funeral accompaniments, though it
may be

> "Not a drum was heard, not a funeral note,
>   As his corse to the rampart we hurried;
> Not a soldier discharged his farewell shot
>   O'er the grave where our hero we buried."

The mass of men serve the State thus, not as men
mainly, but as machines, with their bodies. They are
the standing army, and the militia, jailers, constables,
posse comitatus, &c. In most cases there is no free
exercise whatever of the judgment or of the moral
sense; but they put themselves on a level with wood
and earth and stones, and wooden men can perhaps
be manufactured that will serve the purpose as well.
Such command no more respect than men of straw,
or a lump of dirt. They have the same sort of worth
only as horses and dogs. Yet such as these even are
commonly esteemed good citizens. Others, as most
legislators, politicians, lawyers, ministers, and office-
holders, serve the State chiefly with their heads; and,
as they rarely make any moral distinctions, they are
as likely to serve the devil, without intending it, as
God. A very few, as heroes, patriots, martyrs, reformers in the great sense, and *men*, serve the State with
their consciences also, and so necessarily resist it for
the most part; and they are commonly treated by it as
enemies. A wise man will only be useful as a man,
and will not submit to be "clay," and "stop a hole to
keep the wind away," but leave that office to his dust
at least: —

> "I am too high-born to be propertied,
>   To be a secondary at control,
>   Or useful serving-man and instrument
>   To any sovereign state throughout the world."

He who gives himself entirely to his fellow-men
appears to them useless and selfish; but he who gives

himself partially to them is pronounced a benefactor and philanthropist.

How does it become a man to behave toward this American government to-day? I answer that he cannot without disgrace be associated with it. I cannot for an instant recognize that political organization as *my* government which is the *slave's* government also.

All men recognize the right of revolution; that is, the right to refuse allegiance to and to resist the government, when its tyranny or its inefficiency are great and unendurable. But almost all say that such is not the case now. But such was the case, they think, in the Revolution of '75. If one were to tell me that this was a bad government because it taxed certain foreign commodities brought to its ports, it is most probable that I should not make an ado about it, for I can do without them: all machines have their friction; and possibly this does enough good to counterbalance the evil. At any rate, it is a great evil to make a stir about it. But when the friction comes to have its machine, and oppression and robbery are organized, I say, let us not have such a machine any longer. In other words, when a sixth of the population of a nation which has undertaken to be the refuge of liberty are slaves, and a whole country is unjustly overrun and conquered by a foreign army, and subjected to military law, I think that it is not too soon for honest men to rebel and revolutionize. What makes this duty the more urgent is the fact, that the country so overrun is not our own, but ours is the invading army.

Paley, a common authority with many on moral questions, in his chapter on the "Duty of Submission to Civil Government," resolves all civil obligation into expediency; and he proceeds to say, "that so long as the interest of the whole society requires it, that is, so long as the established government cannot be resisted or changed without public inconveniency, it is the will of God that the established government be obeyed, and no longer." . . . "This principle being admitted, the justice of every particular case of resistance is reduced to a computation of the quantity of the danger and grievance on the one side, and of the probability and expense of redressing it on the other." Of this, he says, every man shall judge for himself. But Paley appears never to have contemplated those cases to which the rule of expediency does not apply, in which a people, as well as an individual, must do justice, cost what it may. If I have unjustly wrested a plank from a drowning man, I must restore it to him though I drown myself. This, according to Paley, would be inconvenient. But he that would save his life, in such a case, shall lose it. This people must cease to hold slaves, and to make war on Mexico, though it cost them their existence as a people.

In their practice, nations agree with Paley; but does any one think that Massachusetts does exactly what is right at the present crisis?

"A drab of state, a cloth-o'-silver slut,
  To have her train borne up, and her soul trail in the dirt."

Practically speaking, the opponents to a reform in Massachusetts are not a hundred thousand politicians at the South, but a hundred thousand merchants and farmers here, who are more interested in commerce and agriculture than they are in humanity, and are not prepared to do justice to the slave and to Mexico, *cost what it may.* I quarrel not with far-off foes, but with those who, near at home, co-operate with, and do the bidding of those far away, and without whom the latter would be harmless. We are accustomed to say, that the mass of men are unprepared; but improvement is slow, because the few are not materially wiser or better than the many. It is not so important that many should be as good as you, as that there be some absolute goodness somewhere; for that will leaven the whole lump. There are thousands who are *in opinion* opposed to slavery and to the war, who yet in effect do nothing to put an end to them; who, esteeming themselves children of Washington and Franklin, sit down with their hands in their pockets, and say that they know not what to do, and do nothing; who even postpone the question of freedom to the question of free-trade, and quietly read the prices-current along with the latest advices from Mexico, after dinner, and, it may be, fall asleep over them both. What is the price-current of an honest man and patriot to-day? They hesitate, and they regret, and sometimes they petition; but they do nothing in earnest and with effect. They will wait, well-disposed, for others to remedy the evil, that they may no longer have it to regret. At most, they give only a cheap vote, and a feeble countenance and God-speed, to the right, as it goes by them. There are nine hundred and ninety-nine patrons of virtue to one virtuous man; but it is easier to deal with the real possessor of a thing than with the temporary guardian of it.

All voting is a sort of gaming, like chequers or back-gammon, with a slight moral tinge to it, a playing with right and wrong, with moral questions; and betting naturally accompanies it. The character of the voters is not staked. I cast my vote, perchance, as I think right; but I am not vitally concerned that that right should prevail. I am willing to leave it to the majority. Its obligation, therefore, never exceeds that of expediency. Even voting *for the right* is *doing* nothing for it. It is only expressing to men feebly your desire that it should prevail. A wise man will not leave the right to the mercy of chance, nor wish it to prevail through the power of the majority. There is but little virtue in the action of masses of men. When the majority shall at length vote for the abolition of slavery, it will be because they are indifferent to slavery, or because there is but little slavery left to be abolished by their vote. *They* will then be the only slaves. Only *his* vote can hasten the abolition of slavery who asserts his own freedom by his vote.

I hear of a convention to be held at Baltimore, or elsewhere, for the selection of a candidate for the Presidency, made up chiefly of editors, and men who are politicians by profession; but I think, what is it to any independent, intelligent, and respectable man what decision they may come to, shall we not have the advantage of his wisdom and honesty, nevertheless? Can we not count upon some independent votes? Are there not many individuals in the country who do not attend conventions? But no: I find that the respectable man, so called, has immediately drifted from his position, and despairs of his country, when his country has more reason to despair of him. He forthwith adopts one of the candidates thus selected as the only *available* one, thus proving that he is himself *available* for any purposes of the demagogue. His vote is of no more worth than that of any unprincipled foreigner or hireling native, who may have been bought. Oh for a man who is a *man*, and, as my neighbor says, has a bone in his back which you cannot pass your hand through! Our statistics are at fault: the population has been returned too large. How many *men* are there to a square thousand miles in this country? Hardly one. Does not America offer any inducement for men to settle here? The American has dwindled into an Odd Fellow,—one who may be known by the development of his organ of gregariousness, and a manifest lack of intellect and cheerful self-reliance; whose first and chief concern, on coming into the world, is to see that the alms-houses are in good repair; and, before yet he has lawfully donned the virile garb, to collect a fund for the support of the widows and orphans that may be; who, in short, ventures to live only by the aid of the mutual insurance company, which has promised to bury him decently.

It is not a man's duty, as a matter of course, to devote himself to the eradication of any, even the most enormous wrong; he may still properly have other concerns to engage him; but it is his duty, at least, to wash his hands of it, and, if he gives it no thought longer, not to give it practically his support. If I devote myself to other pursuits and contemplations, I must first see, at least, that I do not pursue them sitting upon another man's shoulders. I must get off him first, that he may pursue his contemplations too. See what gross inconsistency is tolerated. I have heard some of my townsmen say, "I should like to have them order me out to help put down an insurrection of the slaves, or to march to Mexico,—see if I would go;" and yet these very men have each, directly by their allegiance, and so indirectly, at least, by their money, furnished a substitute. The soldier is applauded who refuses to serve in an unjust war by those who do not refuse to sustain the unjust government which makes the war; is applauded by those whose own act and authority he disregards and sets at nought; as if the State were penitent to that degree that it hired one to scourge it while it sinned, but not to that degree that it left off sinning for a moment. Thus, under the name of order and civil government, we are all made at last to pay homage to and support our own meanness. After the first blush of sin, comes its indifference· and from immoral it becomes, as it were, *un*moral, and not quite unnecessary to that life which we have made.

The broadest and most prevalent error requires the most disinterested virtue to sustain it. The slight reproach to which the virtue of patriotism is commonly liable, the noble are most likely to incur. Those who, while they disapprove of the character and measures of a government, yield to it their allegiance and support, are undoubtedly its most conscientious supporters, and so frequently the most serious obstacles to reform. Some are petitioning the State to dissolve the Union, to disregard the requisitions of the President. Why do they not dissolve it themselves,—the union between themselves and the State,—and refuse to pay their quota into its treasury? Do not they stand in the same relation to the State, that the State does to the Union? And have not the same reasons prevented the State from resisting the Union, which have prevented them from resisting the State?

How can a man be satisfied to entertain an opinion merely, and enjoy *it*? Is there any enjoyment in it, if his opinion is that he is aggrieved? If you are cheated out of a single dollar by your neighbor, you do not rest satisfied with knowing that you are cheated, or with saying that you are cheated, or even with petitioning him to pay you your due; but you take effectual steps at once to obtain the full amount, and see that you are never cheated again. Action from principle,—the perception and the performance of right,—changes things and relations; it is essentially revolutionary, and does not consist wholly with any thing which was. It not only divides states and churches, it divides families; aye, it divides the *individual*, separating the diabolical in him from the divine.

Unjust laws exist: shall we be content to obey them,

or shall we endeavor to amend them, and obey them until we have succeeded, or shall we transgress them at once? Men generally, under such a government as this, think that they ought to wait until they have persuaded the majority to alter them. They think that, if they should resist, the remedy would be worse than the evil. But it is the fault of the government itself that the remedy *is* worse than the evil. *It* makes it worse. Why is it not more apt to anticipate and provide for reform? Why does it not cherish its wise minority? Why does it cry and resist before it is hurt? Why does it not encourage its citizens to be on the alert to point out its faults, and *do* better than it would have them? Why does it always crucify Christ, and excommunicate Copernicus and Luther, and pronounce Washington and Franklin rebels?

One would think, that a deliberate and practical denial of its authority was the only offence never contemplated by government; else, why has it not assigned its definite, its suitable and proportionate penalty? If a man who has no property refuses but once to earn nine shillings for the State, he is put in prison for a period unlimited by any law that I know, and determined only by the discretion of those who placed him there; but if he should steal ninety times nine shillings from the State, he is soon permitted to go at large again.

If the injustice is part of the necessary friction of the machine of government, let it go, let it go: perchance it will wear smooth,—certainly the machine will wear out. If the injustice has a spring, or a pulley, or a rope, or a crank, exclusively for itself, then perhaps you may consider whether the remedy will not be worse than the evil; but if it is of such a nature that it requires you to be the agent of injustice to another, then, I say, break the law. Let your life be a counter friction to stop the machine. What I have to do is to see, at any rate, that I do not lend myself to the wrong which I condemn.

As for adopting the ways which the State has provided for remedying the evil, I know not of such ways. They take too much time, and a man's life will be gone. I have other affairs to attend to. I came into this world, not chiefly to make this a good place to live in, but to live in it, be it good or bad. A man has not every thing to do, but something; and because he cannot do *every thing*, it is not necessary that he should do *something* wrong. It is not my business to be petitioning the governor or the legislature any more than it is theirs to petition me; and, if they should not hear my petition, what should I do then? But in this case the State has provided no way: its very Constitution is the evil. This may seem to be harsh and stubborn and unconciliatory; but it is to treat with the utmost kindness and consideration the only spirit that can appreciate or deserves it. So is all change for the better, like birth and death which convulse the body.

I do not hesitate to say, that those who call themselves abolitionists should at once effectually withdraw their support, both in person and property, from the government of Massachusetts, and not wait till they constitute a majority of one, before they suffer the right to prevail through them. I think that it is enough if they have God on their side, without waiting for that other one. Moreover, any man more right than his neighbors, constitutes a majority of one already.

I meet this American government, or its representative the State government, directly, and face to face, once a year, no more, in the person of its tax-gatherer; this is the only mode in which a man situated as I am necessarily meets it; and it then says distinctly, Recognize me; and the simplest, the most effectual, and, in the present posture of affairs, the indispensablest mode of treating with it on this head, of expressing your little satisfaction with and love for it, is to deny it then. My civil neighbor, the tax-gatherer, is the very man I have to deal with,—for it is, after all, with men and not with parchment that I quarrel,—and he has voluntarily chosen to be an agent of the government. How shall he ever know well what he is and does as an officer of the government, or as a man, until he is obliged to consider whether he shall treat me, his neighbor, for whom he has respect, as a neighbor and well-disposed man, or as a maniac and disturber of the peace, and see if he can get over this obstruction to his neighborliness without a ruder and more impetuous thought or speech corresponding with his action? I know this well, that if one thousand, if one hundred, if ten men whom I could name,—if ten *honest* men only,—aye, if *one* HONEST man, in this State of Massachusetts, *ceasing to hold slaves*, were actually to withdraw from this copartnership, and be locked up in the county jail therefor, it would be the abolition of slavery in America. For it matters not how small the beginning may seem to be: what is once well done is done for ever. But we love better to talk about it: that we say is our mission. Reform keeps many scores of newspapers in its service, but not one man. If my esteemed neighbor, the State's ambassador, who will devote his days to the settlement of the question of human rights in the Council Chamber, instead of being threatened with the prisons of Carolina, were to sit down the prisoner of Massachusetts, that State which is so anxious to foist the sin of slavery upon her sister,—though at present she can discover only an act of inhospitality to be the ground of a quarrel with her,—the Legislature would not wholly waive the subject the following winter.

Under a government which imprisons any unjustly, the true place for a just man is also a prison. The proper place to-day, the only place which Massachusetts has provided for her freer and less desponding spirits, is in her prisons, to be put out and locked out of the State by her own act, as they have already put themselves out by their principles. It is there that the fugitive slave, and the Mexican prisoner on parole, and the Indian come to plead the wrongs of his race, should find them; on that separate, but more free and honorable ground, where the State places those who are not *with* her but *against* her,—the only house in a slave-state in which a free man can abide with honor. If any think that their influence would be lost there, and their voices no longer afflict the ear of the State, that they would not be as an enemy within its walls, they do not know by how much truth is stronger than error, nor how much more eloquently and effectively he can combat injustice who has experienced a little in his own person. Cast your whole vote, not a strip of paper merely, but your whole influence. A minority is powerless while it conforms to the majority; it is not even a minority then; but it is irresistible when it clogs by its whole weight. If the alternative is to keep all just men in prison, or give up war and slavery, the State will not hesitate which to choose. If a thousand men were not to pay their tax-bills this year, that would not be a violent and bloody measure, as it would be to pay them, and enable the State to commit violence and shed innocent blood. This is, in fact, the definition of a peaceable revolution, if any such is possible. If the tax-gatherer, or any other public officer, asks me, as one has done, "But what shall I do?"

my answer is, "If you really wish to do any thing, resign your office." When the subject has refused allegiance, and the officer has resigned his office, then the revolution is accomplished. But even suppose blood should flow. Is there not a sort of blood shed when the conscience is wounded? Through this wound a man's real manhood and immortality flow out, and he bleeds to an everlasting death. I see this blood flowing now.

I have contemplated the imprisonment of the offender, rather than the seizure of his goods,—though both will serve the same purpose,—because they who assert the purest right, and consequently are most dangerous to a corrupt State, commonly have not spent much time in accumulating property. To such the State renders comparatively small service, and a slight tax is wont to appear exorbitant, particularly if they are obliged to earn it by special labor with their hands. If there were one who lived wholly without the use of money, the State itself would hesitate to demand it of him. But the rich man—not to make any invidious comparison—is always sold to the institution which makes him rich. Absolutely speaking, the more money, the less virtue; for money comes between a man and his objects, and obtains them for him; and it was certainly no great virtue to obtain it. It puts to rest many questions which he would otherwise be taxed to answer; while the only new question which it puts is the hard but superfluous one, how to spend it. Thus his moral ground is taken from under his feet. The opportunities of living are diminished in proportion as what are called the "means" are increased. The best thing a man can do for his culture when he is rich is to endeavour to carry out those schemes which he entertained when he was poor. Christ answered the Herodians according to their condition. "Show me the

tribute-money," said he;—and one took a penny out of
his pocket;—If you use money which has the image of
Cæsar on it, and which he has made current and
valuable, that is, *if you are men of the State*, and
gladly enjoy the advantages of Cæsar's government,
then pay him back some of his own when he demands
it; "Render therefore to Cæsar that which is Cæsar's,
and to God those things which are God's,"—leaving
them no wiser than before as to which was which;
for they did not wish to know.

When I converse with the freest of my neighbors,
I perceive that, whatever they may say about the
magnitude and seriousness of the question, and their
regard for the public tranquillity, the long and the
short of the matter is, that they cannot spare the
protection of the existing government, and they dread
the consequences of disobedience to it to their property and families. For my own part, I should not like
to think that I ever rely on the protection of the State.
But, if I deny the authority of the State when it
presents its tax-bill, it will soon take and waste all my
property, and so harass me and my children without
end. This is hard. This makes it impossible for a man
to live honestly and at the same time comfortably in
outward respects. It will not be worth the while to
accumulate property; that would be sure to go again.
You must hire or squat somewhere, and raise but a
small crop, and eat that soon. You must live within
yourself, and depend upon yourself, always tucked up
and ready for a start, and not have many affairs. A
man may grow rich in Turkey even, if he will be in all
respects a good subject of the Turkish government.
Confucius said,—"If a State is governed by the principles of reason, poverty and misery are subjects of
shame; if a State is not governed by the principles of
reason, riches and honors are the subjects of shame."

No: until I want the protection of Massachusetts to be extended to me in some distant southern port, where my liberty is endangered, or until I am bent solely on building up an estate at home by peaceful enterprise, I can afford to refuse allegiance to Massachusetts, and her right to my property and life. It costs me less in every sense to incur the penalty of disobedience to the State, than it would to obey. I should feel as if I were worth less in that case.

Some years ago, the State met me in behalf of the church, and commanded me to pay a certain sum toward the support of a clergyman whose preaching my father attended, but never I myself. "Pay it," it said, "or be locked up in the jail." I declined to pay. But, unfortunately, another man saw fit to pay it. I did not see why the schoolmaster should be taxed to support the priest, and not the priest the schoolmaster; for I was not the State's schoolmaster, but I supported myself by voluntary subscription. I did not see why the lyceum should not present its tax-bill, and have the State to back its demand, as well as the church. However, at the request of the selectmen, I condescended to make some such statement as this in writing:—"Know all men by these presents, that I, Henry Thoreau, do not wish to be regarded as a member of any incorporated society which I have not joined." This I gave to the town-clerk; and he has it. The State, having thus learned that I did not wish to be regarded as a member of that church, has never made a like demand on me since; though it said that it must adhere to its original presumption that time. If I had known how to name them, I should then have signed off in detail from all the societies which I never signed on to; but I did not know where to find a complete list.

I have paid no poll-tax for six years. I was put into

a jail once on this account, for one night; and, as I stood considering the walls of solid stone, two or three feet thick, the door of wood and iron, a foot thick, and the iron grating which strained the light, I could not help being struck with the foolishness of that institution which treated me as if I were mere flesh and blood and bones, to be locked up. I wondered that it should have concluded at length that this was the best use it could put me to, and had never thought to avail itself of my services in some way. I saw that, if there was a wall of stone between me and my townsmen, there was a still more difficult one to climb or break through, before they could get to be as free as I was. I did not for a moment feel confined, and the walls seemed a great waste of stone and mortar. I felt as if I alone of all my townsmen had paid my tax. They plainly did not know how to treat me, but behaved like persons who are underbred. In every threat and in every compliment there was a blunder; for they thought that my chief desire was to stand the other side of that stone wall. I could not but smile to see how industriously they locked the door on my meditations, which followed them out again without let or hinderance, and *they* were really all that was dangerous. As they could not reach me, they had resolved to punish my body; just as boys, if they cannot come at some person against whom they have a spite, will abuse his dog. I saw that the State was half-witted, that it was timid as a lone woman with her silver spoons, and that it did not know its friends from its foes, and I lost all my remaining respect for it, and pitied it.

Thus the State never intentionally confronts a man's sense, intellectual or moral, but only his body, his senses. It is not armed with superior wit or honesty, but with superior physical strength. I was not born to be forced. I will breathe after my own fashion. Let us see who is the strongest. What force has a multitude? They only can force me who obey a higher law than I. They force me to become like themselves. I do not hear of *men* being *forced* to live this way or that by masses of men. What sort of life were that to live? When I meet a government which says to me, "Your money or your life," why should I be in haste to give it my money? It may be in a great strait, and not know what to do: I cannot help that. It must help itself; do as I do. It is not worth the while to snivel about it. I am not responsible for the successful working of the machinery of society. I am not the son of the engineer. I perceive that, when an acorn and a chestnut fall side by side, the one does not remain inert to make way for the other, but both obey their own laws, and spring and grow and flourish as best they can, till one, perchance, overshadows and destroys the other. If a plant cannot live according to its nature, it dies; and so a man.

The night in prison was novel and interesting enough. The prisoners in their shirt-sleeves were enjoying a chat and the evening air in the door-way, when I entered. But the jailer said, "Come, boys, it is time to lock up;" and so they dispersed, and I heard the sound of their steps returning into the hollow apartments. My room-mate was introduced to me by the jailer, as "a first-rate fellow and a clever man." When the door was locked, he showed me where to hang my hat, and how he managed matters there. The rooms were whitewashed once a month; and this one, at least, was the whitest, most simply furnished, and probably the neatest apartment in the town. He naturally wanted to know where I came from, and what brought me there; and, when I had told him, I asked him in my turn how he came there, presuming him to be an honest man, of course; and, as the world goes, I believe he was. "Why," said he, "they accuse me of burning a barn; but I never did it." As near as I could discover, he had probably gone to bed in a barn when drunk, and smoked his pipe there; and so a barn was burnt. He had the reputation of being a clever man, had been there some three months waiting for his trial to come on, and would have to wait as much longer; but he was quite domesticated and contented, since he got his board for nothing, and thought that he was well treated.

He occupied one window, and I the other; and I saw, that, if one stayed there long, his principal business would be to look out the window. I had soon read all the tracts that were left there, and examined where former prisoners had broken out, and where a grate had been sawed off, and heard the history of the various occupants of that room; for I found that even here there was a history and a gossip which never circulated beyond the walls of the jail. Probably this is the only house in the town where verses are composed, which are afterward printed in a circular form, but not published. I was shown quite a long list of verses which were composed by some young men who had been detected in an attempt to escape, who avenged themselves by singing them.

I pumped my fellow-prisoner as dry as I could, for fear I should never see him again; but at length he showed me which was my bed, and left me to blow out the lamp.

It was like travelling into a far country, such as I had never expected to behold, to lie there for one night. It seemed to me that I never had heard the town-clock strike before, nor the evening sounds of the village; for we slept with the windows open, which were inside the grating. It was to see my native village in the light of the middle ages, and our Concord was turned into a Rhine stream, and visions of knights and castles passed before me. They were the voices of old burghers that I heard in the streets. I was an involuntary spectator and auditor of whatever was done and said in the kitchen of the adjacent village-inn,—a wholly new and rare experience to me. It was a closer view of my native town. I was fairly inside of it. I never had seen its institutions before. This is one of its peculiar institutions; for it is a shire town. I began to comprehend what its inhabitants were about.

In the morning, our breakfasts were put through the hole in the door, in small oblong-square tin pans, made to fit, and holding a pint of chocolate, with brown bread, and an iron spoon. When they called for the vessels again, I was green enough to return what bread I had left; but my comrade seized it, and said that I should lay that up for lunch or dinner. Soon after, he was let out to work at haying in a neighboring field, whither he went every day, and would not be back till noon; so he bade me good-day, saying that he doubted if he should see me again.

When I came out of prison,—for some one interfered, and paid the tax,—I did not perceive that great changes had taken place on the common, such as he observed who went in a youth, and emerged a tottering and gray-headed man; and yet a change had to my eyes come over the scene,—the town, and State, and country,—greater than any that mere time could effect. I saw yet more distinctly the State in which I lived. I saw to what extent the people among whom I lived could be trusted as good neighbors and friends; that their friendship was for summer weather only; that they did not greatly purpose to do right; that they were a distinct race from me by their prejudices and superstitions, as the Chinamen and Malays are; that, in their sacrifices to humanity, they ran no risks, not even to their property; that, after all, they were not so noble but they treated the thief as he had treated them, and hoped, by a certain outward observance and a few prayers, and by walking in a particular straight though useless path from time to time, to save their souls. This may be to judge my neighbors harshly; for I believe that most of them are not aware that they have such an institution as the jail in their village.

It was formerly the custom in our village, when a poor debtor came out of jail, for his acquaintances to salute him, looking through their fingers, which were crossed to represent the grating of a jail window, "How do ye do?" My neighbors did not thus salute me, but first looked at me, and then at one another, as if I had returned from a long journey. I was put into jail as I was going to the shoemaker's to get a shoe which was mended. When I was let out the next morning, I proceeded to finish my errand, and, having put on my mended shoe, joined a huckleberry party, who were impatient to put themselves under my conduct; and in half an hour,—for the horse was soon tackled,—was in the midst of a huckleberry field, on one of our highest hills, two miles off; and then the State was nowhere to be seen.

This is the whole history of "My Prisons."

I have never declined paying the highway tax, because I am as desirous of being a good neighbor as I am of being a bad subject; and, as for supporting schools, I am doing my part to educate my fellow-countrymen now. It is for no particular item in the tax-bill that I refuse to pay it. I simply wish to refuse allegiance to the State, to withdraw and stand aloof from it effectually. I do not care to trace the course of my dollar, if I could, till it buys a man, or a musket to shoot one with,—the dollar is innocent,—but I am concerned to trace the effects of my allegiance. In fact, I quietly declare war with the State, after my fashion, though I will still make what use and get what advantage of her I can, as is usual in such cases.

If others pay the tax which is demanded of me, from a sympathy with the State, they do but what they have already done in their own case, or rather they abet injustice to a greater extent than the State requires. If they pay the tax from a mistaken interest in the individual taxed, to save his property or prevent his going to jail, it is because they have not considered wisely how far they let their private feelings interfere with the public good.

This, then, is my position at present. But one cannot be too much on his guard in such a case, lest his action be biassed by obstinacy, or an undue regard for the opinions of men. Let him see that he does only what belongs to himself and to the hour.

I think sometimes, Why, this people mean well; they are only ignorant; they would do better if they knew how: why give your neighbors this pain to treat you as they are not inclined to? But I think, again, this is no reason why I should do as they do, or permit others to suffer much greater pain of a different kind. Again, I sometimes say to myself, When many millions of men, without heat, without ill-will, without personal feeling of any kind, demand of you a few shillings only, without the possibility, such is their constitution, of retracting or altering their present demand, and without the possibility, on your side, of appeal to any other millions, why expose yourself to this overwhelming brute force? You do not resist cold and hunger, the winds and the waves, thus obstinately; you quietly submit to a thousand similar necessities. You do not put your head into the fire. But just in proportion as I regard this as not wholly a brute force, but partly a human force, and consider that I have relations to those millions as to so many millions of men, and not of mere brute or inanimate things, I see that appeal is possible, first and instantaneously, from them to the Maker of them, and, secondly, from them to themselves. But, if I put my head deliberately into the fire, there is no appeal to fire or to the Maker of fire, and I have only myself to blame. If I could convince myself that I have any right to be satisfied with men as they are, and to treat them accordingly, and not according, in some respects, to my requisitions and expectations of what they and I ought to be, then, like a good Mussulman and fatalist, I should endeavor to be satisfied with things as they are, and say it is the will of God. And, above all, there is this difference between resisting this and a purely brute or natural force, that I can resist this with some effect; but I cannot expect, like Orpheus, to change the nature of the rocks and trees and beasts.

I do not wish to quarrel with any man or nation. I do not wish to split hairs, to make fine distinctions, or set myself up as better than my neighbors. I seek rather, I may say, even an excuse for conforming to the laws of the land. I am but too ready to conform to them. Indeed I have reason to suspect myself on this head; and each year, as the tax-gatherer comes round, I find myself disposed to review the acts and position of the general and state governments, and the spirit of the people, to discover a pretext for conformity. I believe that the State will soon be able to take all my work of this sort out of my hands, and then I shall be no better a patriot than my fellow-countrymen. Seen from a lower point of view, the Constitution, with all its faults, is very good; the law and the courts are very respectable; even this State and this American government are, in many respects, very admirable and rare things, to be thankful for, such as a great many have described them; but seen from a point of view a little higher, they are what I have described them; seen from a higher still, and the highest, who shall say what they are, or that they are worth looking at or thinking of at all?

However, the government does not concern me much, and I shall bestow the fewest possible thoughts on it. It is not many moments that I live under a government, even in this world. If a man is thought-free, fancy-free, imagination-free, that which *is not* never for a long time appearing *to be* to him, unwise rulers or reformers cannot fatally interrupt him.

I know that most men think differently from myself; but those whose lives are by profession devoted to the study of these or kindred subjects, content me as little as any. Statesmen and legislators, standing so completely within the institution, never distinctly and nakedly behold it. They speak of moving society, but have no resting-place without it. They may be men of a certain experience and discrimination, and have no doubt invented ingenious and even useful systems, for which we sincerely thank them; but all their wit and usefulness lie within certain not very wide limits. They are wont to forget that the world is not governed by policy and expediency. Webster never goes behind government, and so cannot speak with authority about it. His words are wisdom to those legislators who contemplate no essential reform in the existing government; but for thinkers, and those who legislate for all time, he never once glances at the subject. I know of those whose serene and wise speculations on this theme would soon reveal the limits of his mind's range and hospitality. Yet, compared with the cheap professions of most reformers, and the still cheaper wisdom and eloquence of politicians in general, his are almost the only sensible and valuable words, and we thank Heaven for him. Comparatively, he is always strong, original, and, above all, practical. Still his quality is not wisdom, but prudence. The lawyer's truth is not Truth, but consistency, or a consistent expediency. Truth is always in harmony with herself, and is not concerned chiefly to reveal the justice that may consist with wrong-doing. He well deserves to be called, as he has been called, the Defender of the Constitution. There are really no blows to be given by him but defensive ones. He is not a leader, but a follower. His leaders are the men of '87. "I have never made an effort," he says, "and never propose to make an effort; I have never countenanced an effort, and never mean to countenance an effort, to disturb the arrangement as originally made, by which the various States came into the Union." Still thinking of the sanction which the Constitution gives to slavery, he says, "Because it was

a part of the original compact,—let it stand." Notwithstanding his special acuteness and ability, he is unable to take a fact out of its merely political relations,
and behold it as it lies absolutely to be disposed of by
the intellect,—what, for instance, it behoves a man to
do here in America to-day with regard to slavery,—but
ventures, or is driven, to make some such desperate
answer as the following, while professing to speak
absolutely, and as a private man,—from which what
new and singular code of social duties might be inferred?—"The manner," says he, "in which the governments of those States where slavery exists are to
regulate it, is for their own consideration, under their
responsibility to their constituents, to the general laws
of propriety, humanity, and justice, and to God.
Associations formed elsewhere, springing from a
feeling of humanity, or any other cause, have nothing
whatever to do with it. They have never received any
encouragement from me, and they never will."*

They who know of no purer sources of truth, who
have traced up its stream no higher, stand, and wisely
stand, by the Bible and the Constitution, and drink at
it there with reverence and humility; but they who
behold where it comes trickling into this lake or that
pool, gird up their loins once more, and continue
their pilgrimage toward its fountain-head.

No man with a genius for legislation has appeared
in America. They are rare in the history of the world.
There are orators, politicians, and eloquent men, by
the thousand; but the speaker has not yet opened his
mouth to speak, who is capable of settling the much-
vexed questions of the day. We love eloquence for its
own sake, and not for any truth which it may utter,
or any heroism it may inspire. Our legislators have not

* These extracts have been inserted since the Lecture was
read.

yet learned the comparative value of free-trade and of freedom, of union, and of rectitude, to a nation. They have no genius or talent for comparatively humble questions of taxation and finance, commerce and manufactures and agriculture. If we were left solely to the wordy wit of legislators in Congress for our guidance, uncorrected by the seasonable experience and the effectual complaints of the people, America would not long retain her rank among the nations. For eighteen hundred years, though perchance I have no right to say it, the New Testament has been written; yet where is the legislator who has wisdom and practical talent enough to avail himself of the light which it sheds on the science of legislation?

The authority of government, even such as I am willing to submit to,—for I will cheerfully obey those who know and can do better than I, and in many things even those who neither know nor can do so well,—is still an impure one: to be strictly just, it must have the sanction and consent of the governed. It can have no pure right over my person and property but what I concede to it. The progress from an absolute to a limited monarchy, from a limited monarchy to a democracy, is a progress toward a true respect for the individual. Is a democracy, such as we know it, the last improvement possible in government? Is it not possible to take a step further towards recognizing and organizing the rights of man? There will never be a really free and enlightened State, until the State comes to recognize the individual as a higher and independent power, from which all its own power and authority are derived, and treats him accordingly. I please myself with imagining a State at last which can afford to be just to all men, and to treat the individual with respect as a neighbor; which even would not think it inconsistent with its own repose, if a few were to live aloof from it, not meddling with it, nor embraced by it, who fulfilled all the duties of neighbors and fellow-men. A State which bore this kind of fruit, and suffered it to drop off as fast as it ripened, would prepare the way for a still more perfect and glorious State, which also I have imagined, but not yet anywhere seen.

Slavery in Massachusetts

I LATELY attended a meeting of the citizens of Concord, expecting, as one among many, to speak on the subject of slavery in Massachusetts; but I was surprised and disappointed to find that what had called my townsmen together was the destiny of Nebraska, and not of Massachusetts, and that what I had to say would be entirely out of order. I had thought that the house was on fire, and not the prairie; but though several of the citizens of Massachusetts are now in prison for attempting to rescue a slave from her own clutches, not one of the speakers at that meeting expressed regret for it, not one even referred to it. It was only the disposition of some wild lands a thousand miles off, which appeared to concern them. The inhabitants of Concord are not prepared to stand by one of their own bridges, but talk only of taking up a position on the highlands beyond the Yellowstone river. Our Buttricks, and Davises, and Hosmers are retreating thither, and I fear that they will have no Lexington Common between them and the enemy. There is not one slave in Nebraska; there are perhaps a million slaves in Massachusetts.

They who have been bred in the school of politics fail now and always to face the facts. Their measures are half measures and make-shifts, merely. They put off the day of settlement indefinitely, and meanwhile, the debt accumulates. Though the Fugitive Slave Law had not been the subject of discussion on that occasion, it was at length faintly resolved by my townsmen, at an adjourned meeting, as I learn, that the compromise compact of 1820 having been repudiated by one of the parties, 'Therefore, . . . the Fugitive

Slave Law must be repealed.' But this is not the reason why an iniquitous law should be repealed. The fact which the politician faces is merely, that there is less honor among thieves than was supposed, and not the fact that they are thieves.

As I had no opportunity to express my thoughts at that meeting, will you allow me to do so here?

Again it happens that the Boston Court House is full of armed men, holding prisoner and trying a MAN, to find out if he is not really a SLAVE. Does any one think that Justice or God awaits Mr. Loring's decision? For him to sit there deciding still, when this question is already decided from eternity to eternity, and the unlettered slave himself, and the multitude around, have long since heard and assented to the decision, is simply to make himself ridiculous. We may be tempted to ask from whom he received his commission, and who he is that received it; what novel statutes he obeys, and what precedents are to him of authority. Such an arbiter's very existence is an impertinence. We do not ask him to make up his mind, but to make up his pack.

I listen to hear the voice of a Governor, Commander-in-Chief of the forces of Massachusetts. I hear only the creaking of crickets and the hum of insects which now fill the summer air. The Governor's exploit is to review the troops on muster days. I have seen him on horseback, with his hat off, listening to a chaplain's prayer. It chances that is all I have ever seen of a Governor. I think that I could manage to get along without one. If *he* is not of the least use to prevent my being kidnapped, pray of what important use is he likely to be to me? When freedom is most endangered, he dwells in the deepest obscurity. A distinguished clergyman told me that he chose the profession of a clergyman, because it afforded the most leisure for literary pursuits. I would recommend to him the profession of a Governor.

Three years ago, also, when the Simm's tragedy was acted, I said to myself, there is such an officer, if not such a man, as the Governor of Massachusetts, —what has he been about the last fortnight? Has he had as much as he could do to keep on the fence during this moral earthquake? It seemed to me that no keener satire could have been aimed at, no more cutting insult have been offered to that man, than just what happened—the absence of all inquiry after him in that crisis. The worst and the most I chance to know of him is, that he did not improve that opportunity to make himself known, and worthily known. He could at least have *resigned* himself into fame. It appeared to be forgotten that there was such a man, or such an office. Yet no doubt he was endeavoring to fill the gubernatorial chair all the while. He was no Governor of mine. He did not govern me.

But at last, in the present case, the Governor was heard from. After he and the United States Government had perfectly succeeded in robbing a poor innocent black man of his liberty for life, and, as far as they could, of his Creator's likeness in his breast, he made a speech to his accomplices, at a congratulatory supper!

I have read a recent law of this State, making it penal for 'any officer of the Commonwealth' to 'detain, or aid in the . . . detention,' any where within its limits, 'of any person, for the reason that he is claimed as a fugitive slave.' Also, it was a matter of notoriety that a writ of replevin to take the fugitive out of the custody of the United States Marshal could not be served, for want of sufficient force to aid the officer.

I had thought that the Governor was in some sense the executive officer of the State; that it was his business, as a Governor, to see that the laws of the State were executed; while, as a man, he took care that he did not, by so doing, break the laws of humanity; but when there is any special important use for him, he is useless, or worse than useless, and permits the laws of the State to go unexecuted. Perhaps I do not know what are the duties of a Governor; but if to be a Governor requires to subject one's self to so much ignominy without remedy, if it is to put a restraint upon my manhood, I shall take care never to be Governor of Massachusetts. I have not read far in the statutes of this Commonwealth. It is not profitable reading. They do not always say what is true; and they do not always mean what they say. What I am concerned to know is, that that man's influence and authority were on the side of the slaveholder, and not of the slave—of the guilty, and not of the innocent—of injustice, and not of justice. I never saw him of whom I speak; indeed, I did not know that he was Governor until this event occurred. I heard of him and Anthony Burns at the same time, and thus, undoubtedly, most will hear of him. So far am I from being governed by him. I do not mean that it was any thing to his discredit that I had not heard of him, only that I heard what I did. The worst I shall say of him is, that he proved no better than the majority of his constituents would be likely to prove. In my opinion, he was not equal to the occasion.

The whole military force of the State is at the service of a Mr. Suttle, a slaveholder from Virginia, to enable him to catch a man whom he calls his property; but not a soldier is offered to save a citizen of Massachusetts from being kidnapped! Is this what all these soldiers, all this *training* has been for these seventy-nine years past? Have they been trained merely to rob Mexico, and carry back fugitive slaves to their masters?

These very nights, I heard the sound of a drum in our streets. There were men *training* still; and for what? I could with an effort pardon the cockerels of Concord for crowing still, for they, perchance, had not been beaten that morning; but I could not excuse this rub-a-dub of the 'trainers.' The slave was carried back by exactly such as these, i.e., by the soldier, of whom the best you can say in this connection is, that he is a fool made conspicuous by a painted coat.

Three years ago, also, just a week after the authorities of Boston assembled to carry back a perfectly innocent man, and one whom they knew to be innocent, into slavery, the inhabitants of Concord caused the bells to be rung and the cannons to be fired, to celebrate their liberty—and the courage and love of liberty of their ancestors who fought at the bridge. As if *those* three millions had fought for the right to be free themselves, but to hold in slavery three million others. Now-a-days, men wear a fool's cap, and call it a liberty cap. I do not know but there are some, who, if they were tied to a whipping-post, and could but get one hand free, would use it to ring the bells and fire the cannons, to celebrate *their* liberty. So some of my townsmen took the liberty to ring and fire; that was the extent of their freedom; and when the sound of the bells died away, their liberty died away also; when the powder was all expended, their liberty went off with the smoke.

The joke could be no broader, if the inmates of the prisons were to subscribe for all the powder to be used in such salutes, and hire the jailers to do the firing and ringing for them, while they enjoyed it through the grating.

This is what I thought about my neighbors.

Every humane and intelligent inhabitant of Concord, when he or she heard those bells and those cannons, thought not with pride of the events of the 19th of April, 1775, but with shame of the events of the 12th of April, 1851. But now we have half buried that old shame under a new one.

Massachusetts sat waiting Mr. Loring's decision, as if it could in any way affect her own criminality. Her crime, the most conspicuous and fatal crime of all, was permitting him to be the umpire in such a case. It was really the trial of Massachusetts. Every moment that she hesitated to set this man free—every moment that she now hesitates to atone for her crime, she is convicted. The Commissioner on her case is God; not Edward G. God, but simple God.

I wish my countrymen to consider, that whatever the human law may be, neither an individual nor a nation can ever commit the least act of injustice against the obscurest individual, without having to pay the penalty for it. A government which deliberately enacts injustice, and persists in it, will at length ever become the laughing-stock of the world.

Much has been said about American slavery, but I think that we do not even yet realize what slavery is. If I were seriously to propose to Congress to make mankind into sausages, I have no doubt that most of the members would smile at my proposition, and if any believed me to be in earnest, they would think that I proposed something much worse than Congress had ever done. But if any of them will tell me that to make a man into a sausage would be much worse,—would be any worse, than to make him into a slave,—than it was to enact the Fugitive Slave Law, I will accuse him of foolishness, of intellectual incapacity, of making a distinction without a difference. The one is just as sensible a proposition as the other.

I hear a good deal said about trampling this law under foot. Why, one need not go out of his way to do that. This law rises not to the level of the head or the reason; its natural habitat is in the dirt. It was born and bred, and has its life only in the dust and mire, on a level with the feet, and he who walks with freedom, and does not with Hindoo mercy avoid treading on every venomous reptile, will inevitably tread on it, and so trample it under foot,—and Webster, its maker, with it, like the dirt-bug and its ball.

Recent events will be valuable as a criticism on the administration of justice in our midst, or, rather, as showing what are the true resources of justice in any community. It has come to this, that the friends of liberty, the friends of the slave, have shuddered when they have understood that his fate was left to the legal tribunals of the country to be decided. Free men have no faith that justice will be awarded in such a case; the judge may decide this way or that; it is a kind of accident, at best. It is evident that he is not a competent authority in so important a case. It is no time, then, to be judging according to his precedents, but to establish a precedent for the future. I would much rather trust to the sentiment of the people. In their vote, you would get something of some value, at least, however small; but, in the other case, only the trammelled judgment of an individual, of no significance, be it which way it might.

It is to some extent fatal to the courts, when the people are compelled to go behind them. I do not wish to believe that the courts were made for fair weather, and for very civil cases merely,—but think of leaving it to any court in the land to decide whether more than three millions of people, in this case, a sixth part of a nation, have a right to be freemen or not! But it has been left to the courts of *justice*, so-called— to the Supreme Court of the land—and, as you all know, recognizing no authority but the Constitution, it has decided that the three millions are, and shall continue to be, slaves. Such judges as these are merely the inspectors of a pick-lock and murderer's tools, to tell him whether they are in working order or not, and there they think that their responsibility ends. There was a prior case on the docket, which they, as judges appointed by God, had no right to skip; which having been justly settled, they would have been saved from this humiliation. It was the case of the murderer himself.

The law will never make men free; it is men who have got to make the law free. They are the lovers of law and order, who observe the law when the government breaks it.

Among human beings, the judge whose words seal the fate of a man furthest into eternity, is not he who merely pronounces the verdict of the law, but he, whoever he may be, who, from a love of truth, and unprejudiced by any custom or enactment of men, utters a true opinion or *sentence* concerning him. He it is that *sentences* him. Whoever has discerned truth, has received his commission from a higher source than the chiefest justice in the world, who can discern only law. He finds himself constituted judge of the judge.—Strange that it should be necessary to state such simple truths.

I am more and more convinced that, with reference to any public question, it is more important to know what the country thinks of it, than what the city thinks. The city does not *think* much. On any moral question, I would rather have the opinion of

Boxboro than of Boston and New York put together. When the former speaks, I feel as if somebody *had* spoken, as if *humanity* was yet, and a reasonable being had asserted its rights,—as if some unprejudiced men among the country's hills had at length turned their attention to the subject, and by a few sensible words redeemed the reputation of the race. When, in some obscure country town, the farmers come together to a special town meeting, to express their opinion on some subject which is vexing the land, that, I think, is the true Congress, and the most respectable one that is ever assembled in the United States.

It is evident that there are, in this Commonwealth, at least, two parties, becoming more and more distinct —the party of the city, and the party of the country. I know that the country is mean enough, but I am glad to believe that there is a slight difference in her favor. But as yet, she has few, if any organs, through which to express herself. The editorials which she reads, like the news, come from the sea-board. Let us, the inhabitants of the country, cultivate self-respect. Let us not send to the city for aught more essential than our broadcloths and groceries, or, if we read the opinions of the city, let us entertain opinions of our own.

Among measures to be adopted, I would suggest to make as earnest and vigorous an assault on the Press as has already been made, and with effect, on the Church. The Church has much improved within a few years; but the Press is almost, without exception, corrupt. I believe that, in this country, the press exerts a greater and a more pernicious influence than the Church did in its worst period. We are not a religious people, but we are a nation of politicians. We do not care for the Bible, but we do care for the newspaper. At any meeting of politicians,—like that at Concord the other evening, for instance,—how impertinent it would be to quote from the Bible! how pertinent to quote from a newspaper or from the Constitution! The newspaper is a Bible which we read every morning and every afternoon, standing and sitting, riding and walking. It is a Bible which every man carries in his pocket, which lies on every table and counter, and which the mail, and thousands of missionaries, are continually dispensing. It is, in short, the only book which America has printed, and which America reads. So wide is its influence. The editor is a preacher whom you voluntarily support. Your tax is commonly one cent daily, and it costs nothing for pew hire. But how many of these preachers preach the truth? I repeat the testimony of many an intelligent foreigner, as well as my own convictions, when I say, that probably no country was ever ruled by so mean a class of tyrants as, with a few noble exceptions, are the editors of the periodical press in *this* country. And as they live and rule only by their servility, and appealing to the worst, and not the better nature of man, the people who read them are in the condition of the dog that returns to his vomit.

The *Liberator* and the *Commonwealth* were the only papers in Boston, as far as I know, which made themselves heard in condemnation of the cowardice and meanness of the authorities of that city, as exhibited in '51. The other journals, almost without exception, by their manner of referring to and speaking of the Fugitive Slave Law, and the carrying back of the slave Simms, insulted the common sense of the country, at least. And, for the most part, they did this, one would say, because they thought so to secure the approbation of their patrons, not being aware that a sounder sentiment prevailed to any extent in the heart of the Commonwealth. I am told that some of them have improved of late; but they are still eminently time-serving. Such is the character they have won.

But, thank fortune, this preacher can be even more easily reached by the weapons of the reformer than could the recreant priest. The free men of New England have only to refrain from purchasing and reading these sheets, have only to withhold their cents, to kill a score of them at once. One whom I respect told me that he purchased Mitchell's *Citizen* in the cars, and then threw it out the window. But would not his contempt have been more fatally expressed, if he had not bought it?

Are they Americans? are they New Englanders? are they inhabitants of Lexington, and Concord, and Framingham, who read and support the Boston *Post*, *Mail*, *Journal*, *Advertiser*, *Courier*, and *Times*? Are these the Flags of our Union? I am not a newspaper reader, and may omit to name the worst.

Could slavery suggest a more complete servility than some of these journals exhibit? Is there any dust which their conduct does not lick, and make fouler still with its slime? I do not know whether the Boston *Herald* is still in existence, but I remember to have seen it about the streets when Simms was carried off. Did it not act its part well—serve its master faithfully? How could it have gone lower on its belly? How can a man stoop lower than he is low? do more than put his extremities in the place of the head he has? than make his head his lower extremity? When I have taken up this paper with my cuffs turned up, I have heard the gurgling of the sewer through every column. I have felt that I was handling a paper picked out of the public gutters, a leaf from the gospel of the gambling-house, the groggery and the brothel, harmonizing with the gospel of the Merchants' Exchange.

The majority of the men of the North, and of the South, and East, and West, are not men of principle. If they vote, they do not send men to Congress on errands of humanity, but while their brothers and sisters are being scourged and hung for loving liberty, while——I might here insert all that slavery implies and is,——it is the mismanagement of wood and iron and stone and gold which concerns them. Do what you will, O Government! with my wife and children, my mother and brother, my father and sister, I will obey your commands to the letter. It will indeed grieve me if you hurt them, if you deliver them to overseers to be hunted by hounds or to be whipped to death; but nevertheless, I will peaceably pursue my chosen calling on this fair earth, until perchance, one day, when I have put on mourning for them dead, I shall have persuaded you to relent. Such is the attitude, such are the words of Massachusetts.

Rather than do thus, I need not say what match I would touch, what system endeavor to blow up,—but as I love my life, I would side with the light, and let the dark earth roll from under me, calling my mother and my brother to follow.

I would remind my countrymen, that they are to be men first, and Americans only at a late and convenient hour. No matter how valuable law may be to protect your property, even to keep soul and body together, if it do not keep you and humanity together.

I am sorry to say, that I doubt if there is a judge in Massachusetts who is prepared to resign his office, and get his living innocently, whenever it is required of him to pass sentence under a law which is merely contrary to the law of God. I am compelled to see that they put themselves, or rather, are by character, in this respect, exactly on a level with the marine who discharges his musket in any direction he is ordered to. They are just as much tools and as little men. Certainly, they are not the more to be respected, because their master enslaves their understandings and consciences, instead of their bodies.

The judges and lawyers,—simply as such, I mean, —and all men of expediency, try this case by a very low and incompetent standard. They consider, not whether the Fugitive Slave Law is right, but whether it is what they call *constitutional*. Is virtue constitutional, or vice? Is equity constitutional, or iniquity? In important moral and vital questions like this, it is just as impertinent to ask whether a law is constitutional or not, as to ask whether it is profitable or not. They persist in being the servants of the worst of men, and not the servants of humanity. The question is not whether you or your grandfather, seventy years ago, did not enter into an agreement to serve the devil, and that service is not accordingly now due; but whether you will not now, for once and at last, serve God,—in spite of your own past recreancy, or that of your ancestor,—by obeying that eternal and only just CONSTITUTION, which He, and not any Jefferson or Adams, has written in your being.

The amount of it is, if the majority vote the devil to be God, the minority will live and behave accordingly, and obey the successful candidate, trusting that some time or other, by some Speaker's casting vote, perhaps, they may reinstate God. This is the highest principle I can get out of or invent for my neighbors. These men act as if they believed that they could safely slide down hill a little way—or a good way—and would surely come to a place, by and by, where they could begin to slide up again. This is expediency, or choosing that course which offers the slightest obstacles to the feet, that is, a down-hill one. But there is no such thing as accomplishing a right-eous reform by the use of 'expediency.' There is no such thing as sliding up hill. In morals, the only sliders are backsliders.

Thus we steadily worship Mammon, both School, and State, and Church, and the Seventh Day curse God with a tintamar from one end of the Union to the other.

Will mankind never learn that policy is not moral-ity—that it never secures any moral right, but con-siders merely what is expedient? chooses the available candidate, who is invariably the devil,—and what right have his constituents to be surprised, because the devil does not behave like an angel of light? What is wanted is men, not of policy, but of probity—who recognize a higher law than the Constitution, or the decision of the majority. The fate of the country does not depend on how you vote at the polls—the worst man is as strong as the best at that game; it does not depend on what kind of paper you drop into the ballot-box once a year, but on what kind of man you drop from your chamber into the street every morn-ing.

What should concern Massachusetts is not the Nebraska Bill, nor the Fugitive Slave Bill, but her own slaveholding and servility. Let the State dissolve her union with the slaveholder. She may wriggle and hesitate, and ask leave to read the Constitution once more; but she can find no respectable law or prec-edent which sanctions the continuance of such a Union for an instant.

Let each inhabitant of the State dissolve his union with her, as long as she delays to do her duty.

The events of the past month teach me to distrust Fame. I see that she does not finely discriminate, but

coarsely hurrahs. She considers not the simple heroism of an action, but only as it is connected with its
apparent consequences. She praises till she is hoarse
the easy exploit of the Boston tea party, but will be
comparatively silent about the braver and more dis-
interestedly heroic attack on the Boston Court-House,
simply because it was unsuccessful!

Covered with disgrace, the State has sat down
coolly to try for their lives and liberties the men
who attempted to do its duty for it. And this is called
justice! They who have shown that they can behave
particularly well may perchance be put under bonds
for *their good behavior.* They whom truth requires
at present to plead guilty, are of all the inhabitants of
the State, pre-eminently innocent. While the Governor, and the Mayor, and countless officers of the
Commonwealth, are at large, the champions of liberty
are imprisoned.

Only they are guiltless, who commit the crime of
contempt of such a Court. It behoves every man to
see that his influence is on the side of justice, and let
the courts make their own characters. My sympathies
in this case are wholly with the accused, and wholly
against the accusers and their judges. Justice is sweet
and musical; but injustice is harsh and discordant.
The judge still sits grinding at his organ, but it yields
no music, and we hear only the sound of the handle.
He believes that all the music resides in the handle,
and the crowd toss him their coppers the same as
before.

Do you suppose that that Massachusetts which is
now doing these things,—which hesitates to crown
these men, some of whose lawyers, and even judges,
perchance, may be driven to take refuge in some poor
quibble, that they may not wholly outrage their in-
stinctive sense of justice,—do you suppose that she is

any thing but base and servile? that she is the champion of liberty?

Show me a free State, and a court truly of justice, and I will fight for them, if need be; but show me Massachusetts, and I refuse her my allegiance, and express contempt for her courts.

The effect of a good government is to make life more valuable,—of a bad one, to make it less valuable. We can afford that railroad, and all merely material stock, should lose some of its value, for that only compels us to live more simply and economically; but suppose that the value of life itself should be diminished! How can we make a less demand on man and nature, how live more economically in respect to virtue and all noble qualities, than we do? I have lived for the last month,—and I think that every man in Massachusetts capable of the sentiment of patriotism must have had a similar experience,—with the sense of having suffered a vast and indefinite loss. I did not know at first what ailed me. At last it occurred to me that what I had lost was a country. I had never respected the Government near to which I had lived, but I had foolishly thought that I might manage to live here, minding my private affairs, and forget it. For my part, my old and worthiest pursuits have lost I cannot say how much of their attraction, and I feel that my investment in life here is worth many per cent. less since Massachusetts last deliberately sent back an innocent man, Anthony Burns, to slavery. I dwelt before, perhaps, in the illusion that my life passed somewhere only *between* heaven and hell, but now I cannot persuade myself that I do not dwell *wholly within* hell. The site of that political organization called Massachusetts is to me morally covered with volcanic scoriæ and cinders, such as Milton describes in the infernal regions. If there is any hell more unprincipled than our rulers, and we, the ruled, I feel curious to see it. Life itself being worth less, all things with it, which minister to it, are worth less. Suppose you have a small library, with pictures to adorn the walls—a garden laid out around—and contemplate scientific and literary pursuits, &c., and discover all at once that your villa, with all its contents, is located in hell, and that the justice of the peace has a cloven foot and a forked tail—do not these things suddenly lose their value in your eyes?

I feel that, to some extent, the State has fatally interfered with my lawful business. It has not only interrupted me in my passage through Court street on errands of trade, but it has interrupted me and every man on his onward and upward path, on which he had trusted soon to leave Court street far behind. What right had it to remind me of Court street? I have found that hollow which even I had relied on for solid.

I am surprised to see men going about their business as if nothing had happened. I say to myself— Unfortunates! they have not heard the news. I am surprised that the man whom I just met on horseback should be so earnest to overtake his newly-bought cows running away—since all property is insecure—and if they do not run away again, they may be taken away from him when he gets them. Fool! does he not know that his seed-corn is worth less this year—that all beneficent harvests fail as you approach the empire of hell? No prudent man will build a stone house under these circumstances, or engage in any peaceful enterprise which it requires a long time to accomplish. Art is as long as ever, but life is more interrupted and less available for a man's proper pur-

suits. It is not an era of repose. We have used up all
our inherited freedom. If we would save our lives, we
must fight for them.

I walk toward one of our ponds, but what signifies
the beauty of nature when men are base? We walk to
lakes to see our serenity reflected in them; when we
are not serene, we go not to them. Who can be serene
in a country where both the rulers and the ruled are
without principle? The remembrance of my country
spoils my walk. My thoughts are murder to the State,
and involuntarily go plotting against her.

But it chanced the other day that I scented a white
water-lily, and a season I had waited for had arrived.
It is the emblem of purity. It bursts up so pure and
fair to the eye, and so sweet to the scent, as if to show
us what purity and sweetness reside in, and can be
extracted from, the slime and muck of earth. I think
I have plucked the first one that has opened for a
mile. What confirmation of our hopes is in the fragrance of this flower! I shall not so soon despair of
the world for it, notwithstanding slavery, and the
cowardice and want of principle of Northern men. It
suggests what kind of laws have prevailed longest
and widest, and still prevail, and that the time may
come when man's deeds will smell as sweet. Such is
the odor which the plant emits. If Nature can compound this fragrance still annually, I shall believe her
still young and full of vigor, her integrity and genius
unimpaired, and that there is virtue even in man, too,
who is fitted to perceive and love it. It reminds me
that Nature has been partner to no Missouri Compromise. I scent no compromise in the fragrance of
the water-lily. It is not a *Nymphœa Douglassii*. In it,
the sweet, and pure, and innocent, are wholly sun-
dered from the obscene and baleful. I do not scent in
this the time-serving irresolution of a Massachusetts

Governor, nor of a Boston Mayor. So behave that the odor of your actions may enhance the general sweetness of the atmosphere, that when we behold or scent a flower, we may not be reminded how inconsistent your deeds are with it; for all odor is but one form of advertisement of a moral quality, and if fair actions had not been performed, the lily would not smell sweet. The foul slime stands for the sloth and vice of man, the decay of humanity; the fragrant flower that springs from it, for the purity and courage which are immortal.

Slavery and servility have produced no sweet-scented flower annually, to charm the senses of men, for they have no real life: they are merely a decaying and a death, offensive to all healthy nostrils. We do not complain that they *live*, but that they do not *get buried*. Let the living bury them; even they are good for manure.

A Plea for Captain John Brown[*]

I TRUST that you will pardon me for being here. I do not wish to force my thoughts upon you, but I feel forced myself. Little as I know of Captain Brown, I would fain do my part to correct the tone and the statements of the newspapers, and of my countrymen generally, respecting his character and actions. It costs us nothing to be just. We can at least express our sympathy with, and admiration of, him and his companions, and that is what I now propose to do.

First, as to his history.

I will endeavor to omit, as much as possible, what you have already read. I need not describe his person to you, for probably most of you have seen and will not soon forget him. I am told that his grandfather, John Brown, was an officer in the Revolution; that he himself was born in Connecticut about the beginning of this century, but early went with his father to Ohio. I heard him say that his father was a contractor who furnished beef to the army there, in the war of 1812; that he accompanied him to the camp, and assisted him in that employment, seeing a good deal of military life, more, perhaps, than if he had been a soldier, for he was often present at the councils of the officers. Especially, he learned by experience how armies are supplied and maintained in the field—a work which, he observed, requires at least as much experience and skill as to lead them in battle. He said that few persons had any conception of the cost, even the pecuniary cost, of firing a single bullet in war. He saw

[*] Read to the citizens of Concord, Mass., Sunday Evening, October 30, 1859. Also as the fifth lecture of the Fraternity Course in Boston, November 1; and at Worcester, November 3.

enough, at any rate, to disgust him with a military life, indeed to excite in him a great abhorrence of it; so much so, that though he was tempted by the offer of some petty office in the army, when he was about eighteen, he not only declined that, but he also refused to train when warned, and was fined for it. He then resolved that he would never have anything to do with any war, unless it were a war for liberty.

When the troubles in Kansas began, he sent several of his sons thither to strengthen the party of the Free State men, fitting them out with such weapons as he had; telling them that if the troubles should increase, and there should be need of him, he would follow to assist them with his hand and counsel. This, as you all know, he soon after did; and it was through his agency, far more than any other's, that Kansas was made free.

For a part of his life he was a surveyor, and at one time he was engaged in wool-growing, and he went to Europe as an agent about that business. There, as every where, he had his eyes about him, and made many original observations. He said, for instance, that he saw why the soil of England was so rich, and that of Germany (I think it was) so poor, and he thought of writing to some of the crowned heads about it. It was because in England the peasantry live on the soil which they cultivate, but in Germany they are gathered into villages, at night. It is a pity that he did not make a book of his observations.

I should say that he was an old-fashioned man in his respect for the Constitution, and his faith in the permanence of this Union. Slavery he deemed to be wholly opposed to these, and he was its determined foe.

He was by descent and birth a New England farmer, a man of great common sense, deliberate and practical as that class is, and tenfold more so. He was like the best of those who stood at Concord Bridge once, on Lexington Common, and on Bunker Hill, only he was firmer and higher principled than any that I have chanced to hear of as there. It was no abolition lecturer that converted him. Ethan Allen and Stark, with whom he may in some respects be compared, were rangers in a lower and less important field. They could bravely face their country's foes, but he had the courage to face his country herself, when she was in the wrong. A Western writer says, to account for his escape from so many perils, that he was concealed under a "rural exterior;" as if, in that prairie land, a hero should, by good rights, wear a citizen's dress only.

He did not go to the college called Harvard, good old Alma Mater as she is. He was not fed on the pap that is there furnished. As he phrased it, "I know no more of grammar than one of your calves." But he went to the great university of the West, where he sedulously pursued the study of Liberty, for which he had early betrayed a fondness, and having taken many degrees, he finally commenced the public practice of Humanity in Kansas, as you all know. Such were *his humanities*, and not any study of grammar. He would have left a Greek accent slanting the wrong way, and righted up a falling man.

He was one of that class of whom we hear a great deal, but, for the most part, see nothing at all—the Puritans. It would be in vain to kill him. He died lately in the time of Cromwell, but he reappeared here. Why should he not? Some of the Puritan stock are said to have come over and settled in New England. They were a class that did something else than celebrate their forefathers' day, and eat parched corn in remembrance of that time. They were neither Democrats nor Republicans, but men of simple habits, straightforward, prayerful; not thinking much of rulers who did not fear God, not making many compromises, nor seeking after available candidates.

"In his camp," as one has recently written, and as I have myself heard him state, "he permitted no profanity; no man of loose morals was suffered to remain there, unless, indeed, as a prisoner of war. 'I would rather,' said he, 'have the small-pox, yellow fever, and cholera, all together in my camp, than a man without principle. . . . It is a mistake, sir, that our people make, when they think that bullies are the best fighters, or that they are the fit men to oppose these Southerners. Give me men of good principles,— God-fearing men,—men who respect themselves, and with a dozen of them I will oppose any hundred such men as these Buford ruffians.' " He said that if one offered himself to be a soldier under him, who was forward to tell what he could or would do, if he could only get sight of the enemy, he had but little confidence in him.

He was never able to find more than a score or so of recruits whom he would accept, and only about a dozen, among them his sons, in whom he had perfect faith. When he was here, some years ago, he showed to a few a little manuscript book,—his "orderly book" I think he called it,—containing the names of his company in Kansas, and the rules by which they bound themselves; and he stated that several of them had already sealed the contract with their blood. When some one remarked that, with the addition of a chaplain, it would have been a perfect Cromwellian troop, he observed that he would have been glad to add a chaplain to the list, if he could have found one who could fill that office worthily. It is easy enough to find one for the United States army. I believe that he had prayers in his camp morning and evening, nevertheless.

He was a man of Spartan habits, and at sixty was scrupulous about his diet at your table, excusing himself by saying that he must eat sparingly and fare hard, as became a soldier or one who was fitting himself for difficult enterprises, a life of exposure.

A man of rare common sense and directness of speech, as of action; a transcendentalist above all, a man of ideas and principles,—that was what distinguished him. Not yielding to a whim or transient impulse, but carrying out the purpose of a life. I noticed that he did not overstate any thing, but spoke within bounds. I remember, particularly, how, in his speech here, he referred to what his family had suffered in Kansas, without ever giving the least vent to his pent-up fire. It was a volcano with an ordinary chimney-flue. Also referring to the deeds of certain Border Ruffians, he said, rapidly paring away his speech, like an experienced soldier, keeping a reserve of force and meaning, "They had a perfect right to be hung." He was not in the least a rhetorician, was not talking to Buncombe or his constituents any where, had no need to invent any thing, but to tell the simple truth, and communicate his own resolution; therefore he appeared incomparably strong, and eloquence in Congress and elsewhere seemed to me at a discount. It was like the speeches of Cromwell compared with those of an ordinary king.

As for his tact and prudence, I will merely say, that at a time when scarcely a man from the Free States was able to reach Kansas by any direct route, at least without having his arms taken from him, he, carrying what imperfect guns and other weapons he could collect, openly and slowly drove an ox-cart through Missouri, apparently in the capacity of a surveyor, with his surveying compass exposed in it, and so passed unsuspected, and had ample opportunity to learn the designs of the enemy. For some time after his arrival he still followed the same profession. When, for instance, he saw a knot of the ruffians on the prairie, discussing, of course, the single topic which then occupied their minds, he would, perhaps, take his compass and one of his sons, and proceed to run an imaginary line right through the very spot on which that conclave had assembled, and when he came up to them, he would naturally pause and have some talk with them, learning their news, and, at last, all their plans perfectly; and having thus completed his real survey, he would resume his imaginary one, and run on his line till he was out of sight.

When I expressed surprise that he could live in Kansas at all, with a price set upon his head, and so large a number, including the authorities, exasperated against him, he accounted for it by saying, "It is perfectly well understood that I will not be taken." Much of the time for some years he has had to skulk in swamps, suffering from poverty and from sickness, which was the consequence of exposure, befriended only by Indians and a few whites. But though it might be known that he was lurking in a particular swamp, his foes commonly did not care to go in after him. He could even come out into a town where there were more Border Ruffians than Free State men, and transact some business, without delaying long, and yet not be molested; for said he, "No little handful of men were willing to undertake it, and a large body could not be got together in season."

As for his recent failure, we do not know the facts about it. It was evidently far from being a wild and desperate attempt. His enemy, Mr. Vallandigham, is compelled to say, tht t "it was among the best planned and executed conspiracies that ever failed."

Not to mention his other successes, was it a failure, or did it show a want of good management, to deliver from bondage a dozen human beings, and walk off with them by broad daylight, for weeks if not months, at a leisurely pace, through one State after another, for half the length of the North, conspicuous to all parties, with a price set upon his head, going into a court room on his way and telling what he had done, thus convincing Missouri that it was not profitable to try to hold slaves in his neighborhood?—and this, not because the government menials were lenient, but because they were afraid of him.

Yet he did not attribute his success, foolishly, to "his star," or to any magic. He said, truly, that the reason why such greatly superior numbers quailed before him, was, as one of his prisoners confessed, because they *lacked a cause*—a kind of armor which he and his party never lacked. When the time came, few men were found willing to lay down their lives in defence of what they knew to be wrong; they did not like that this should be their last act in this world.

But to make haste to *his* last act, and its effects.

The newspapers seem to ignore, or perhaps are really ignorant of the fact, that there are at least as many as two or three individuals to a town throughout the North, who think much as the present speaker does about him and his enterprise. I do not hesitate to say that they are an important and growing party. We aspire to be something more than stupid and timid chattels, pretending to read history and our bibles, but desecrating every house and every day we breathe in. Perhaps anxious politicians may prove that only seventeen white men and five negroes were concerned in the late enterprise, but their very anxiety to prove this might suggest to themselves that all is not told. Why do they still dodge the truth? They are so anxious because of a dim consciousness of the fact, which they do not distinctly face, that at least a million of the free inhabitants of the United States would have rejoiced if it had succeeded. They at most only criticise the tactics. Though we wear no crape, the thought of that man's position and probable fate is spoiling many a man's day here at the North for other thinking. If any one who has seen him here can pursue successfully any other train of thought, I do not know what he is made of. If there is any such who gets his usual allowance of sleep, I will warrant him to fatten easily under any circumstances which do not touch his body or purse. I put a piece of paper and a pencil under my pillow, and when I could not sleep, I wrote in the dark.

On the whole, my respect for my fellow-men, except as one may outweigh a million, is not being increased these days. I have noticed the cold-blooded way in which newspaper writers and men generally speak of this event, as if an ordinary malefactor, though one of unusual "pluck,"—as the Governor of Virginia is reported to have said, using the language of the cock-pit, "the gamest man he ever saw,"—had been caught, and were about to be hung. He was not dreaming of his foes when the governor thought he looked so brave. It turns what sweetness I have to gall, to hear, or hear of, the remarks of some of my neighbors. When we heard at first that he was dead, one of my townsmen observed that "he died as the fool dieth;" which, pardon me, for an instant suggested a likeness in him dying to my neighbor living. Others, craven-hearted, said disparagingly, that "he threw his life away," because he resisted the government. Which way have they thrown *their* lives, pray? —Such as would praise a man for attacking singly an ordinary band of thieves or murderers. I hear another ask, Yankee-like, "What will he gain by it?" as if he expected to fill his pockets by this enterprise. Such a one has no idea of gain but in this worldly sense. If it does not lead to a "surprise" party, if he does not get a new pair of boots, or a vote of thanks, it must be a failure. "But he won't gain any thing by it." Well, no, I don't suppose he could get four-and-sixpence a day for being hung, take the year round; but then he stands a chance to save a considerable part of his soul—and *such* a soul!—when *you* do not. No doubt you can get more in your market for a quart of milk than for a quart of blood, but that is not the market that heroes carry their blood to.

Such do not know that like the seed is the fruit, and that, in the moral world, when good seed is planted, good fruit is inevitable, and does not depend on our watering and cultivating; that when you plant, or bury, a hero in his field, a crop of heroes is sure to spring up. This is a seed of such force and vitality, that it does not ask our leave to germinate.

The momentary charge at Balaclava, in obedience to a blundering command, proving what a perfect machine the soldier is, has, properly enough, been celebrated by a poet laureate; but the steady, and for the most part successful charge of this man, for some years, against the legions of Slavery, in obedience to an infinitely higher command, is as much more memorable than that, as an intelligent and conscientious man is superior to a machine. Do you think that that will go unsung?

"Served him right"—"A dangerous man"—"He is undoubtedly insane." So they proceed to live their sane, and wise, and altogether admirable lives, reading

their Plutarch a little, but chiefly pausing at that feat
of Putnam, who was let down into a wolf's den; and
in this wise they nourish themselves for brave and
patriotic deeds some time or other. The Tract Society could afford to print that story of Putnam. You
might open the district schools with the reading of it,
for there is nothing about Slavery or the Church in it;
unless it occurs to the reader that some pastors are
wolves in sheep's clothing. "The American Board of
Commissioners for Foreign Missions" even, might
dare to protest against *that* wolf. I have heard of
boards, and of American boards, but it chances that I
never heard of this particular lumber till lately. And
yet I hear of Northern men, women, and children,
by families, buying a "life membership" in such societies as these;—a life-membership in the grave! You
can get buried cheaper than that.

Our foes are in our midst and all about us. There is
hardly a house but is divided against itself, for our
foe is the all but universal woodenness of both head
and heart, the want of vitality in man, which is the
effect of our vice; and hence are begotten fear, superstition, bigotry, persecution, and slavery of all kinds.
We are mere figure-heads upon a hulk, with livers in
the place of hearts. The curse is the worship of idols,
which at length changes the worshipper into a stone
image himself; and the New Englander is just as
much an idolater as the Hindoo. This man was an
exception, for he did not set up even a political graven
image between him and his God.

A church that can never have done with excom-
municating Christ while it exists! Away with your
broad and flat churches, and your narrow and tall
churches! Take a step forward, and invent a new
style of out-houses. Invent a salt that will save you,
and defend our nostrils.

The modern Christian is a man who has consented to say all the prayers in the liturgy, provided you will let him go straight to bed and sleep quietly afterward. All his prayers begin with "Now I lay me down to sleep," and he is forever looking forward to the time when he shall go to his "*long* rest." He has consented to perform certain old established charities, too, after a fashion, but he does not wish to hear of any new-fangled ones; he doesn't wish to have any supplementary articles added to the contract, to fit it to the present time. He shows the whites of his eyes on the Sabbath, and the blacks all the rest of the week. The evil is not merely a stagnation of blood, but a stagnation of spirit. Many, no doubt, are well disposed, but sluggish by constitution and by habit, and they cannot conceive of a man who is actuated by higher motives than they are. Accordingly they pronounce this man insane, for they know that *they* could never act as he does, as long as they are themselves.

We dream of foreign countries, of other times and races of men, placing them at a distance in history or space; but let some significant event like the present occur in our midst, and we discover, often, this distance and this strangeness between us and our nearest neighbors. *They* are our Austrias, and Chinas, and South Sea Islands. Our crowded society becomes well spaced all at once, clean and handsome to the eye, a city of magnificent distances. We discover why it was that we never got beyond compliments and surfaces with them before; we become aware of as many versts between us and them as there are between a wandering Tartar and a Chinese town. The thoughtful man becomes a hermit in the thoroughfares of the market-place. Impassable seas suddenly find their level between us, or dumb steppes stretch themselves out there. It is the difference of constitution, of intelligence, and faith, and not streams and mountains, that make the true and impassable boundaries between individuals and between states. None but the like-minded can come plenipotentiary to our court.

I read all the newspapers I could get within a week after this event, and I do not remember in them a single expression of sympathy for these men. I have since seen one noble statement, in a Boston paper, not editorial. Some voluminous sheets decided not to print the full report of Brown's words to the exclusion of other matter. It was as if a publisher should reject the manuscript of the New Testament, and print Wilson's last speech. The same journal which contained this pregnant news, was chiefly filled, in parallel columns, with the reports of the political conventions that were being held. But the descent to them was too steep. They should have been spared this contrast, been printed in an extra at least. To turn from the voices and deeds of earnest men to the *cackling* of political conventions! Office seekers and speechmakers, who do not so much as lay an honest egg, but wear their breasts bare upon an egg of chalk! Their great game is the game of straws, or rather that universal aboriginal game of the platter, at which the Indians cried *hub, bub!* Exclude the reports of religious and political conventions, and publish the words of a living man.

But I object not so much to what they have omitted as to what they have inserted. Even the *Liberator* called it "a misguided, wild, and apparently insane . . . effort." As for the herd of newspapers and magazines, I do not chance to know an editor in the country who will deliberately print anything which he knows will ultimately and permanently reduce the number of his subscribers. They do not believe that it would be expedient. How then can they print truth? If we do not say pleasant things, they argue, nobody will attend to us. And so they do like some travelling auctioneers, who sing an obscene song in order to draw a crowd around them. Republican editors, obliged to get their sentences ready for the morning edition, and accustomed to look at every thing by the twilight of politics, express no admiration, nor true sorrow even, but call these men "deluded fanatics"– "mistaken men"–"insane," or "crazed." It suggests what a *sane* set of editors we are blessed with, *not* "mistaken men"; who know very well on which side their bread is buttered, at least.

A man does a brave and humane deed, and at once, on all sides, we hear people and parties declaring, "I didn't do it, nor countenance *him* to do it, in any conceivable way. It can't be fairly inferred from my past career." I, for one, am not interested to hear you define your position. I don't know that I ever was, or ever shall be. I think it is mere egotism, or impertinent at this time. Ye needn't take so much pains to wash your skirts of him. No intelligent man will ever be convinced that he was any creature of yours. He went and came, as he himself informs us, "under the auspices of John Brown and nobody else." The Republican party does not perceive how many his *failure* will make to vote more correctly than they would have them. They have counted the votes of Pennsylvania &. Co., but they have not correctly counted Captain Brown's vote. He has taken the wind out of their sails, the little wind they had, and they may as well lie to and repair.

What though he did not belong to your clique! Though you may not approve of his method or his principles, recognize his magnanimity. Would you not like to claim kindredship with him in that, though in no other thing he is like, or likely, to you? Do you think that you would lose your reputation so? What you lost at the spile, you would gain at the bung.

If they do not mean all this, then they do not speak the truth, and say what they mean. They are simply at their old tricks still.

"It was always conceded to him," *says one who calls him crazy*, "that he was a conscientious man, very modest in his demeanor, apparently inoffensive, until the subject of Slavery was introduced, when he would exhibit a feeling of indignation unparalleled."

The slave-ship is on her way, crowded with its dying victims; new cargoes are being added in mid ocean; a small crew of slaveholders, countenanced by a large body of passengers, is smothering four millions under the hatches, and yet the politician asserts that the only proper way by which deliverance is to be obtained, is by "the quiet diffusion of the sentiments of humanity," without any "outbreak." As if the sentiments of humanity were ever found unaccompanied by its deeds, and you could disperse them, all finished to order, the pure article, as easily as water with a watering-pot, and so lay the dust. What is that that I hear cast overboard? The bodies of the dead that have found deliverance. That is the way we are "diffusing" humanity, and its sentiments with it.

Prominent and influential editors, accustomed to deal with politicians, men of an infinitely lower grade, say, in their ignorance, that he acted "on the principle of revenge." They do not know the man. They must enlarge themselves to conceive of him. I have no doubt that the time will come when they will begin to see him as he was. They have got to conceive of a man of faith and of religious principle, and not a politician or an Indian; of a man who did not wait till he was personally interfered with, or thwarted in some harmless business, before he gave his life to the cause of the oppressed.

If Walker may be considered the representative of the South, I wish I could say that Brown was the representative of the North. He was a superior man. He did not value his bodily life in comparison with ideal things. He did not recognize unjust human laws, but resisted them as he was bid. For once we are lifted out of the trivialness and dust of politics into the region of truth and manhood. No man in America has ever stood up so persistently and effectively for the dignity of human nature, knowing himself for a man, and the equal of any and all governments. In that sense he was the most American of us all. He needed no babbling lawyer, making false issues, to defend him. He was more than a match for all the judges that American voters, or office-holders of whatever grade, can create. He could not have been tried by a jury of his peers, because his peers did not exist. When a man stands up serenely against the condemnation and vengeance of mankind, rising above them literally *by a whole body*,—even though he were of late the vilest murderer, who has settled that matter with himself,—the spectacle is a sublime one,—didn't ye know it, ye Liberators, ye Tribunes, ye Republicans?—and we become criminal in comparison. Do yourselves the honor to recognize him. He needs none of your respect.

As for the Democratic journals, they are not human enough to affect me at all. I do not feel indignation at any thing they may say.

I am aware that I anticipate a little, that he was still, at the last accounts, alive in the hands of his foes; but that being the case, I have all along found myself thinking and speaking of him as physically dead.

I do not believe in erecting statues to those who still live in our hearts, whose bones have not yet crumbled in the earth around us, but I would rather see the statue of Captain Brown in the Massachusetts State-House yard, than that of any other man whom I know. I rejoice that I live in this age—that I am his contemporary.

What a contrast, when we turn to that political party which is so anxiously shuffling him and his plot out of its way, and looking around for some available slaveholder, perhaps, to be its candidate, at least for one who will execute the Fugitive Slave Law, and all those other unjust laws which he took up arms to annul!

Insane! A father and six sons, and one son-in-law, and several more men besides,—as many at least as twelve disciples,—all struck with insanity at once; while the sane tyrant holds with a firmer gripe than ever his four millions of slaves, and a thousand sane editors, his abettors, are saving their country and their bacon! Just as insane were his efforts in Kansas. Ask the tyrant who is his most dangerous foe, the sane man or the insane. Do the thousands who know him best, who have rejoiced at his deeds in Kansas, and have afforded him material aid there, think him insane? Such a use of this word is a mere trope with most who persist in using it, and I have no doubt that many of the rest have already in silence retracted their words.

Read his admirable answers to Mason and others. How they are dwarfed and defeated by the contrast! On the one side, half brutish, half timid questioning; on the other, truth, clear as lightning, crashing into their obscene temples. They are made to stand with Pilate, and Gessler, and the Inquisition. How ineffectual their speech and action! and what a void their silence! They are but helpless tools in this great work. It was no human power that gathered them about this preacher.

What have Massachusetts and the North sent a few *sane* representatives to Congress for, of late years?— to declare with effect what kind of sentiments? All their speeches put together and boiled down,—and probably they themselves will confess it,—do not match for manly directness and force, and for simple truth, the few casual remarks of crazy John Brown, on the floor of the Harper's Ferry engine house;— that man whom you are about to hang, to send to the other world, though not to represent *you* there. No, he was not our representative in any sense. He was too fair a specimen of a man to represent the like of us. Who, then, *were* his constituents? If you read his words understandingly you will find out. In his case there is no idle eloquence, no made, nor maiden speech, no compliments to the oppressor. Truth is his inspirer, and earnestness the polisher of his sentences. He could afford to lose his Sharps' rifles, while he retained his faculty of speech, a Sharps' rifle of infinitely surer and longer range.

And the *New York Herald* reports the conversation "*verbatim*"! It does not know of what undying words it is made the vehicle.

I have no respect for the penetration of any man who can read the report of that conversation, and still call the principal in it insane. It has the ring of a saner sanity than an ordinary discipline and habits of life, than an ordinary organization, secure. Take any sentence of it—"Any questions that I can honorably answer, I will; not otherwise. So far as I am myself concerned, I have told every thing truthfully. I value my word, sir." The few who talk about his vindictive spirit, while they really admire his heroism, have no test by which to detect a noble man, no amalgam to combine with his pure gold. They mix their own dross with it.

It is a relief to turn from these slanders to the testimony of his more truthful, but frightened, jailers and hangmen. Governor Wise speaks far more justly and appreciatingly of him than any Northern editor, or politician, or public personage, that I chance to have heard from. I know that you can afford to hear him again on this subject. He says: "They are themselves mistaken who take him to be a madman. . . . He is cool, collected, and indomitable, and it is but just to him to say, that he was humane to his prisoners. . . . And he inspired me with great trust in his integrity as a man of truth. He is a fanatic, vain and garrulous," (I leave that part to Mr. Wise) "but firm, truthful, and intelligent. His men, too, who survive, are like him. . . . Colonel Washington says that he was the coolest and firmest man he ever saw in defying danger and death. With one son dead by his side, and another shot through, he felt the pulse of his dying son with one hand, and held his rifle with the other, and commanded his men with the utmost composure, encouraging them to be firm, and to sell their lives as dear as they could. Of the three white prisoners, Brown, Stevens, and Coppoc, it was hard to say which was most firm. . . ."

Almost the first Northern men whom the slaveholder has learned to respect!

The testimony of Mr. Vallandigham, though less valuable, is of the same purport, that "it is vain to underrate either the man or his conspiracy. . . . He is the farthest possible remove from the ordinary ruffian, fanatic, or madman."

"All is quiet at Harper's Ferry," say the journals. What is the character of that calm which follows when the law and the slaveholder prevail? I regard this event as a touchstone designed to bring out, with glaring distinctness, the character of this government. We needed to be thus assisted to see it by the light of history. It needed to see itself. When a government puts forth its strength on the side of injustice, as ours to maintain Slavery and kill the liberators of the slave, it reveals itself a merely brute force, or worse, a demoniacal force. It is the head of the Plug Uglies. It is more manifest than ever that tyranny rules. I see this government to be effectually allied with France and Austria in oppressing mankind. There sits a tyrant holding fettered four millions of slaves; here comes their heroic liberator. This most hypocritical and diabolical government looks up from its seat on the gasping four millions, and inquires with an assumption of innocence, "What do you assault me for? Am I not an honest man? Cease agitation on this subject, or I will make a slave of you, too, or else hang you."

We talk about a *representative* government; but what a monster of a government is that where the noblest faculties of the mind, and the *whole* heart, are not *represented*. A semi-human tiger or ox, stalking over the earth, with its heart taken out and the top of its brain shot away. Heroes have fought well on their stumps when their legs were shot off, but I never heard of any good done by such a government as that.

The only government that I recognize,—and it matters not how few are at the head of it, or how small its army,—is that power that establishes justice in the land, never that which establishes injustice. What shall we think of a government to which all the truly brave and just men in the land are enemies, standing between it and those whom it oppresses? A government that pretends to be Christian and crucifies a million Christs every day!

Treason! Where does such treason take its rise? I cannot help thinking of you as you deserve, ye governments. Can you dry up the fountains of thought? High treason, when it is resistance to tyranny here below, has its origin in, and is first committed by the power that makes and forever recreates man. When you have caught and hung all these human rebels, you have accomplished nothing but your own guilt, for you have not struck at the fountain head. You presume to contend with a foe against whom West Point cadets and rifled cannon *point* not. Can all the art of the cannon-founder tempt matter to turn against its maker? Is the form in which the founder thinks he casts it more essential than the constitution of it and of himself?

The United States have a coffle of four millions of slaves. They are determined to keep them in this condition; and Massachusetts is one of the confederated overseers to prevent their escape. Such are not all the inhabitants of Massachusetts, but such are they who rule and are obeyed here. It was Massachusetts, as well as Virginia, that put down this insurrection at Harper's Ferry. She sent the marines there, and she will have to pay the penalty of her sin.

Suppose that there is a society in this State that out of its own purse and magnanimity saves all the fugitive slaves that run to us, and protects our colored fellow-citizens, and leaves the other work to the Government, so-called. Is not that government fast losing its occupation, and becoming contemptible to mankind? If private men are obliged to perform the offices of government, to protect the weak and dispense justice, then the government becomes only a hired man, or clerk, to perform menial or indifferent services. Of course, that is but the shadow of a government whose existence necessitates a Vigilant Committee. What should we think of the oriental Cadi even, behind whom worked in secret a Vigilant Committee? But such is the character of our Northern States generally; each has its Vigilant Committee. And, to a certain extent, these crazy governments recognize and accept this relation. They say, virtually, "We'll be glad to work for you on these terms, only don't make a noise about it." And thus the government, its salary being insured, withdraws into the back shop, taking the constitution with it, and bestows most of its labor on repairing that. When I hear it at work sometimes, as I go by, it reminds me, at best, of those farmers who in winter contrive to turn a penny by following the coopering business. And what kind of spirit is their barrel made to hold? They speculate in stocks, and bore holes in mountains, but they are not competent to lay out even a decent highway. The only *free* road, the Underground Railroad, is owned and managed by the Vigilant Committee. *They* have tunnelled under the whole breadth of the land. Such a government is losing its power and respectability as surely as water runs out of a leaky vessel, and is held by one that can contain it.

I hear many condemn these men because they were so few. When were the good and the brave ever in a majority? Would you have had him wait till that time came?—till you and I came over to him? The very fact that he had no rabble or troop of hirelings about him would alone distinguish him from ordinary heroes. His company was small indeed, because few could be found worthy to pass muster. Each one who there laid down his life for the poor and oppressed, was a picked man, called out of many thousands, if not

millions; apparently a man of principle, of rare courage and devoted humanity, ready to sacrifice his life at
any moment for the benefit of his fellow man. It may
be doubted if there were as many more their equals
in these respects in all the country—I speak of his
followers only—for their leader, no doubt, scoured the
land far and wide, seeking to swell his troop. These
alone were ready to step between the oppressor and
the oppressed. Surely, they were the very best men
you could select to be hung. That was the greatest
compliment which this country could pay them. They
were ripe for her gallows. She has tried a long time,
she has hung a good many, but never found the
right one before.

When I think of him, and his six sons, and his
son in law,—not to enumerate the others,—enlisted for
this fight; proceeding coolly, reverently, humanely to
work, for months if not years, sleeping and waking
upon it, summering and wintering the thought, without expecting any reward but a good conscience,
while almost all America stood ranked on the other
side, I say again that it affects me as a sublime spectacle. If he had had any journal advocating *"his
cause,"* any organ as the phrase is, monotonously and
wearisomely playing the same old tune, and then
passing round the hat, it would have been fatal to
his efficiency. If he had acted in any way so as to be
let alone by the government, he might have been
suspected. It was the fact that the tyrant must give
place to him, or he to the tyrant, that distinguished
him from all the reformers of the day that I know.

It was his peculiar doctrine that a man has a perfect right to interfere by force with the slaveholder, in
order to rescue the slave. I agree with him. They who
are continually shocked by slavery have some right to
be shocked by the violent death of the slaveholder,

but no others. Such will be more shocked by his life than by his death. I shall not be forward to think him mistaken in his method who quickest succeeds to liberate the slave. I speak for the slave when I say, that I prefer the philanthropy of Captain Brown to that philanthropy which neither shoots me nor liberates me. At any rate, I do not think it is quite sane for one to spend his whole life in talking or writing about this matter, unless he is continuously inspired, and I have not done so. A man may have other affairs to attend to. I do not wish to kill nor to be killed, but I can foresee circumstances in which both these things would be by me unavoidable. We preserve the so-called "peace" of our community by deeds of petty violence every day. Look at the policeman's billy and hand cuffs! Look at the jail! Look at the gallows! Look at the chaplain of the regiment! We are hoping only to live safely on the outskirts of *this* provisional army. So we defend ourselves and our hen roosts, and maintain slavery. I know that the mass of my countrymen think that the only righteous use that can be made of Sharps' rifles and revolvers is to fight duels with them, when we are insulted by other nations, or to hunt Indians, or shoot fugitive slaves with them, or the like. I think that for once the Sharps' rifles and the revolvers were employed in a righteous cause. The tools were in the hands of one who could use them.

The same indignation that is said to have cleared the temple once will clear it again. The question is not about the weapon, but the spirit in which you use it. No man has appeared in America as yet who loved his fellow man so well, and treated him so tenderly. He lived for him. He took up his life and he laid it down for him. What sort of violence is that which is encouraged, not by soldiers but by peaceable citizens, not so much by lay-men as by ministers of the gospel, not so much by the fighting sects as by the Quakers, and not so much by Quaker men as by Quaker women?

This event advertises me that there is such a fact as death—the possibility of a man's dying. It seems as if no man had ever died in America before, for in order to die you must first have lived. I dont believe in the hearses and palls and funerals that they have had. There was no death in the case, because there had been no life; they merely rotted or sloughed off, pretty much as they had rotted or sloughed along. No temple's vail was rent, only a hole dug somewhere. Let the dead bury their dead. The best of them fairly ran down like a clock. Franklin—Washington—they were let off without dying; they were merely missing one day. I hear a good many pretend that they are going to die;—or that they have died for aught that I know. Nonsense! I'll defy them to do it. They haven't got life enough in them. They'll deliquesce like fungi, and keep a hundred eulogists mopping the spot where they left off. Only half a dozen or so have died since the world began. Do you think that you are going to die, sir? No! there's no hope of you. You haven't got your lesson yet. You've got to stay after school. We make a needless ado about capital punishment—taking lives, when there is no life to take. *Memento mori!* We don't understand that sublime sentence which some worthy got sculptured on his gravestone once. We've interpreted it in a grovelling and snivelling sense; we've wholly forgotten how to die.

But be sure you do die, nevertheless. Do your work, and finish it. If you know how to begin, you will know when to end.

These men, in teaching us how to die, have at the same time taught us how to live. If this man's acts and words do not create a revival, it will be the severest possible satire on the acts and words that do. It is the best news that America has ever heard. It has already quickened the feeble pulse of the North, and infused more and more generous blood into her veins and heart, than any number of years of what is called commercial and political prosperity could. How many a man who was lately contemplating suicide has now something to live for!

One writer says that Brown's peculiar monomania made him to be "dreaded by the Missourians as a supernatural being." Sure enough, a hero in the midst of us cowards is always so dreaded. He is just that thing. He shows himself superior to nature. He has a spark of divinity in him.

> "Unless above himself he can
> Erect himself, how poor a thing is man!"

Newspaper editors argue also that it is a proof of his *insanity* that he thought he was appointed to do this work which he did—that he did not suspect himself for a moment! They talk as if it were impossible that a man could be "divinely appointed" in these days to do any work whatever; as if vows and religion were out of date as connected with any man's daily work,—as if the agent to abolish Slavery could only be somebody appointed by the President, or by some political party. They talk as if a man's death were a failure, and his continued life, be it of whatever character, were a success.

When I reflect to what a cause this man devoted himself, and how religiously, and then reflect to what cause his judges and all who condemn him so angrily and fluently devote themselves, I see that they are as far apart as the heavens and earth are asunder.

The amount of it is, our *"leading men"* are a harmless kind of folk, and they know *well enough* that *they* were not divinely appointed, but elected by the votes of their party.

Who is it whose safety requires that Captain Brown be hung? Is it indispensable to any Northern man? Is there no resource but to cast these men also to the Minotaur? If you do not wish it say so distinctly. While these things are being done, beauty stands veiled and music is a screeching lie. Think of him— of his rare qualities! such a man as it takes ages to make, and ages to understand; no mock hero, nor the representative of any party. A man such as the sun may not rise upon again in this benighted land. To whose making went the costliest material, the finest adamant; sent to be the redeemer of those in captivity. And the only use to which you can put him is to hang him at the end of a rope! You who pretend to care for Christ crucified, consider what you are about to do to him who offered himself to be the savior of four millions of men.

Any man knows when he is justified, and all the wits in the world cannot enlighten him on that point. The murderer always knows that he is justly punished; but when a government takes the life of a man without the consent of his conscience, it is an audacious government, and is taking a step towards its own dissolution. Is it not possible that an individual may be right and a government wrong? Are laws to be enforced simply because they were made? or declared by any number of men to be good, if they are *not* good? Is there any necessity for a man's being a tool to perform a deed of which his better nature disapproves? Is it the intention of law-makers that *good* men shall be hung ever? Are judges to interpret the law according to the letter, and not the spirit? What right have *you* to enter into a compact with yourself that you *will* do thus or so, against the light within you? Is it for *you* to *make up* your mind—to form any resolution whatever—and not accept the convictions that are forced upon you, and which ever pass your understanding? I do not believe in lawyers, in that mode of attacking or defending a man, because you descend to meet the judge on his own ground, and, in cases of the highest importance, it is of no consequence whether a man breaks a human law or not. Let lawyers decide trivial cases. Business men may arrange that among themselves. If they were the interpreters of the everlasting laws which rightfully bind man, that would be another thing. A counterfeiting law-factory, standing half in a slave land and half in a free! What kind of laws for free men can you expect from that?

I am here to plead his cause with you. I plead not for his life, but for his character—his immortal life; and so it becomes your cause wholly, and is not his in the least. Some eighteen hundred years ago Christ was crucified; this morning, perchance, Captain Brown was hung. These are the two ends of a chain which is not without its links. He is not Old Brown any longer; he is an Angel of Light.

I see now that it was necessary that the bravest and humanest man in all the country should be hung. Perhaps he saw it himself. I *almost fear* that I may yet hear of his deliverance, doubting if a prolonged life, if *any* life, can do as much good as his death.

"Misguided"! "Garrulous"! "Insane"! "Vindictive"! So ye write in your easy chairs, and thus he wounded responds from the floor of the Armory, clear as a cloudless sky, true as the voice of nature is: "No man sent me here; it was my own prompting and that of my Maker. I acknowledge no master in human form."

And in what a sweet and noble strain he proceeds, addressing his captors, who stand over him: "I think, my friends, you are guilty of a great wrong against God and humanity, and it would be perfectly right for any one to interfere with you so far as to free those you wilfully and wickedly hold in bondage."

And referring to his movement: "It is, in my opinion, the greatest service a man can render to God."

"I pity the poor in bondage that have none to help them; that is why I am here; not to gratify any personal animosity, revenge, or vindictive spirit. It is my sympathy with the oppressed and the wronged, that are as good as you, and as precious in the sight of God."

You don't know your testament when you see it.

"I want you to understand that I respect the rights of the poorest and weakest of colored people, oppressed by the slave power, just as much as I do those of the most wealthy and powerful."

"I wish to say, furthermore, that you had better, all you people at the South, prepare yourselves for a settlement of that question, that must come up for settlement sooner than you are prepared for it. The sooner you are prepared the better. You may dispose of me very easily. I am nearly disposed of now; but this question is still to be settled—this negro question, I mean; the end of that is not yet."

I foresee the time when the painter will paint that scene, no longer going to Rome for a subject; the poet will sing it; the historian record it; and, with the Landing of the Pilgrims and the Declaration of Independence, it will be the ornament of some future national gallery, when at least the present form of Slavery shall be no more here. We shall then be at liberty to weep for Captain Brown. Then, and not till then, we will take our revenge.

Martyrdom of John Brown

So universal and widely related is any transcendent moral greatness—so nearly identical with greatness every where and in every age, as a pyramid contracts the nearer you approach its apex—that, when I now look over my commonplace book of poetry, I find that the best of it is oftenest applicable, in part or wholly, to the case of Captain Brown. Only what is true, and strong, and solemnly earnest will recommend itself to our mood at this time. Almost any noble verse may be read, either as his elegy, or eulogy, or be made the text of an oration on him. Indeed, such are now discerned to be the parts of a universal liturgy, applicable to those rare cases of heroes and martyrs, for which the ritual of no church has provided. This is the formula established on high, —their burial service—to which every great genius has contributed its stanza or line. As Marvell wrote,

> "When the sword glitters o'er the judge's head,
> And fear has coward churchmen silenced,
> Then is the poet's time; 'tis then he draws,
> And single fights forsaken virtue's cause.
> He when the wheel of empire whirleth back,
> And though the world's disjointed axel crack,
> Sings still of ancient rights and better times,
> Seeks suff'ring good, arraigns successful crimes."

The sense of grand poetry, read by the light of this event, is brought out distinctly, like an invisible writing held to the fire.

> "All heads must come
> To the cold tomb,
> Only the actions of the just
> Smell sweet and blossom in the dust."

We have heard that the Boston lady who recently visited our hero in prison found him wearing still the clothes all cut and torn by sabres and by bayonet thrusts, in which he had been taken prisoner; and thus he had gone to his trial, and without a hat. She spent her time in the prison mending those clothes, and, for a memento, brought home a pin covered with blood.—What are the clothes that endure?

> "The garments lasting evermore
>   Are works of mercy to the poor;
>   And neither tetter, time, nor moth
>   Shall fray that silk, or fret this cloth."

The well known verses called "The Soul's Errand," supposed, by some, to have been written by Sir Walter Raleigh, when he was expecting to be executed the following day, are at least worthy of such an origin, and are equally applicable to the present case. Hear them.

> Go, Soul, the body's guest,
>   Upon a thankless arrant;
> Fear not to touch the best,
>   The truth shall be thy warrant:
>   Go, since I needs must die,
>   And give the world the lie.
>
> Go, tell the court it glows
>   And shines like rotten wood;
> Go, tell the church it shows
>   What's good, and doth no good;
>   If church and court reply,
>   Then give them both the lie.
>
> Tell potentates they live
>   Acting by others' actions;
> Not loved unless they give,
>   Not strong but by their factions:
>   If potentates reply,
>   Give potentates the lie.

Tell men of high condition,
   That rule affairs of state,
Their purpose is ambition,
   Their practice only hate;
      And if they once reply,
      Then give them all the lie.

Tell zeal, it lacks devotion;
   Tell love, it is but lust;
Tell time, it is but motion;
   Tell flesh, it is but dust;
      And wish them not reply,
      For thou must give the lie.

Tell age, it daily wasteth;
   Tell honor, how it alters;
Tell beauty, how she blasteth;
   Tell favor, how she falters;
      And as they shall reply,
      Give each of them the lie.

Tell fortune of her blindness;
   Tell nature of decay;
Tell friendship of unkindness;
   Tell justice of delay;
      And if they dare reply,
      Then give them all the lie.

And when thou hast, as I
   Commanded thee, done blabbing,
Although to give the lie
   Deserves no less than stabbing,
      Yet stab at thee who will,
      No stab the soul can kill.

   "When I am dead,
      Let not the day be writ—"
   *Nor bell be tolled—**
         "Love will remember it"
   When hate is cold.

* The selectmen of the town refused to allow the bell to be
tolled on this occasion.

You, Agricola, are fortunate, not only because your life was glorious, but because your death was timely. As they tell us who heard your last words, unchanged and willing you accepted your fate; as if, as far as in your power, you would make the emperor appear innocent. But, besides the bitterness of having lost a parent, it adds to our grief, that it was not permitted us to minister to your health, . . . to gaze on your countenance, and receive your last embrace; surely, we might have caught some words and commands which we could have treasured in the inmost part of our souls. This is our pain, this our wound. . . . You were buried with the fewer tears, and in your last earthly light, your eyes looked around for something which they did not see.

If there is any abode for the spirits of the pious; if, as wise men suppose, great souls are not extinguished with the body, may you rest placidly, and call your family from weak regrets, and womanly laments, to the contemplation of your virtues, which must not be lamented, either silently or aloud. Let us honor you by our admiration, rather than by short-lived praises, and, if nature aid us, by our emulation of you. That is true honor, that the piety of whoever is most akin to you. This also I would teach your family, so to venerate your memory, as to call to mind all your actions and words, and embrace your character and the form of your soul, rather than of your body; not because I think that statues which are made of marble or brass are to be condemned, but as the features of men, so images of the features, are frail and perishable. The form of the soul is eternal; and this we can retain and express, not by a foreign material and art, but by our own lives. Whatever of Agricola we have loved, whatever we have admired, remains, and will remain, in the minds of men, and the records of history, through the eternity of ages. For oblivion will overtake many of the ancients, as if they were inglorious and ignoble: Agricola, described and transmitted to posterity, will survive.[1]

[1] Translated by Thoreau from Tacitus [editor's note].

The Last Days of John Brown

JOHN Brown's career for the last six weeks of his life was meteor-like, flashing through the darkness in which we live. I know of nothing so miraculous in our history.

If any person, in a lecture or conversation at that time, cited any ancient example of heroism, such as Cato or Tell or Winkelried, passing over the recent deeds and words of Brown, it was felt by any intelligent audience of Northern men to be tame and inexcusably far-fetched.

For my own part, I commonly attend more to nature than to man, but any affecting human event may blind our eyes to natural objects. I was so absorbed in him as to be surprised whenever I detected the routine of the natural world surviving still, or met persons going about their affairs indifferent. It appeared strange to me that the 'little dipper' should be still diving quietly in the river, as of yore; and it suggested that this bird might continue to dive here when Concord should be no more.

I felt that he, a prisoner in the midst of his enemies, and under sentence of death, if consulted as to his next step or resource, could answer more wisely than all his countrymen beside. He best understood his position; he contemplated it most calmly. Comparatively, all other men, North and South, were beside themselves. Our thoughts could not revert to any greater or wiser or better man with whom to contrast him, for he, then and there, was above them all. The man this country was about to hang appeared the greatest and best in it.

Years were not required for a revolution of public opinion; days, nay, hours, produced marked changes in this case. Fifty who were ready to say on going into our meeting in honor of him in Concord, that he ought to be hung, would not say it when they came out. They heard his words read, they saw the earnest faces of the congregation; and perhaps they joined at last in singing the hymn in his praise.

The order of instructors was reversed. I heard that one preacher, who at first was shocked and stood aloof, felt obliged at last, after he was hung, to make him the subject of a sermon, in which, to some extent, he eulogized the man, but said that his act was a failure. An influential class-teacher thought it necessary, after the services, to tell his grown-up pupils, that at first he thought as the preacher did then, but now he thought that John Brown was right. But it was understood that his pupils were as much ahead of the teacher, as he was ahead of the priest; and I know for a certainty, that very little boys at home had already asked their parents, in a tone of surprise, why God did not interfere to save him. In each case, the constituted teachers were only half conscious that they were not *leading*, but being *dragged*, with some loss of time and power.

The more conscientious preachers, the Bible men, they who talk about principle, and doing to others as you would that they should do unto you,—how could they fail to recognize him, by far the greatest preacher of them all, with the Bible in his life and in his acts, the embodiment of principle, who actually carried out the golden rule? All whose moral sense had been aroused, who had a calling from on high to preach, sided with him. What confessions he extracted from the cold and conservative! It is remarkable, but on the whole it is well, that it did not prove the occasion for a new sect of *Brownites* being formed in our midst.

They, whether within the Church or out of it, who adhere to the spirit and let go the letter, and are accordingly called infidel, were as usual foremost to recognize him. Men have been hung in the South before for attempting to rescue slaves, and the North was not much stirred by it. Whence, then, this wonderful difference? We were not so sure of *their* devotion to principle. We made a subtle distinction, forgot human laws, and did homage to an idea. The North, I mean the *living* North, was suddenly all transcendental. It went behind the human law, it went behind the apparent failure, and recognized eternal justice and glory. Commonly, men live according to a formula, and are satisfied if the order of law is observed, but in this instance they, to some extent, returned to original perceptions, and there was a slight revival of old religion. They saw that what was called order was confusion, what was called justice, injustice, and that the best was deemed the worst. This attitude suggested a more intelligent and generous spirit than that which actuated our forefathers, and the possibility, in the course of ages, of a revolution in behalf of another and an oppressed people.

Most Northern men, and a few Southern ones, were wonderfully stirred by Brown's behavior and words. They saw and felt that they were heroic and noble, and that there had been nothing quite equal to them in their kind in this country, or in the recent history of the world. But the minority were unmoved by them. They were only surprised and provoked by the attitude of their neighbors. They saw that Brown was Brave, and that he believed that he had done right, but they did not detect any further peculiarity in him. Not being accustomed to make fine distinctions, or to appreciate magnanimity, they read his letters and speeches as if they read them not. They were

not aware when they approached a heroic statement
—they did not know when they *burned*. They did not
feel that he spoke with authority, and hence they
only remembered that the *law* must be executed.
They remembered the old formula, but did not hear
the new revelation. The man who does not recognize
in Brown's words a wisdom and nobleness, and therefore an authority, superior to our laws, is a modern
Democrat. This is the test by which to discover him.
He is not wilfully but constitutionally blind on this
side, and he is consistent with himself. Such has been
his past life; no doubt of it. In like manner he has
read history and his Bible, and he accepts, or seems
to accept, the last only as an established formula, and
not because he has been convicted by it. You will not
find kindred sentiments in his common-place book,
if he has one.

When a noble deed is done, who is likely to appreciate it? They who are noble themselves. I was not
surprised that certain of my neighbors spoke of John
Brown as an ordinary felon, for who are they? They
have either much flesh, or much office, or much
coarseness of some kind. They are not etherial natures in any sense. The dark qualities predominate
in them. Several of them are decidedly pachyder-
matous. I say it in sorrow, not in anger. How can a
man behold the light, who has no answering inward
light? They are true to their *right*, but when they
look this way they *see* nothing, they are blind. For
the children of the light to contend with them is as
if there should be a contest between eagles and owls.
Show me a man who feels bitterly toward John
Brown, and let me hear what noble verse he can
repeat. He'll be as dumb as if his lips were stone.

It is not every man who can be a Christian, even
in a very moderate sense, whatever education you

give him. It is a matter of constitution and temperament, after all. He may have to be born again many times. I have known many a man who pretended to be a Christian, in whom it was ridiculous, for he had no genius for it. It is not every man who can be a freeman, even.

Editors persevered for a good while in saying that Brown was crazy: but at last they said only that it was 'a crazy scheme,' and the only evidence brought to prove it was that it cost him his life. I have no doubt that if he had gone with five thousand men, liberated a thousand slaves, killed a hundred or two slaveholders, and had as many more killed on his own side, but not lost his own life, these same editors would have called it by a more respectable name. Yet he has been far more successful than that. He has liberated many thousands of slaves, both North and South. They seem to have known nothing about living or dying for a principle. They all called him crazy then; who calls him crazy now?

All through the excitement occasioned by his remarkable attempt and subsequent behavior, the Massachusetts Legislature, not taking any steps for the defence of her citizens who were likely to be carried to Virginia as witnesses and exposed to the violence of a slaveholding mob, was wholly absorbed in a liquor-agency question, and indulging in poor jokes on the word 'extension.' Bad spirits occupied their thoughts. I am sure that no statesman up to the occasion could have attended to that question at all at that time,–a very vulgar question to attend to at any time.

When I looked into a liturgy of the Church of England, printed near the end of the last century, in order to find a service applicable to the case of Brown, I found that the only martyr recognized and provided for by it was King Charles the First, an eminent scamp. Of all the inhabitants of England and of the world, he was the only one according to this authority, whom that church had made a martyr and saint of; and for more than a century it had celebrated his martyrdom, so called, by an annual service. What a satire on the Church is that!

Look not to legislatures and churches for your guidance, nor to any soulless, *incorporated* bodies, but to *inspirited* or inspired ones.

What avail all your scholarly accomplishments and learning, compared with wisdom and manhood? To omit his other behavior, see what a work this comparatively unread and unlettered man wrote within six weeks. Where is our professor of *belles lettres* or of logic and rhetoric, who can write so well? He wrote in prison, not a history of the world, like Raleigh, but an American book which I think will live longer than that. I do not know of such words, uttered under such circumstances, and so copiously withal, in Roman or English or any history. What a variety of themes he touched on in that short space! There are words in that letter to his wife, respecting the education of his daughters, which deserve to be framed and hung over every mantlepiece in the land. Compare this earnest wisdom with that of Poor Richard.

The death of Irving, which at any other time would have attracted universal attention, having occurred while these things were transpiring, went almost unobserved. I shall have to read of it in the biography of authors.

Literary gentlemen, editors and critics, think that they know how to write, because they have studied grammar and rhetoric; but they are egregiously mistaken. The *art* of composition is as simple as the discharge of a bullet from a rifle, and its master-pieces imply an infinitely greater force behind them. This unlettered man's speaking and writing are standard English. Some words and phrases deemed vulgarisms and Americanisms before, he has made standard American; such as '*It will pay.*' It suggests that the one great rule of composition—and if I were a professor of rhetoric, I should insist on this—is to *speak the truth.* This first, this second, this third; pebbles in your mouth or not. This demands earnestness and manhood chiefly.

We seem to have forgotten that the expression, a *liberal* education, originally meant among the Romans one worthy of *free* men; while the learning of trades and professions by which to get your livelihood merely, was considered worthy of *slaves* only. But taking a hint from the word, I would go a step further and say, that it is not the man of wealth and leisure simply, though devoted to art, or science, or literature, who, in a true sense, is *liberally* educated, but only the earnest and *free* man. In a slaveholding country like this, there can be no such thing as a *liberal* education tolerated by the State; and those scholars of Austria and France who, however learned they may be, are contented under their tyrannies, have received only a *servile* education.

Nothing could his enemies do, but it redounded to his infinite advantage—that is, to the advantage of his cause. They did not hang him at once, but reserved him to preach to them. And then there was another great blunder. They did not hang his four followers with him; that scene was still postponed; and so his victory was prolonged and completed. No theatrical manager could have arranged things so wisely to give effect to his behavior and words. And who, think you, *was* the manager? Who placed the slave woman and her child, whom he stooped to kiss for a symbol, between his prison and the gallows?

We soon saw, as he saw, that he was not to be pardoned or rescued by men. That would have been to disarm him, to restore to him a material weapon, a Sharps' rifle, when he had taken up the sword of the spirit—the sword with which he has really won his greatest and most memorable victories. Now he has not laid aside the sword of the spirit, for he is pure spirit himself, and his sword is pure spirit also.

> 'He nothing common did or mean
> Upon that memorable scene,
> Nor called the gods with vulgar spite,
> To vindicate his helpless right;
> But bowed his comely head
> Down as upon a bed.'

What a transit was that of his horizontal body alone, but just cut down from the gallows-tree! We read, that at such a time it passed through Philadelphia, and by Saturday night had reached New York. Thus, like a meteor it shot through the Union from the southern regions toward the north! No such freight had the cars borne since they carried him southward alive.

On the day of his translation, I heard, to be sure, that he was *hung*, but I did not know what that meant; I felt no sorrow on that account; but not for a day or two did I even *hear* that he was *dead*, and not after any number of days shall I believe it. Of all the men who were said to be my contemporaries, it seemed to me that John Brown was the only one who *had not died*. I never hear of a man named Brown now,—and I hear of them pretty often,—I never hear of any particularly brave and earnest man, but my first thought is of John Brown, and what relation he may be to him. I meet him at every turn. He is more alive than ever he was. He has earned immortality. He is not confined to North Elba nor to Kansas. He is no longer working in secret. He works in public, and in the clearest light that shines on this land.

Life without Principle

AT a lyceum, not long since, I felt that the lecturer had chosen a theme too foreign to himself, and so failed to interest me as much as he might have done. He described things not in or near to his heart, but toward his extremities and superficies. There was, in this sense, no truly central or centralizing thought in the lecture. I would have had him deal with his privatest experience, as the poet does. The greatest compliment that was ever paid me was when one asked me what I *thought*, and attended to my answer. I am surprised, as well as delighted, when this happens, it is such a rare use he would make of me, as if he were acquainted with the tool. Commonly, if men want anything of me, it is only to know how many acres I make of their land,—since I am a surveyor,—or, at most, what trivial news I have burdened myself with. They never will go to law for my meat; they prefer the shell. A man once came a considerable distance to ask me to lecture on Slavery; but on conversing with him, I found that he and his clique expected seven-eighths of the lecture to be theirs, and only one-eighth mine; so I declined. I take it for granted, when I am invited to lecture anywhere,—for I have had a little experience in that business,—that there is a desire to hear what I *think* on some subject, though I may be the greatest fool in the country,—and not that I should say pleasant things merely, or such as the audience will assent to; and I resolve, accordingly, that I will give them a strong dose of myself. They have sent for me, and engaged to pay for me, and I am determined that they shall have me, though I bore them beyond all precedent.

So now I would say something similar to you, my

readers. Since *you* are my readers, and I have not been much of a traveller, I will not talk about people a thousand miles off, but come as near home as I can. As the time is short, I will leave out all the flattery, and retain all the criticism.

Let us consider the way in which we spend our lives.

This world is a place of business. What an infinite bustle! I am awaked almost every night by the panting of the locomotive. It interrupts my dreams. There is no sabbath. It would be glorious to see mankind at leisure for once. It is nothing but work, work, work. I cannot easily buy a blank-book to write thoughts in; they are commonly ruled for dollars and cents. An Irishman, seeing me making a minute in the fields, took it for granted that I was calculating my wages. If a man was tossed out of a window when an infant, and so made a cripple for life, or scared out of his wits by the Indians, it is regretted chiefly because he was thus incapacitated for—business! I think that there is nothing, not even crime, more opposed to poetry, to philosophy, ay, to life itself, than this incessant business.

There is a coarse and boisterous money-making fellow in the outskirts of our town, who is going to build a bank-wall under the hill along the edge of his meadow. The powers have put this into his head to keep him out of mischief, and he wishes me to spend three weeks digging there with him. The result will be that he will perhaps get some more money to hoard, and leave for his heirs to spend foolishly. If I do this, most will commend me as an industrious and hard-working man; but if I choose to devote myself to certain labors which yield more real profit, though but little money, they may be inclined to look on me as an idler. Nevertheless, as I do not need the police of meaningless labor to regulate me, and do not see anything absolutely praiseworthy in this fellow's undertaking, any more than in many an enterprise of our own or foreign governments, however amusing it may be to him or them, I prefer to finish my education at a different school.

If a man walk in the woods for love of them half of each day, he is in danger of being regarded as a loafer; but if he spends his whole day as a speculator, shearing off those woods and making earth bald before her time, he is esteemed an industrious and enterprising citizen. As if a town had no interest in its forests but to cut them down!

Most men would feel insulted, if it were proposed to employ them in throwing stones over a wall, and then in throwing them back, merely that they might earn their wages. But many are no more worthily employed now. For instance: just after sunrise, one summer morning, I noticed one of my neighbors walking beside his team, which was slowly drawing a heavy hewn stone swung under the axle, surrounded by an atmosphere of industry,—his day's work begun, —his brow commenced to sweat,—a reproach to all sluggards and idlers,—pausing abreast the shoulders of his oxen, and half turning round with a flourish of his merciful whip, while they gained their length on him. And I thought, Such is the labor which the American Congress exists to protect,—honest, manly toil,—honest as the day is long,—that makes his bread taste sweet, and keeps society sweet,—which all men respect and have consecrated: one of the sacred band, doing the needful, but irksome drudgery. Indeed, I felt a slight reproach, because I observed this from the window, and was not abroad and stirring about a similar business. The day went by, and at evening I passed the yard of another neighbor, who keeps many servants, and spends much money foolishly, while he adds nothing to the common stock, and there I saw the stone of the morning lying beside a whimsical structure intended to adorn this Lord Timothy Dexter's premises, and the dignity forthwith departed from the teamster's labor, in my eyes. In my opinion, the sun was made to light worthier toil than this. I may add, that his employer has since run off, in debt to a good part of the town, and, after passing through Chancery, has settled somewhere else, there to become once more a patron of the arts.

The ways by which you may get money almost without exception lead downward. To have done anything by which you earned money *merely* is to have been truly idle or worse. If the laborer gets no more than the wages which his employer pays him, he is cheated, he cheats himself. If you would get money as a writer or lecturer, you must be popular, which is to go down perpendicularly. Those services which the community will most readily pay for it is most disagreeable to render. You are paid for being something less than a man. The State does not commonly reward a genius any more wisely. Even the poet-laureate would rather not have to celebrate the accidents of royalty. He must be bribed with a pipe of wine; and perhaps another poet is called away from his muse to gauge that very pipe. As for my own business, even that kind of surveying which I could do with most satisfaction my employers do not want. They would prefer that I should do my work coarsely and not too well, ay, not well enough. When I observe that there are different ways of surveying, my employer commonly asks which will give him the most land, not which is most correct. I once invented a rule for measuring cord-wood, and tried to introduce it in Boston; but the measurer there told me that the sellers did not wish to have their wood measured correctly,—that he was already too accurate for them, and therefore they commonly got their wood measured in Charlestown before crossing the bridge.

The aim of the laborer should be, not to get his living, to get "a good job," but to perform well a certain work; and, even in a pecuniary sense, it would be economy for a town to pay its laborers so well that they would not feel that they were working for low ends, as for a livelihood merely, but for scientific, or even moral ends. Do not hire a man who does your work for money, but him who does it for love of it.

It is remarkable that there are few men so well employed, so much to their minds, but that a little money or fame would commonly buy them off from their present pursuit. I see advertisements for *active* young men, as if activity were the whole of a young man's capital. Yet I have been surprised when one has with confidence proposed to me, a grown man, to embark in some enterprise of his, as if I had absolutely nothing to do, my life having been a complete failure hitherto. What a doubtful compliment this is to pay me! As if he had met me half-way across the ocean beating up against the wind, but bound nowhere, and proposed to me to go along with him! If I did, what do you think the underwriters would say? No, no! I am not without employment at this stage of the voyage. To tell the truth, I saw an advertisement for able-bodied seamen, when I was a boy, sauntering in my native port, and as soon as I came of age I embarked.

The community has no bribe that will tempt a wise man. You may raise money enough to tunnel a mountain, but you cannot raise money enough to hire a man who is minding *his own* business. An efficient and valuable man does what he can, whether the community pay him for it or not. The inefficient offer their inefficiency to the highest bidder, and are forever expecting to be put into office. One would suppose that they were rarely disappointed.

Perhaps I am more than usually jealous with respect to my freedom. I feel that my connection with and obligation to society are still very slight and transient. Those slight labors which afford me a livelihood, and by which it is allowed that I am to some extent serviceable to my contemporaries, are as yet commonly a pleasure to me, and I am not often reminded that they are a necessity. So far I am successful. But I foresee, that, if my wants should be much increased, the labor required to supply them would become a drudgery. If I should sell both my forenoons and afternoons to society, as most appear to do, I am sure, that, for me, there would be nothing left worth living for. I trust that I shall never thus sell my birthright for a mess of pottage. I wish to suggest that a man may be very industrious, and yet not spend his time well. There is no more fatal blunderer than he who consumes the greater part of his life getting his living. All great enterprises are self-supporting. The poet, for instance, must sustain his body by his poetry, as a steam planing-mill feeds its boilers with the shavings it makes. You must get your living by loving. But as it is said of the merchants that ninety-seven in a hundred fail, so the life of men generally, tried by this standard, is a failure, and bankruptcy may be surely prophesied.

Merely to come into the world the heir of a fortune is not to be born, but to be still-born, rather. To be supported by the charity of friends, or a government-pension,—provided you continue to breathe,—by whatever fine synonymes you describe these relations, is to go into the almshouse. On Sundays the poor debtor goes to church to take an account of stock, and finds, of course, that his outgoes have been greater than his income. In the Catholic Church, especially, they go into Chancery, make a clean confession, give up all, and think to start again. Thus men will lie on their backs, talking about the fall of man, and never make an effort to get up.

As for the comparative demand which men make on life, it is an important difference between two, that the one is satisfied with a level success, that his marks can all be hit by point-blank shots, but the other, however low and unsuccessful his life may be, constantly elevates his aim, though at a very slight angle to the horizon. I should much rather be the last man, —though, as the Orientals say, "Greatness doth not approach him who is forever looking down; and all those who are looking high are growing poor."

It is remarkable that there is little or nothing to be remembered written on the subject of getting a living: how to make getting a living not merely honest and honorable, but altogether inviting and glorious; for if *getting* a living is not so, then living is not. One would think, from looking at literature, that this question had never disturbed a solitary individual's musings. Is it that men are too much disgusted with their experience to speak of it? The lesson of value which money teaches, which the Author of the Universe has taken so much pains to teach us, we are inclined to skip altogether. As for the means of living, it is wonderful how indifferent men of all classes are about it, even reformers, so called,—whether they inherit, or earn, or steal it. I think that society has done nothing for us in this respect, or at least has undone what she has done. Cold and hunger seem more friendly to my nature than those methods which men have adopted and advise to ward them off.

The title *wise* is, for the most part, falsely applied. How can one be a wise man, if he does not know any better how to live than other men?—if he is only more cunning and intellectually subtle? Does Wisdom work in a tread-mill? or does she teach how to succeed *by her example*? Is there any such thing as wisdom not applied to life? Is she merely the miller who grinds the finest logic? It is pertinent to ask if Plato got his *living* in a better way or more successfully than his contemporaries,—or did he succumb to the difficulties of life like other men? Did he seem to prevail over some of them merely by indifference, or by assuming grand airs? or find it easier to live, because his aunt remembered him in her will? The ways in which most men get their living, that is, live, are mere make-shifts, and a shirking of the real business of life,—chiefly because they do not know, but partly because they do not mean, any better.

The rush to California, for instance, and the attitude, not merely of merchants, but of philosophers and prophets, so called, in relation to it, reflect the greatest disgrace on mankind. That so many are ready to live by luck, and so get the means of commanding the labor of others less lucky, without contributing any value to society! And that is called enterprise! I know of no more startling development of the immorality of trade, and all the common modes of getting a living. The philosophy and poetry and religion of such a mankind are not worth the dust of a puff-ball. The hog that gets his living by rooting, stirring up the soil so, would be ashamed of such company. If I could command the wealth of all the worlds by lifting my finger, I would not pay *such* a price for it. Even Mahomet knew that God did not make this world in jest. It makes God to be a moneyed gentleman who scatters a handful of pennies in order to see mankind scramble for them. The world's raffle! A subsistence in the domains of Nature a thing to be raffled for! What a comment, what a satire on our institutions! The conclusion will be, that mankind will hang itself upon a tree. And have all the precepts in all the Bibles taught men only this? and is the last and most admirable invention of the human race only an improved muck-rake? Is this the ground on which Orientals and Occidentals meet? Did God direct us so to get our living, digging where we never planted,— and He would, perchance, reward us with lumps of gold?

God gave the righteous man a certificate entitling him to food and raiment, but the unrighteous man found a *facsimile* of the same in God's coffers, and appropriated it, and obtained food and raiment like the former. It is one of the most extensive systems of counterfeiting that the world has seen. I did not know that mankind were suffering for want of gold. I have seen a little of it. I know that it is very malleable, but not so malleable as wit. A grain of gold will gild a great surface, but not so much as a grain of wisdom.

The gold-digger in the ravines of the mountains is as much a gambler as his fellow in the saloons of San Francisco. What difference does it make, whether you shake dirt or shake dice? If you win, society is the loser. The gold-digger is the enemy of the honest laborer, whatever checks and compensations there may be. It is not enough to tell me that you worked hard to get your gold. So does the Devil work hard. The way of transgressors may be hard in many respects. The humblest observer who goes to the mines sees and says that gold-digging is of the character of a lottery; the gold thus obtained is not the same thing with the wages of honest toil. But, practically, he forgets what he has seen, for he has seen only the fact, not the principle, and goes into trade there, that is, buys a ticket in what commonly proves another lottery, where the fact is not so obvious.

After reading Howitt's account of the Australian gold-diggings one evening, I had in my mind's eye, all night, the numerous valleys, with their streams, all cut up with foul pits, from ten to one hundred feet deep, and half a dozen feet across, as close as they can be dug, and partly filled with water,—the locality to which men furiously rush to probe for their fortunes,—uncertain where they shall break ground,—not knowing but the gold is under their camp itself,—sometimes digging one hundred and sixty feet before they strike the vein, or then missing it by a foot,—turned into demons, and regardless of each other's rights, in their thirst for riches,—whole valleys, for thirty miles, suddenly honey-combed by the pits of the miners, so that even hundreds are drowned in them,—standing in water, and covered with mud and clay, they work night and day, dying of exposure and disease. Having read this, and partly forgotten it, I was thinking, accidentally, of my own unsatisfactory life, doing as others do; and with that vision of the diggings still before me, I asked myself, why *I* might not be washing some gold daily, though it were only the finest particles,—why *I* might not sink a shaft down to the gold within me, and work that mine. *There* is a Ballarat, a Bendigo for you,—what though it were a Sulky Gully? At any rate, I might pursue some path, however solitary and narrow and crooked, in which I could walk with love and reverence. Wherever a man separates from the multitude, and goes his own way in this mood, there indeed is a fork in the road, though ordinary travellers may see only a gap in the paling. His solitary path across-lots will turn out the *higher way* of the two.

Men rush to California and Australia as if the true gold were to be found in that direction; but that is to go to the very opposite extreme to where it lies. They go prospecting farther and farther away from the true lead, and are most unfortunate when they think themselves most successful. Is not our *native* soil auriferous? Does not a stream from the golden mountains flow through our native valley? and has not this for more than geologic ages been bringing down the shining particles and forming the nuggets for us? Yet, strange to tell, if a digger steal away, prospecting for this true gold, into the unexplored solitudes around us, there is no danger that any will dog his steps, and endeavor to supplant him. He may claim and undermine the whole valley even, both the cultivated and the uncultivated portions, his whole life long in peace, for no one will ever dispute his claim. They will not mind his cradles or his toms. He is not confined to a claim twelve feet square, as at Ballarat, but may mine anywhere, and wash the whole wide world in his tom.

Howitt says of the man who found the great nugget which weighed twenty-eight pounds, at the Bendigo diggings in Australia:—"He soon began to drink; got a horse and rode all about, generally at full gallop, and when he met people, called out to inquire if they knew who he was, and then kindly informed them that he was 'the bloody wretch that had found the nugget.' At last he rode full speed against a tree, and nearly knocked his brains out." I think, however, there was no danger of that, for he had already knocked his brains out against the nugget. Howitt adds, "He is a hopelessly ruined man." But he is a type of the class. They are all fast men. Hear some of the names of the places where they dig:—"Jackass Flat,"—"Sheep's-Head Gully,"—"Murderer's Bar," etc.

Is there no satire in these names? Let them carry their ill-gotten wealth where they will, I am thinking it will still be "Jackass Flat," if not "Murderer's Bar," where they live.

The last resource of our energy has been the robbing of graveyards on the Isthmus of Darien, an enterprise which appears to be but in its infancy; for, according to late accounts, an act has passed its second reading in the legislature of New Granada, regulating this kind of mining; and a correspondent of the *Tribune* writes:—"In the dry season, when the weather will permit of the country being properly prospected, no doubt other rich '*guacas*' [that is, graveyards] will be found." To emigrants he says:—"Do not come before December; take the Isthmus route in preference to the Boca del Toro one; bring no useless baggage, and do not cumber yourself with a tent; but a good pair of blankets will be necessary; a pick, shovel, and axe of good material will be almost all that is required": advice which might have been taken from the "Burker's Guide." And he concludes with this line in Italics and small capitals: "*If you are doing well at home*, STAY THERE," which may fairly be interpreted to mean, "If you are getting a good living by robbing graveyards at home, stay there."

But why go to California for a text? She is the child of New England, bred at her own school and church.

It is remarkable that among all the preachers there are so few moral teachers. The prophets are employed in excusing the ways of men. Most reverend seniors, the *illuminati* of the age, tell me, with a gracious, reminiscent smile, betwixt an aspiration and a shudder, not to be too tender about these things,—to lump all that, that is, make a lump of gold of it. The highest advice I have heard on these subjects was grovelling. The burden of it was,—It is not worth your while to undertake to reform the world in this particular. Do not ask how your bread is buttered; it will make you sick, if you do,—and the like. A man had better starve at once than lose his innocence in the process of getting his bread. If within the sophisticated man there is not an unsophisticated one, then he is but one of the Devil's angels. As we grow old, we live more coarsely, we relax a little in our disciplines, and, to some extent, cease to obey our finest instincts. But we should be fastidious to the extreme of sanity, disregarding the gibes of those who are more unfortunate than ourselves.

In our science and philosophy, even, there is commonly no true and absolute account of things. The spirit of sect and bigotry has planted its hoof amid the stars. You have only to discuss the problem, whether the stars are inhabited or not, in order to discover it. Why must we daub the heavens as well as the earth? It was an unfortunate discovery that Dr. Kane was a Mason, and that Sir John Franklin was another. But it was a more cruel suggestion that possibly that was the reason why the former went in search of the latter. There is not a popular magazine in this country that would dare to print a child's thought on important subjects without comment. It must be submitted to the D. D.s. I would it were the chickadee-dees.

You come from attending the funeral of mankind to attend to a natural phenomenon. A little thought is sexton to all the world.

I hardly know an *intellectual* man, even, who is so broad and truly liberal that you can think aloud in his society. Most with whom you endeavor to talk soon come to a stand against some institution in which they appear to hold stock,—that is, some particular, not universal, way of viewing things. They will continually thrust their own low roof, with its narrow skylight, between you and the sky, when it is the unobstructed heavens you would view. Get out of the way with your cobwebs, wash your windows, I say! In some lyceums they tell me that they have voted to exclude the subject of religion. But how do I know what their religion is, and when I am near to or far from it? I have walked into such an arena and done my best to make a clean breast of what religion I have experienced, and the audience never suspected what I was about. The lecture was as harmless as moonshine to them. Whereas, if I had read to them the biography of the greatest scamps in history, they might have thought that I had written the lives of the deacons of their church. Ordinarily, the inquiry is, Where did you come from? or, Where are you going? That was a more pertinent question which I overheard one of my auditors put to another once,— "What does he lecture for?" It made me quake in my shoes.

To speak impartially, the best men that I know are not serene, a world in themselves. For the most part, they dwell in forms, and flatter and study effect only more finely than the rest. We select granite for the underpinning of our houses and barns; we build fences of stone; but we do not ourselves rest on an under-pinning of granitic truth, the lowest primitive rock. Our sills are rotten. What stuff is the man made of who is not coexistent in our thought with the purest and subtilest truth? I often accuse my finest acquaint-ances of an immense frivolity; for, while there are manners and compliments we do not meet, we do not teach one another the lessons of honesty and sincerity that the brutes do, or of steadiness and solidity that the rocks do. The fault is commonly mutual, however;

for we do not habitually demand any more of each other.

That excitement about Kossuth, consider how characteristic, but superficial, it was!—only another kind of politics or dancing. Men were making speeches to him all over the country, but each expressed only the thought, or the want of thought, of the multitude. No man stood on truth. They were merely banded together, as usual, one leaning on another, and all together on nothing; as the Hindoos made the world rest on an elephant, the elephant on a tortoise, and the tortoise on a serpent, and had nothing to put under the serpent. For all fruit of that stir we have the Kossuth hat.

Just so hollow and ineffectual, for the most part, is our ordinary conversation. Surface meets surface. When our life ceases to be inward and private, conversation degenerates into mere gossip. We rarely meet a man who can tell us any news which he has not read in a newspaper, or been told by his neighbor; and, for the most part, the only difference between us and our fellow is, that he has seen the newspaper, or been out to tea, and we have not. In proportion as our inward life fails, we go more constantly and desperately to the post-office. You may depend on it, that the poor fellow who walks away with the greatest number of letters, proud of his extensive correspondence, has not heard from himself this long while.

I do not know but it is too much to read one newspaper a week. I have tried it recently, and for so long it seems to me that I have not dwelt in my native region. The sun, the clouds, the snow, the trees say not so much to me. You cannot serve two masters. It requires more than a day's devotion to know and to possess the wealth of a day.

We may well be ashamed to tell what things we have read or heard in our day. I do not know why my news should be so trivial,—considering what one's dreams and expectations are, why the developments should be so paltry. The news we hear, for the most part, is not news to our genius. It is the stalest repetition. You are often tempted to ask, why such stress is laid on a particular experience which you have had,—that, after twenty-five years, you should meet Hobbins, Registrar of Deeds, again on the sidewalk. Have you not budged an inch, then? Such is the daily news. Its facts appear to float in the atmosphere, insignificant as the sporules of fungi, and impinge on some neglected *thallus*, or surface of our minds, which affords a basis for them, and hence a parasitic growth. We should wash ourselves clean of such news. Of what consequence, though our planet explode, if there is no character involved in the explosion? In health we have not the least curiosity about such events. We do not live for idle amusement. I would not run round a corner to see the world blow up.

All summer, and far into the autumn, perchance, you unconsciously went by the newspapers and the news, and now you find it was because the morning and the evening were full of news to you. Your walks were full of incidents. You attended, not to the affairs of Europe, but to your own affairs in Massachusetts fields. If you chance to live and move and have your being in that thin stratum in which the events that make the news transpire,—thinner than the paper on which it is printed,—then these things will fill the world for you; but if you soar above or dive below that plane, you cannot remember nor be reminded of them. Really to see the sun rise or go down every day, so to relate ourselves to a universal fact, would preserve us sane forever. Nations! What are nations? Tartars, and Huns, and Chinamen! Like insects, they swarm. The historian strives in vain to make them memorable. It is for want of a man that there are so many men. It is individuals that populate the world. Any man thinking may say with the Spirit of Lodin,—

> "I look down from my height on nations,
> And they become ashes before me;—
> Calm is my dwelling in the clouds;
> Pleasant are the great fields of my rest."

Pray, let us live without being drawn by dogs, Esquimaux-fashion, tearing over hill and dale, and biting each other's ears.

Not without a slight shudder at the danger, I often perceive how near I had come to admitting into my mind the details of some trivial affair,—the news of the street; and I am astonished to observe how willing men are to lumber their minds with such rubbish,—to permit idle rumors and incidents of the most insignificant kind to intrude on ground which should be sacred to thought. Shall the mind be a public arena, where the affairs of the street and the gossip of the tea-table chiefly are discussed? Or shall it be a quarter of heaven itself,—an hypæthral temple, consecrated to the service of the gods? I find it so difficult to dispose of the few facts which to me are significant, that I hesitate to burden my attention with those which are insignificant, which only a divine mind could illustrate. Such is, for the most part, the news in newspapers and conversation. It is important to preserve the mind's chastity in this respect. Think of admitting the details of a single case of the criminal court into our thoughts, to stalk profanely through their very *sanctum sanctorum* for an hour, ay, for many hours! to make a very bar-room of the mind's inmost apartment, as if for so long the dust of the street had occupied us,—the very street itself, with all its travel, its bustle, and filth had passed through our thoughts' shrine! Would it not be an intellectual and moral suicide? When I have been compelled to sit spectator and auditor in a court-room for some hours, and have seen my neighbors, who were not compelled, stealing in from time to time, and tiptoeing about with washed hands and faces, it has appeared to my mind's eye, that, when they took off their hats, their ears suddenly expanded into vast hoppers for sound, between which even their narrow heads were crowded. Like the vanes of windmills, they caught the broad, but shallow stream of sound, which, after a few titillating gyrations in their coggy brains, passed out the other side. I wondered if, when they got home, they were as careful to wash their ears as before their hands and faces. It has seemed to me, at such a time, that the auditors and the witnesses, the jury and the counsel, the judge and the criminal at the bar,—if I may presume him guilty before he is convicted,—were all equally criminal, and a thunderbolt might be expected to descend and consume them all together.

By all kinds of traps and sign-boards, threatening the extreme penalty of the divine law, exclude such trespassers from the only ground which can be sacred to you. It is so hard to forget what it is worse than useless to remember! If I am to be a thoroughfare, I prefer that it be of the mountain-brooks, the Parnassian streams, and not the town-sewers. There is inspiration, that gossip which comes to the ear of the attentive mind from the courts of heaven. There is the profane and stale revelation of the bar-room and the police court. The same ear is fitted to receive both communications. Only the character of the hearer determines to which it shall be open, and to which closed. I believe that the mind can be permanently profaned by the habit of attending to trivial things, so that all our thoughts shall be tinged with triviality. Our very intellect shall be macadamized, as it were,— its foundation broken into fragments for the wheels of travel to roll over; and if you would know what will make the most durable pavement, surpassing rolled stones, spruce blocks, and asphaltum, you have only to look into some of our minds which have been subjected to this treatment so long.

If we have thus desecrated ourselves,—as who has not?—the remedy will be by wariness and devotion to reconsecrate ourselves, and make once more a fane of the mind. We should treat our minds, that is, our-selves, as innocent and ingenuous children, whose guardians we are, and be careful what objects and what subjects we thrust on their attention. Read not the Times. Read the Eternities. Conventionalities are at length as bad as impurities. Even the facts of sci-ence may dust the mind by their dryness, unless they are in a sense effaced each morning, or rather ren-dered fertile by the dews of fresh and living truth. Knowledge does not come to us by details, but in flashes of light from heaven. Yes, every thought that passes through the mind helps to wear and tear it, and to deepen the ruts, which, as in the streets of Pompeii, evince how much it has been used. How many things there are concerning which we might well deliberate, whether we had better know them,— had better let their peddling-carts be driven, even at the slowest trot or walk, over that bridge of glorious span by which we trust to pass at last from the far-thest brink of time to the nearest shore of eternity! Have we no culture, no refinement,—but skill only to live coarsely and serve the Devil?—to acquire a little worldly wealth, or fame, or liberty, and make a false show with it, as if we were all husk and shell, with no tender and living kernel to us? Shall our institutions be like those chestnut-burs which contain abortive nuts, perfect only to prick the fingers?

America is said to be the arena on which the battle of freedom is to be fought; but surely it cannot be freedom in a merely political sense that is meant. Even if we grant that the American has freed himself from a political tyrant, he is still the slave of an economical and moral tyrant. Now that the republic— the *res-publica*—has been settled, it is time to look after the *res-privata*,—the private state,—to see, as the Roman senate charged its consuls, *"ne quid res-*PRIVATA *detrimenti caperet,"* that the *private* state receive no detriment.

Do we call this the land of the free? What is it to be free from King George and continue the slaves of King Prejudice? What is it to be born free and not to live free? What is the value of any political freedom, but as a means to moral freedom? Is it a freedom to be slaves, or a freedom to be free, of which we boast? We are a nation of politicians, concerned about the outmost defences only of freedom. It is our children's children who may perchance be really free. We tax ourselves unjustly. There is a part of us which is not represented. It is taxation without representation. We quarter troops, we quarter fools and cattle of all sorts upon ourselves. We quarter our gross bodies on our poor souls, till the former eat up all the latter's substance.

With respect to a true culture and manhood, we are essentially provincial still, not metropolitan,—mere Jonathans. We are provincial, because we do not find at home our standards,—because we do not worship truth, but the reflection of truth,—because we are warped and narrowed by an exclusive devotion to trade and commerce and manufactures and agriculture and the like, which are but means, and not the end.

So is the English Parliament provincial. Mere country-bumpkins, they betray themselves, when any more important question arises for them to settle, the Irish question, for instance,—the English question why did I not say? Their natures are subdued to what they work in. Their "good breeding" respects only secondary objects. The finest manners in the world are awkwardness and fatuity, when contrasted with a finer intelligence. They appear but as the fashions of past days,—mere courtliness, knee-buckles and small-clothes, out of date. It is the vice, but not the excellence of manners, that they are continually being deserted by the character; they are cast-off clothes or shells, claiming the respect which belonged to the living creature. You are presented with the shells instead of the meat, and it is no excuse generally, that, in the case of some fishes, the shells are of more worth than the meat. The man who thrusts his manners upon me does as if he were to insist on introducing me to his cabinet of curiosities, when I wished to see himself. It was not in this sense that the poet Decker called Christ "the first true gentleman that ever breathed." I repeat that in this sense the most splendid court in Christendom is provincial, having authority to consult about Transalpine interests only, and not the affairs of Rome. A praetor or proconsul would suffice to settle the questions which absorb the attention of the English Parliament and the American Congress.

Government and legislation! these I thought were respectable professions. We have heard of heaven-born Numas, Lycurguses, and Solons, in the history

of the world, whose *names* at least may stand for
ideal legislators; but think of legislating to *regulate*
the breeding of slaves, or the exportation of tobacco!
What have divine legislators to do with the exportation or the importation of tobacco? what humane
ones with the breeding of slaves? Suppose you were
to submit the question to any son of God,—and has
He no children in the nineteenth century? is it a
family which is extinct?—in what condition would
you get it again? What shall a State like Virginia say
for itself at the last day, in which these have been
the principal, the staple productions? What ground is
there for patriotism in such a State? I derive my facts
from statistical tables which the States themselves
have published.

A commerce that whitens every sea in quest of
nuts and raisins, and makes slaves of its sailors for
this purpose! I saw, the other day, a vessel which had
been wrecked, and many lives lost, and her cargo of
rags, juniper-berries, and bitter almonds were strewn
along the shore. It seemed hardly worth the while to
tempt the dangers of the sea between Leghorn and
New York for the sake of a cargo of juniper-berries
and bitter almonds. America sending to the Old World
for her bitters! Is not the sea-brine, is not shipwreck,
bitter enough to make the cup of life go down here?
Yet such, to a great extent, is our boasted commerce;
and there are those who style themselves statesmen
and philosophers who are so blind as to think that
progress and civilization depend on precisely this
kind of interchange and activity,—the activity of flies
about a molasses-hogshead. Very well, observes one,
if men were oysters. And very well, answer I, if men
were mosquitoes.

Lieutenant Herndon, whom our Government sent
to explore the Amazon, and, it is said, to extend the

area of Slavery, observed that there was wanting there "an industrious and active population, who know what the comforts of life are, and who have artificial wants to draw out the great resources of the country." But what are the "artificial wants" to be encouraged? Not the love of luxuries, like the tobacco and slaves of, I believe, his native Virginia, nor the ice and granite and other material wealth of our native New England; nor are "the great resources of a country" that fertility or barrenness of soil which produces these. The chief want, in every State that I have been into, was a high and earnest purpose in its inhabitants. This alone draws out "the great resources" of Nature, and at last taxes her beyond her resources; for man naturally dies out of her. When we want culture more than potatoes, and illumination more than sugar-plums, then the great resources of a world are taxed and drawn out, and the result, or staple production, is, not slaves, nor operatives, but men,— those rare fruits called heroes, saints, poets, philosophers, and redeemers.

In short, as a snow-drift is formed where there is a lull in the wind, so, one would say, where there is a lull of truth, an institution springs up. But the truth blows right on over it, nevertheless, and at length blows it down.

What is called politics is comparatively something so superficial and inhuman, that, practically, I have never fairly recognized that it concerns me at all. The newspapers, I perceive, devote some of their columns specially to politics or government without charge; and this, one would say, is all that saves it; but, as I love literature, and, to some extent, the truth also, I never read those columns at any rate. I do not wish to blunt my sense of right so much. I have not got to answer for having read a single President's Message,

A strange age of the world this, when empires, king-
doms, and republics come a-begging to a private man's
door, and utter their complaints at his elbow! I cannot
take up a newspaper but I find that some wretched
government or other, hard pushed, and on its last
legs, is interceding with me, the reader, to vote for
it,—more importunate than an Italian beggar; and if
I have a mind to look at its certificate, made, perchance, by some benevolent merchant's clerk, or the
skipper that brought it over, for it cannot speak a
word of English itself, I shall probably read of the
eruption of some Vesuvius, or the overflowing of some
Po, true or forged, which brought it into this condition. I do not hesitate, in such a case, to suggest work,
or the almshouse; or why not keep its castle in silence,
as I do commonly? The poor President, what with
preserving his popularity and doing his duty, is completely bewildered. The newspapers are the ruling
power. Any other government is reduced to a few marines at Fort Independence. If a man neglects to read
the Daily Times, Government will go down on its
knees to him, for this is the only treason in these days.

Those things which now most engage the attention
of men, as politics and the daily routine, are, it is
true, vital functions of human society, but should be
unconsciously performed, like the corresponding functions of the physical body. They are *infra*-human, a
kind of vegetation. I sometimes awake to a half-
consciousness of them going on about me, as a man
may become conscious of some of the processes of
digestion in a morbid state, and so have the dyspepsia,
as it is called. It is as if a thinker submitted himself
to be rasped by the great gizzard of creation. Politics
is, as it were, the gizzard of society, full of grit and
gravel, and the two political parties are its two opposite halves,—sometimes split into quarters, it may be,

which grind on each other. Not only individuals, but States, have thus a confirmed dyspepsia, which expresses itself, you can imagine by what sort of eloquence. Thus our life is not altogether a forgetting, but also, alas! to a great extent, a remembering of that which we should never have been conscious of, certainly not in our waking hours. Why should we not meet, not always as dyspeptics, to tell our bad dreams, but sometimes as *eu*peptics, to congratulate each other on the ever glorious morning? I do not make an exorbitant demand, surely.

Reform and the Reformers

THE Reformers are no doubt the true ancestors of the next generation; the Conservative belongs to a decaying family, and has not learned that he who seeks to save his 'life' shall lose it. Both are sick, but the one is already convalescent. His disease is not organic but acute, and he looks forward to coming springs with hope. He is not sick of any incurable disorder, of plague or consumption; but of tradition and conformity and infidelity; but the other is still taking his bitters and quack medicines patiently, and will grow worse yet. The heads of conservatives have a puny and deficient look, a certain callowness and concavity, as if they were prematurely exposed on one or both sides, or were made to lie or pack together, as when several nuts are formed under the same burr where only one should have been. We wonder to see such a head wear a whole hat. Such as these naturally herd together for mutual protection. They say *We* and *Our*, as if they had never been assured of an individual existence. *Our* Indian policy; *our* coast defences, *our* national character. They are what are called public men, fashionable men, ambitious men, chaplains of the army or navy; men of property, standing and respectability, for the most part, and in all cases created by society. Sometimes even they are embarked in "Great Causes" which have been stranded on the shores of society in a previous age, carrying them through with a kind of reflected and traditionary nobleness, certainly disinterestedness. The Conservative has many virtues which the Reformer has not,— ofttimes a singular and unexpected liberality and courtesy, a decided practicalness and reverence for facts, and with a little less irritability, or more indif-

ference would be the more tolerable companion. He is
the steward of society, and in this office at least is
faithful and generous. He is a dutiful son but a tyrannical father, and does not foresee that unimaginable
epoch when the rising generation will have attained
to a level with the risen. Rather he is himself a son
all his days, and never arrives at such maturity as to
be informed that he and such as he are now mankind
and the latest generation, the occupants and proprie-
tors of the globe, but he still feels it to be his chief
duty to preserve the law and order and institutions
which he finds existing.

It is remarkable how well men train. The teamster
rolls out of his cradle into a Tom-and-Jerry—and goes
at once to look after his team—to fodder and water
his horses, without standing agape at his position.
What is the destiny of man, compared with the
shipping interests? What does he care for—his creator? does'nt he drive for Squire Make-a-Stir?

The ladies of the land with equal bravery are
weavers of toilet cushions and tidies not to betray too
green an interest in their fates. Men now take snuff
into their noses, but if they had been so advised in
season, they would have put it into their ears and
eyes. They may gravely deny this, but do not believe them.

In the midst of all this disorder and imperfection
in human affairs which he would rather avoid to
think of comes the Reformer, the impersonation of
disorder and imperfection; to heal and reform them;
seeking to discover the divine order and conform to
it; and earnestly asking the cooperation of men.

No doubt the evil is great and manifest, and something must certainly be done; and his zeal is in proportion to the urgency of the case,—but I know of
few radicals as yet who are radical enough, and have

not got this name ratner by meddling with the exposed roots of innocent institutions than with their own.

The disease and disorder in society are wont to be referred to the false relations in which men live one to another, but strictly speaking there can be no such thing as a false relation; if the condition of the things related is true. False relations grow out of false conditions. The inmate of a poorhouse would be more pauper still on a desolate island, and the convict would find his prison and prison discipline there.

It is not the worst reason why the reform should be a private and individual enterprise, that perchance the evil may be private also. From what southern plains comes up the voice of wailing,—under what latitudes reside the heathen to whom we would send light,—and who is that intemperate and brutal man whom he would redeem?

Now, if anything ail a man so that he does not perform his functions; especially if his digestion is poor, though he may have considerable nervous strength left; if he has failed in all his undertakings hitherto; if he has committed some heinous sin and partially repents, what does he do? He sets about reforming the world. Do ye hear it, ye Woloffs, ye Patagonians, ye Tartars, ye Nez Percés? The world is going to be reformed, formed once for all. Presto — Change! Methinks I hear the glad tidings spreading over the green prairies of the west; over the silent South American pampas, parched African deserts, and stretching Siberian versts; through the populous Indian and Chinese villages, along the Indus, the Ganges, and Hydaspes.

There is no reformer on the globe, no such philanthropic—benevolent and charitable man—now engaged in any good work anywhere, sorely afflicted by the sight of misery around him, and animated by the desire to relieve it, who would not instantly and unconsciously sign off from these pure labors, and betake himself to purer, if he had but righted some obscure, and perhaps unrecognized private grievance. Let but the spring come to him, let the morning rise over his couch, and he will forsake his generous companions, without apology or explanation!

The Reformer who comes recommending any institution or system to the adoption of men, must not rely solely on logic and argument, or on eloquence and oratory for his success, but see that he represents one pretty perfect institution in himself, the centre and circumference of all others, an erect man.

I ask of all Reformers, of all who are recommending Temperance—Justice—Charity—Peace, the Family, Community or Associative life, not to give us their theory and wisdom only, for these are no proof, but to carry around with them each a small specimen of his own manufactures, and to despair of ever recommending anything of which a small sample at least cannot be exhibited:—that the Temperance man let me know the savor of Temperance, if it be good, the Just man permit to enjoy the blessings of liberty while with him, the Community man allow me to taste the sweets of the Community life in his society.

I cannot bear to be told to wait for good results, I pine as much for good beginnings. We never come to final results, and it is too late to start from perennial beginnings.

But alas, when we ask the schemer to show us the material of which his structure is to be built. He exhibits only fair looking words, resolute and solid words for the underpinning, convenient and homely words for the body of the edifice, poems and flights of the imagination for the dome and cupola.

Men know very well how to distinguish barren words from those which are cousin to a deed, and the promising or threatening speaker is only rated at his faculty and resolution to do what he says. The phlegmatic audience which sits near the doors know that the speaker does not mean to abolish property or dissolve the family tie, or do without human governments all over the world to-night, but that simply, he has agreed to be the speaker and—they have agreed to be the audience. They may chance to know that the lecturer against the use of money is paid for his lecture, and that is the precept which they hear and believe, and they have a great deal of sympathy with him.

After all the peace lectures and non resistance meetings it was never yet learned from them how any of the speakers would conduct in an emergency, because a very important disputant, one Mr Resistance was not present to offer his arguments.

There are not only books, but lectures and sermons of fiction, whether written or extemporaneous. The modern Reformers are a class of *improvvisánti* more wonderful and amusing than the Italians.

What the prophets even have said is forgotten, and the oracles are decayed, but what heroes and saints have done is still remembered, and posterity will tell it again and again.

We rarely see the Reformer who is fairly launched in his enterprise, bringing about the right state of things with hearty and effective tugs, and not rather preparing and grading the way through the minds of the people. What if the community were to pull altogether says he!—Aye, what if two—what if one even were to work harmoniously and with all his energies! say I. No wonder you plead for my cooperation—I could exert myself considerably. It would be worth the while methinks to have my traces hitched to some good institution.

There certainly can be no greater folly than for men to set about to prove a truth at their leisure who have no other business with it. As if one were to proclaim that he was going a long journey, and because one of his neighbors was inattentive or did not believe it, should put it off. To the man of industry and work it is not quite essential that I should *think* with him. When my neighbor is going to build a house, whether for me or for himself, he does not come to me and re-proach or pity me for living in a shed, but he digs the cellar and raises the frame, and makes haste to get the roof done, that he may do the inside-work more comfortably, and he knows very well what as-sistance he can count upon in these labors.

For the most part by simply agreeing in opinion with the preacher and Reformer I defend myself and get rid of him, for he really asks for no sympathy with deeds,—and this trick it would be well for the irritable Conservative to know and practise.

The great benefactors of their race have been single and singular and not masses of men. Whether in poetry or history it is the same: Minerva – Ceres – Nep-tune – Prometheus – Socrates – Christ – Luther – Co-lumbus – Arkwright.

There is no objection to action in societies or com-munities when it is the individual using the society as his instrument, rather than the society using the individual. While one's inspiration is so high and pure as to be necessarily solitary and not to be made a subject of sympathy or congratulation, he may safely use any instrument in his way, whether wood or iron or masses of men. But when the vote of the so-ciety rises to a level with his own prayers, and its reso-lution in the least confirms his own, he may suspect

himself, or he may suspect his companions. There
have been meetings, religious, political and reforma-
tory, to which men came a hundred miles—though all
they had to offer were—some resolutions! What becomes of resolutions that have been offered?

In every society there is or was at least one individual, its founder and leader, who did not belong to
it, but who imparted to it whatever life and efficiency
it had, and sad indeed is the condition of that society,
and it is the condition of most, which is deprived of
its head—and soul—for the members can still vote,—
and as it were by force of galvanism, a spasmodic
action be kept up in the body, and men call it life,
and expect virtue and character from senseless nerves
and muscles. Such societies, as they prize life, will
have recourse to dinners and tea-parties that the
members may not utterly fail for want of a belly also.

Consider, after all, how very private and silent an
affair it is to lead a life—that we do not consider our
duties, or the actions of our life, as in a caucus or
convention of men, where the subject has been before
the meeting a long time, and many resolutions have
been proposed and passed, and now one speaker has
the floor and then another, and the subject is fairly
under discussion; but the convention where our most
private and intimate affairs are discussed is very
thinly attended, almost we are not there ourselves,
that is the go-to-meeting part of us. It is very still,
and few resolutions get passed. Few words are spoken,
and the hours are not counted!

Next and nearest to that unfortunate man even
whom we would stand by in our philanthropy is the
mystery of his life. It is nearer than cold or hunger
for they are but the outside of it—it is between him
and them, and do what we will, we must leave him
alone with that.

The information which the gods vouchsafe to give us is never concerning anything which we wished to know. We are not wise enough to put a question to them. Tell me some truth about society and you will annihilate it. What though we are its ailing members and prisoners. We cannot always be detained by your measures for reform. All that is called hindrance without is but occasion within. The prisoner who is free in spirit, on whose innocent life some rays of light and hope still fall, will not delay to be a reformer of prisons, an inventor of superior prison disciplines, but walks forth free on the path by which those rays penetrated to his cell. Has the Green Mountain boy made no better nor more thrilling discovery than that the church is rotten and the state corrupt? Thank heaven, we have not to choose our calling out of those enterprises which society has to offer. Is he then indeed called, who chooses to what he is called? Obey your calling rather, and it will not be whither your neighbors and kind friends and patrons expect or desire, but be true nevertheless, and choose not, nor go whither they call you. "Thy lot or portion of life, is seeking after thee; therefore be at rest from seeking after it."

From the side to which all eyes are turned, and the hue and cry leads, from the effort which the state abets, and the church prays for, the least profitable result comes, the least performance issues.

We would have some pure product of man's hands, some pure labor, some life got in this old trade of getting a living—some work done which shall not be a mending, a cobbling, a reforming. Show me the mountain boy, the city boy, who never heard of an abuse, who has not *chosen* his calling. It is the delight of the ages, the free labor of man, even the creative and beautiful arts.

Be sure your fate
Doth keep apart its state;
Not linked with any band,
Even the nobles of the land;
In tented fields with cloth of gold
No place doth hold,
But is more chivalrous than they are,
And sigheth for a nobler war;
A finer strain its trumpet sings,
A brighter gleam its armor flings.
The life that I aspire to live
No man proposeth me,
Only the promise of my heart
Wears its emblazonry.

How long shall vice give a home to virtue? One generation abandons the enterprises of another. Many an institution which was thought to be an essential part of the order of society, has, in the true order of events, been left like a stranded vessel on the sand.

When a zealous Reformer would fain discourse to me, I would have him consider first if he has anything to say to me. All simple and necessary speech between men is sweet; but it takes calamity, it takes death or great good fortune commonly to bring them together. We are sages and proud to speak when we are the bearers of great news, even though it be hard; to tell a man of the welfare of his kindred in foreign parts, or even that his house is on fire, is a great good fortune, and seems to relate us to him by a worthier tie.

It is a great blessing to have to do with men, to be called to them as simply as into the field of your occupation. It refreshes and invigorates us. But this happiness is rare. For the most part we can only treat one another to our wit, our good manners and equanimity, and though we have eagles to give we demand of each other only coppers. We pray that our companion will demand of us truth, sincerity, love and noble behavior, for now these virtues lie impossible to us, and we only know them by their names. Only lovers know the value and magnanimity of truth, while traders prize a cheap honesty, and neighbors and acquaintances a cheap civility.

If you have nothing to say let me have your silence, for that is good and fertile. Silence is the ambrosial night in the intercourse of men in which their sincerity is recruited and takes deeper root.—There are such vices as frivolity, garrulity, and verbosity, not to mention prophanity, growing out of the abuse of speech which does not belong wholly to antiquity, and none have imparted a more cheerless aspect to society.

A man must serve another and a better use than any he can consciously render. Every class and order in the universe is the heaven of certain gifts to men. There is a whole class of musk bearing animals, and each flower has its peculiar odor. And all these together go to make the general wholesome and invigorating atmosphere. So each man should take care to emit his fragrance, and after all perform some such office as hemlock boughs, or dried and healing herbs. Though you are a Reformer we want not your reasons, your good roots and foundations—nor your uprightness and benevolence which are your stem and leaves—but we want the flower and fruit of the man—that some fragrance at least as of fresh spring life be wafted over from thee to me. This is consolation and that charity that hides a multitude of sins. Our companion must be a sort of appreciable wealth to us or at least make us sensible of our own riches—in his degree an apostle á Mercury, á Ceres, á Minerva, the bearer of diverse gifts to us. He must bring me the morning light untarnished, and the evening red undimmed. There must be the hilarity of spring in his mirth, the summer's serenity in his joy, the autumnal ripeness in his wisdom, and the repose and abundance of winter in his silence. He should impart his courage and not his despair; his health and ease, and not his disease, and take care that this does not spread by contagion.

It is rare that we are able to impart wealth to our fellows, and do not surround them with our own cast off griefs as an atmosphere, and name it sympathy. If we would indeed reform mankind by truly Indian, botanic, magnetic, or *natural* means, let us strive first to be as simple and well as nature ourselves.

I would say therefore to the anxious speculator and philanthropist—Let us dispel the clouds which hang over our own brows—take up a little life into your pores, endeavor to encourage the flow of sap in your veins, find your soil, strike root and grow—Apollo's waters and God will give the increase. Help to clothe the human field with green. Be green and flourishing plants in God's nursery, and not such complaining bleeding trees as Dante saw in the Infernal Regions.

If your branches wither, send out your fibres into every kingdom of nature for its contribution—lift up your boughs into the heavens for etherial and starry influences, let your roots like those of the willow wander wider, deeper, to some moist and fertile spot in the earth, and make firm your trunk against the elements.

Be fast rooted withal in your native soil of originality and independence, your virgin mould of un-exhausted strength and fertility—Nor suffer yourself ever to be transplanted again into the foreign and ungenial regions of tradition and conformity, or the lean and sandy soils of public opinion.

What! to be blown about, a creature of the affections, preaching love and good will and charity, with these tender fibres all bare in a cold world, and not a brother kind enough to throw a spade-full of earth over them! Better try what virtue there is in sand even, and cover your roots with the first exhausted soil you can find.

Who shall tell what blossoms, what fruits, what public and private advantage may push up through this rind we call a man? The traveller may stand by him as a perennial fountain in the desert and slake his thirst forever.

The wind rustling the leaves, the brags of some children have thrilled me more than the lives of the greatest and holiest men. What idle sorrow and stereotyped despair in the saints! What wavering performance in the heroes! Even the prophets and redeemers have rather consoled the fears than satisfied the free demands and hopes of man! We know nowhere recorded a simple and irrepressible satisfaction with the gift of life, a memorable and unbribed praise of God. So long as the Reformers are earnest enough and pleased with their own conceptions, they may entertain me, but when the time comes that their theme is exhausted, and only the sad alternative is left to do the things they have said; and they would rather that I should do them, then they are intolerable companions.

I like the old world and I like the new—winter and summer, hay and grass,—but the death that presumes to give laws to life, and persists in affirming essential disease and disorder to the child who has just begun to bathe his senses and his understanding in the perception of order and beauty—that perseveres in maturing its schemes of life till its last days are come, is not to be compared to anything in nature. The growing man or youth, is a fact which commonly we do not enough allow for in our speculations—but to remember which would be fatal to many a fine theory. Speak for yourself, old man. When we are oppressed by the heat and turmoil of the noon, we should remember that the sun which scorches us with his beams, is gilding the hills of morning and awaking the woodland quires for other men. So too it must not be forgotten, the evening exhibits in the still rear of day a beauty to which the morning and the noon are strangers.

It is hard to make those who have talked much, especially preachers and lecturers, deepen their speech, and give it fresh sincerity and significance. It will be a long time before they understand what you mean. They will wonder if you don't value fluency. But the drains flow. Turn your back, and wait till you hear their words ring solid, and they will have cause to thank you! How infinitely trackless yet passable are we. Is not our own interior white on the chart? Inward is a direction which no traveller has taken. Inward is the bourne which all travellers seek and from which none desire to return. There are the sources of the Nile and Niger.

Every man is the lord of a realm beside which the earthly empire of the Czars is but a petty state—with its ocean borders—its mountain ranges, and its trackless paradises of unfallen nature. And, O ye Reformers! if the good Gods have given ye any high ray of truth to be wrought into life, here in your own realms without let or hindrance is the application to be made.

Those who dwell in Oregon and the far west are not so solitary as the enterprising and independent thinker, applying his discoveries to his own life. This is the way we would see a man striving with his axe and kettle to take up his abode. To this rich soil should the New Englander wend his way. Here is

Wisconsin and the farthest west. It is simple, independent, original, natural life.

Most whom I meet in the streets are, so to speak, outward bound, they live out and out, are going and coming, looking before and behind, all out of doors and in the air. I would fain see them inward bound, retiring in and in, farther and farther every day, and when I inquired for them I should not hear, that they had gone abroad anywhere, to Rondont or Sackets Harbor, but that they had withdrawn deeper within the folds of being.

England and France, Spain and Portugal, Gold Coast and Slave Coast, all front upon this private sea, but no bark from them has ventured out of sight of land,—though it is without a doubt the direct way to India.

I would say then to my vagrant countrymen—Go not to any foreign theater for spectacles, but consider first that there is nothing which can delight or astonish the eyes, but you may discover it all in yourselves. One hastens to Southern Africa perchance to chase the giraffe; but that is not the game he would be after. How long, pray, would a man hunt giraffes, if he could?— What was the meaning of that Exploring Expedition with all its parade and expense, but a recognition of the fact that there are continents and seas in the moral world to which every man is an inlet, yet unexplored by him; but that it is easier to sail many thousand miles through cold and storms and savage cannibals, in a government ship, with 500 men and boys to steer and sail for one, than it is to explore the private sea, the Atlantic and Pacific ocean of one's being alone.

> Erret, et extremos alter scrutetur Iberos.
> Plus habet hic vitae, plus habet ille viae.

> Let the other wander and scrutinize the
>   outlandish Australians.
> This one has more of God, that one has
>   more of the road.

Here is demanded the eye and the nerve. Only the defeated and deserters go to the wars—Cowards that run away and enlist. O ye Chivalry, ye could not fight a duel with your lives, and so ye challenged a man!

I met a pilgrim travel-worn, who could speak all tongues and conform himself to the customs of all nations;—who carried a passport to all countries, and was naturalized in all climes, who had vanquished all the chimeras and caused the Sphinx to go and dash her head against a stone—who never retraced his steps nor returned to his native land, and was reputed to have travelled further than all the travellers. He bore for device on his shield these words only—"Know Thyself."

> "Direct your eye sight inward, and you'll find
>   A thousand regions in your mind
> Yet undiscovered. Travel them, and be
>   Expert in home-cosmographie."

Most revolutions in society have not power to interest, still less alarm us, but tell me that our rivers are drying up, or the genus pine dying out in the country, and I might attend. Some events in history are more remarkable than important, like eclipses of the sun by which all are attracted, but whose effects no one takes the trouble to calculate. Revolutions are never sudden. The most important is commonly some silent and unobtrusive fact in history. In the year 449 three Saxon cyules arrived on the British coast. "Three scipen gode comen mid than flode."

To the sick the doctors wisely recommend a change of air and scenery. Who chains me to this dull town?

There is this moment proposed to me every kind of life that men lead anywhere or at any time—or that imagination can paint. By another spring I may be a mail carrier in Peru, or a South African planter, or a Siberian exile, or a Greenland whaler, or a settler on the Columbia River—or a Canton merchant, or a soldier in Mexico, or a mackerel fisher off Cape Sable, or a Robinson Crusoe in the Pacific, or a silent navigator of any sea.

How many are now standing on the European coast whom another spring will find located on the Wisconsin or the Sacramento!

I can move away from public opinion, from government, from religion, from education, from society. Shall I be reckoned a rateable poll in the county of Middlesex, or be rated at one spear under the palm trees of Guinea? Shall I raise corn and potatoes in Massachusetts, or figs and olives in Asia Minor? Sit out the day in my office in State street, or ride it out on the steppes of Tartary? For my Brobdingnag I may sail to Patagonia, for my Lilliput to Lapland. In Arabia and Persia my days' adventures may surpass the Arabian Nights entertainments. I may be a logger on the head waters of the Penobscot, to be recorded in fable hereafter as an amphibious river God by as sounding a name as Triton or Proteus.—Carry furs from Nootka to China and so be more renowned than Jason and his Golden Fleece, or join a South Sea exploring expedition to be recounted hereafter along with the Periplus of Hanno.

And how many more things may I do with which there is none to be compared!

Thank Heaven here is not all the world. The buckeye does not grow in New England, and the mocking bird is rarely heard here. Why should I fall behind the summer and the migrations of birds? Shall we not compete with the buffalo who keeps pace with the seasons, cropping the pastures of the Colorado till a greener and sweeter grass awaits him by the Yellow-stone? The wild-goose is more a cosmopolite than we, —he breaks his fast in Canada—takes a luncheon in the Susquehanna, and plumes himself for the night in a Louisiana bayou. The pigeon carries an acorn in his crop from the King of Holland's to Mason and Dixon's Line. Yet we think if rail-fences are pulled down and stone walls set up on our farms, bounds are henceforth set to our lives and our fates decided. If you are chosen town-clerk forsooth, you cannot go to Tierra del Fuego this summer.

But what would all this activity amount to—?

> Goosey goosey gander
> Where shall I wander?
> Up stairs down stairs
> In a lady's chamber?

Shall we not stretch our legs?—Why shall we pause this side of sundown? We will not then be immigrants still further into our native country. Let us start now on that fartherest western way which does not pause at the Mississippi or the Pacific, pushing on by day and night, sun down—moon down—stars down—and at last earth down too.

Index

intelligent citizens' shame
in, 96; meeting for John
Brown in, 146; seen from
jail, 82
Concord (N. H.), 49
Concord Bridge, 113
Concord fight, 91, 113
Concord monument, 61
Confucius, quoted, 78
Congress, United States, 89,
96, 115, 127, 157, 175;
compared to town meeting,
99
Connecticut, John Brown
born in, 111
conscience, above govern-
ment, 65; corporation and,
65; hero serves state with,
66
Conservative, irritable, 186
Conservatives, heads of, 181;
qualities of, 181-82
Constitution, United States,
86, 88, 98, 100, 112;
Defender of, 87; evil in,
74; framers of, 60; higher
law than, 104
constitution for association,
Etzler's, 43
constitutionality, distinction
from rightness of, 103
convention, 70
conventionalities, compared
to impurities, 173
conversation, ineffectuality
of, 169
Copernicus, 73
Coppoc, [Edwin], 128
cord-wood, measuring, 158
corporation and conscience,
65
correspondence, ineffectuality
of, 169
Council Chamber, 75
court, truly of justice, 106
Court street, 107
court-room, auditors in, 172

courts, true function of, 97
coward, 3-6; discord of, 11
cowards, 135, 195; Northern
men as, 108
crank within, 40
Cromwell, Oliver, 113, 115
Cromwellian troop, 114
culture, true, 174
Cyclon, 5

Dante, 191
Darien, Isthmus of, 166
Decker, [Thomas], 175
Declaration of Independence,
138
deed, noble, 148
deeds, importance of, 16
democracy, not ultimate, 89
Democrat, modern, 148
Democratic journals, 125
Democrats, 113-14
Devil, hard work of, 163
Devil's angels, one of the, 167
Dexter, Lord Timothy, 158
distance, related to strange-
ness, 121
Divine, the, 43. See also
God, Author of the
Universe
dog, on treadmill, 23
dwellings, constant repair
of, 36; Etzler's concepts
of, 35-38
"Duty of Submission to Civil
Government," 67
dyspepsia, politics as, 179;
reform as caused by, 183

Eden, no sign of, 42
editor, Northern, 128
editors, newspaper, 135; on
John Brown, 124, 149;
Republican, 123; tyranny
of, 100
education, liberal, 151;
Thoreau's preference in,
157

Editorial Appendix

Notes on Illustrations

"The Service," a manuscript page of Thoreau's
      printer's copy   following page 232

> The third page, recto of sheet 2, of the manuscript
> Thoreau dated "July–1840" and submitted for Mar-
> garet Fuller's consideration for publication in *The
> Dial*. The text appears on pages 4-5 of the present
> edition. The neat script is characteristic of Thoreau's
> early fair-copy drafts. The small "2" in the upper
> right hand corner and the light marginal pencillings
> are in a foreign hand. In her covering letter to
> Thoreau, enclosing the manuscript, Miss Fuller re-
> marked that "the thoughts seem to me so out of their
> natural order, that I cannot read it through without
> pain."–Pierpont Morgan Library

"Reform and the Reformers," a manuscript page of
      Thoreau's final draft

> The matter on this page, verso of sheet 1, Thoreau
> succeeded in bringing to fair copy. On no other page
> of the essay, however, did he enjoy comparable
> success; and his copy reflects on some pages as many
> as four levels of revision and expansion. The script
> is typical of the period preceding the publication of
> *Walden*. The text appears on pages 181-182 of the
> present edition.–Houghton Library, Harvard Uni-
> versity.

"A Plea for Captain John Brown," a manuscript
page of Thoreau's reading draft and
printer's copy

The heavy script of this page is typical of the John
Brown period. Text appears on page 111 of the
present edition. Thoreau's cancellation of "Sold for
the benefit of Capt. Brown's Family" and his interlineation in pencil of the record of his readings at
Boston and Worcester were in response to the thwart-
ing of his initial purpose in writing the essay. The
non-authorial "Miscell. p. 196" pencilled in the upper
right hand corner locates the essay in Volume x of
the Riverside Edition (1893).—The Henry E. Huntington Library and Art Gallery.

John Brown broadside

The announcement of the service in the Concord
Town Hall held simultaneously with the hanging
of John Brown in Virginia on December 2, 1859. The
"Dirge" was written for the occasion by Franklin B.
Sanborn, but the hand that altered in ink the date at
the bottom of the sheet is unknown.—Berg Collection,
New York Public Library.

Acknowledgments

THE ISSUANCE of THE WRITINGS OF HENRY D. THOREAU is a cooperative effort, product of the collaboration of a multitude of Thoreau readers and scholars, who have for many years hoped for an authoritative edition of Thoreau's writings. The editor of this volume has, therefore, solicited the help of the other editors of the edition, and particularly that of Editor-in-Chief William L. Howarth and former Editor-in-Chief Walter Harding, who have supplied aid of many kinds. Professors Harrison Hayford and Hershel Parker, representing the Center for Editions of American Authors, have generously read and criticized the entire manuscript to its great benefit. To them the editor's debt is very great.

Acknowledgment for diverse kinds of assistance is made also to the following: the secretaries of the edition, Sally Catanzariti and Marsha Britt; the staff of the library of the University of Minnesota, Duluth, and particularly Mrs. Ellen Oswald; the staff of the Wilson Library of the University of Minnesota, Minneapolis; Mr. Thomas Blanding of Princeton University; Mrs. Frieda Gardner; Mrs. Ruth Wheeler of Concord, Massachusetts; Mrs. Robert Owens of the staff of the Duluth Public Library; Mr. Julian P. Boyd, Editor of *The Papers of Thomas Jefferson*; Professor Walter H. Merrill of Drexel Institute of Technology; Mr. Malcolm M. Ferguson of West Concord, Massachusetts; Mr. Edmund Berkeley, Jr., Curator of Manuscripts of the Clifton Waller Barrett Library of the University of Virginia; Mr. Herbert Cahoon of the Pierpont Morgan Library; Dr. Lola L. Szladits of the Berg Collection of the New York Public Library; Miss Carolyn Jakeman of the Manuscript Division of the Houghton Library;

Mr. Herbert C. Schultz, Curator of Manuscripts of the Henry E. Huntington Library and Art Gallery; Professor Robert Sonkowsky of the University of Minnesota; and Miss Janice Jolly, Miss Jean Johnson, Miss Barbara Harris, and Miss Catherine Glick, all indefatigable collators. I wish also to acknowledge the care, concern, and good judgment of Ms. Carol Orr of Princeton University Press.

I am indebted to the administration of the University of Minnesota and its Board of Regents for granting me a sabbatical leave for the academic year 1969-1970 to enable me to devote full time to this project; to my department for collectively subsidizing me by taking over my work in my absence; and to the National Endowment for the Humanities and the Center for Editions of American Authors for support for the twelve-month period beginning September 1969. I am grateful also to the Graduate School of the University of Minnesota (particularly Dean Bryce Crawford) for grants-in-aid to defray expenses of collation, photo-copying, and travel.

Above all, I thank my wife, Barbara, for devoting time to tedious comparison of texts and for putting up with me when progress was slow.

For the preparation of this volume, permission has been generously given by: Mr. Herbert Cahoon and the Pierpont Morgan Library to publish the manuscripts of "The Service," MA 607, and of "Martyrdom of John Brown," MA 884, to quote from holograph letters preserved with these manuscripts and from the manuscript journals of Thoreau, MA 1302, and to allude to MA 1303 and scattered working forms of "Life without Principle" and other essays; Mr. W. H. Bond and the Harvard College Library to publish the holograph matter of folder 18B of bMS AM 278.5 under the title of "Reform and the Reformers," to quote from folders 2, 4D, 11, 14, 17F, 18A, and 20 of bMS AM 278.5, and to allude to the manuscript cost-books of Ticknor and Fields, MS AM 1185.6; Mr. Clifton Waller Barrett and the Clifton Waller Barrett Library of the University of Virginia to quote from one manuscript leaf of "A Plea for Captain John Brown" in the Thoreau Collection; Mr. Malcolm M. Ferguson, West Concord, Massachusetts, to quote from one manuscript leaf of "A Plea for Captain John Brown"; Mr. Robert O. Dougan, Librarian of the Henry E. Huntington Library and Art Gallery, to quote from twelve leaves of "A Plea for Captain John Brown" in HM 13202 and HM 13203, and from the pencilled draft of an unpublished Thoreau letter in HM 13193; and the officers of the Henry W. and Albert A. Berg Collection of the New York Public Library, Astor, Lenox and Tilden Foundations, to refer to the Thoreau commonplace book in that collection.

To the dozens of other private individuals and libraries that have supplied me with photocopies of preliminary forms of the essays published in this volume, and to Professor Paul O. Williams for compiling the index, I am grateful.

General Introduction

SCANT evidence can be evoked to support the theory—and a theory is all it is—that Thoreau ever envisioned bringing his anti-slavery and reform essays together in a single volume. It was not until 1866, four years after his death, that most of the short pieces appearing here were collected under the title *A Yankee in Canada, with Anti-Slavery and Reform Papers*, the fifth of the posthumous volumes to be issued by Ticknor and Fields; and even then they were pendulously attached to the more highly esteemed record of Thoreau's Canadian trip. Whether Thoreau projected such a volume with his sister Sophia in the months of confinement preceding his death when he was editing such papers as "The Allegash and East Branch," "Autumnal Tints," and "Life without Principle" is a moot question; it seems extremely doubtful that he looked beyond the first two posthumous volumes: *Excursions* (1863) and *The Maine Woods* (1864). Patently, he did not list for Sophia the papers he desired to be included in such a volume, else the short selection "Prayers," the prose text of which was Emerson's, would not have appeared there. The impetus for creating this collection may have come from neither Thoreau nor his sister but from the publisher James T. Fields, who had earlier failed to win Sophia's consent to print Thoreau's journal.

Of what the printer's copy for *A Yankee* consisted, who prepared it, whether Thoreau left marked copies of earlier printings for some of the selections, or who saw the volume through the press—little is known. Sophia's role as copyist, custodian of Thoreau's manu-

scripts following his death, and editor of the posthumous *Excursions*, *The Maine Woods*, and *Cape
Cod* (1864), suggests of course that she had a hand
in editing *A Yankee* as well. According to Bronson
Alcott, in February of 1865 she was planning to edit
"a book or two of *Politics* [and] one or more of
Morals."[1] "*Politics*" and "*Morals*" possibly became the
text for *A Yankee*, and since Ellery Channing assisted her with the earlier volumes, he may have collaborated with her on this one. But the editors of the
volume are not named, though the names of the editors of the four posthumous volumes issued earlier by
Ticknor and Fields appear on the title pages. And
testimony about the volume is conflicting. F. B. Sanborn in January 1909, accounting to C. E. Goodspeed
for his possession of the papers of the John Brown
Memorial Service of December 2, 1859, designated
Sophia as sole editor.[2] Sanborn, however, was often
inaccurate, and his testimony in this instance follows
publication of the book by forty-three years. S. A.
Jones, in his "A Contribution Towards a Bibliography
of Thoreau," attributed the editorship to Emerson.[3]
Since he also attributed *Excursions*, *The Maine Woods*,
and *Cape Cod* to Emerson, though they were demonstrably the work of Sophia Thoreau and Ellery

[1] *The Letters of A. Bronson Alcott*, Richard L. Herrnstadt,
ed. (Ames, Iowa: Iowa State University Press, 1969), pp. 362-
63.

[2] MA 884 in the Pierpont Morgan Library, p. 24. Sanborn's
testimony is supported by a letter from Sophia Thoreau to
Daniel Ricketson, May 26, 1866, discovered by Thomas Blanding in the Concord Antiquarian Museum. "Mr Channing
leaves our neighborhood tomorrow," she wrote, "but we shall
not miss him for he *never* comes to see us." [*The Concord
Saunterer*, 7 (Sept. 1972), 2-6]. Since Bronson Alcott had
observed in his Journal for July 28, 1865, that Sophia had
begun work on "a book or two," it is of course possible that
Channing collaborated in the early stages.

[3] *The Unitarian*, 5 (March 1890), 127.

Channing, his testimony is also suspect. Francis Allen, Thoreau's first comprehensive bibliographer and an editor of great conscientiousness, admitted that he had "no information as to who made up the volume."[4] The Berg Collection of the New York Public Library contains Channing's presentation copy of *A Yankee* from Sophia, obtained by the library at the Wakeman dispersal sale of 1924, but the inscription gives no hint as to whether he participated in issuing the volume.

The first edition of *A Yankee* was printed in an impression of 1,546 copies from stereotype plates cast by Welch, Bigelow, & Company of Cambridge. Total cost of the impression was $1114.11 or 74½ cents per copy; and the selling price was $1.50.[5] The volume was cloth-bound in varying colors, the leaves 16mo in size, paged [*i-iv*] 1-286 [+ 2]. Page *i* is the title page; page *ii* bears the copyright and imprint; page *iii* provides the table of contents; page *iv* is blank; page 1 bears the half-title for "A Yankee in Canada"; page 2 is blank; page 3 begins the text of "A Yankee in Canada"; page 94 is blank; page 95 bears the half-title for "Anti-Slavery and Reform Papers." After blank page 96, "Slavery in Massachusetts" begins on page 97; "Prayers" on page 117; "Civil Disobedience" on page 123; "A Plea for Captain John Brown" on page 152; "Paradise (To Be) Regained" on page 182; "Herald of Freedom" on page 206; "Thomas Carlyle and His Works" on page 211; "Life without Principle" on page 248; "Wendell Phillips Before the Concord Lyceum" on page 274; and "The Last Days of John

---

[4] *Thoreau's Editors / History and Reminiscence*, Thoreau Society Booklet Number Seven (1950), p. 10.

[5] This and the following data on the first printing and the reimpressions of *A Yankee* may be found in the manuscript cost-books of Ticknor and Fields in the Houghton Library (MS AM 1185.6).

Brown" on page 278. The printer and binder used different sets of signatures; gatherings are printed [A]^{10} B-R^8 (using the full English alphabet), but bound [1]^{14} 2-12^{12}, 146 leaves, pages [i-iv] 1-286 [+ 2] = 292. In gatherings 2-12, leaf 5 is signed "$*," but 12$_5$ is missigned "10*," and no correction of the error is made in subsequent impressions.

The first impression was apparently sold out quickly. In early October, a scarce six weeks after the first issuance, Ticknor and Fields ordered from Welch, Bigelow & Company 500 additional copies of *A Yankee*, which the printer supplied on October 29 at a cost of $256.15 or fifty-three cents per copy. This second impression was in every way identical with the first. Subsequent impressions followed in this order: June 21, 1869 (100 copies); November 20, 1872 (108 copies); February 10, 1874 (150 copies); September 26, [1880?] (150 copies). A copy has been discovered dated 1878, though no impression of that date is listed in the cost-books. The cost-book record terminates in 1880 with the establishment of Houghton, Mifflin and Company, but an impression was issued in 1881 and another in 1891 (sizes unknown) under the imprint of *The Riverside Press*, Cambridge. The plates were by this time well battered, and collation reveals no evidence of renewal. Words that had disappeared from line ends as early as 1878 were never replaced; gathering signatures and punctuation marks that had disappeared were not restored. No impression after that of 1891 has been found to come from the original 1866 Welch, Bigelow & Company stereotype plates.

Before the final impression from the 1866 stereotype plates was issued, a second collection containing five selections from the 1866 *Yankee* appeared in England. Henry S. Salt was editor of the volume published in London in 1890 under the title *Anti-Slavery and Reform Papers*. Included were (in this order) "Civil Disobedience," "A Plea for Captain John Brown," "The Last Days of John Brown," "Paradise (To Be) Regained," and "Life without Principle," all based on one of the impressions issued from the 1866 plates. What arrangements Salt made with Houghton, Mifflin, if any, this editor has not been able to determine. Collation bears out, however, what the title "Civil Disobedience" suggests, that Salt did not return to the first printings for the texts of any of the selections that he included in his volume. Salt's use of the 1866 sub-title was the last until the appearance of Walter Harding's Canadian edition (Montreal: Harvest House, 1963). The potpourri of Thoreau's essays, letters, and poems issued by the Camelot Press in London in 1891, and edited by Will H. Dircks, this editor has not examined. Entitled *Essays and Other Writings*, the collection included four essays Salt had reprinted the year before and added "Thomas Carlyle and His Works."

Horace Scudder does not disclose in his preface to Volume x of the Riverside Edition (1893) the sources of his texts. Collation establishes, however, that *A Yankee* was his source for all selections that had hitherto appeared there. Scudder's collection acquired a new name, *Miscellanies*, and included enough new selections (including Emerson's biographical sketch and a sixty-five-page index to the entire Riverside Edition) to make an 8vo volume of *xii*, 429 pages. Scudder added to the grouping of the essays from the 1866 printing an excerpt from "The Service" Sanborn had read at the Concord Summer School of Philosophy in 1882, having extracted it haphazardly from the manuscript rejected by Margaret Fuller for *The Dial* in 1840. The text of the fragment used by Scudder— a text as corrupt as it was brief—was that supplied by Sanborn to Raymond L. Bridgman for the volume *Concord Lectures on Philosophy*, published by Moses King (Cambridge, 1883). Emerson's essay, "Prayers," no longer appeared with the collection; Edward Emerson had removed it. Added, however, was "After the Death of John Brown," designated in the present edition "Martyrdom of John Brown." For the text of this selection Scudder went to the first and only printing in James Redpath's *Echoes of Harper's Ferry* (1860). The first printing of "A Plea for Captain John Brown" was also available in Redpath, but Scudder passed it over for the more corrupt version in *A Yankee*. "The Prometheus Bound of Aeschylus," "Translations from Pindar," and a group of ten poems completed the volume. For such a diverse collection, only a broad rubric like *Miscellanies* would serve.

Scudder's failure to attempt more than the reduplication of existing texts in the Riverside Edition had grave consequences, for this opportunity once missed would never come again. The great dispersal of Thoreau's autograph manuscripts, to be signaled by the death of H. G. O. Blake in 1898, had not yet begun. The materials on which the most authoritative texts of these fugitive selections could be based were still concentrated in few hands. George S. Hellman and C. E. Goodspeed had not begun their acquisition of the cache of material preserved by Sophia Thoreau until her death in 1876, and afterwards by Blake, Thoreau's correspondent and confidant. By the time Francis Allen and Bradford Torrey set to work on the Walden and Manuscript editions, which were to be published at a cost of $300,000 in 1906, the liquidation, which was to be climaxed by the Wakeman sale in 1924, was well under way. Accessories to the dispersion of the manuscripts, ironically, were the Houghton, Mifflin editors themselves. Their binding a holograph sheet into the first volume of each of the sets of the Manuscript Edition—one presumes to insure the recovery of their heavy investment in issuing the works of a not-yet-established American author—probably doomed forever the full genetic reconstruction of the texts of such late essays as "Autumnal Tints" and "Life without Principle." A vigorous, still continuing search has located a bare tithe of the original sets of the Manuscript Edition, and from some of them the holograph sheet has been detached. Some of these sheets, now of great value, have found their way through autograph dealers into the Houghton, Huntington, Morgan, and Abernethy libraries. But as a conservative estimate, 500 such sheets of Thoreau manuscript material remain unlocated.

Though he is well known for his conscientiousness, Francis Allen's handling of the texts of the present selections in the 1906 Walden Edition is difficult to explain. Of course, he had to confront Scudder's problem of deciding in what company to lodge the anti-slavery and reform papers: they did not bulk enough to fill a volume of the Edition. For his own reasons, Allen preferred not to use the same ballast of translations and poems that Scudder had chosen, nor did he wish to recombine the anti-slavery and reform papers with "A Yankee in Canada." His final decision, as to grouping and title, was to preserve Scudder's rubric for the essays ("Miscellanies") and to append them to the "Cape Cod" narrative. Collation reveals that the texts of the Walden and Manuscript editions, and even a portion of the "Introductory Note" of

Volume ıv, *Cape Cod and Miscellanies*, were set from the Riverside text. What Allen succeeded in doing as editor of Volume ıv of the Walden Edition was to corrupt further the text of Volume x of the Riverside Edition, itself lacking authority. Fully aware as he was of the untrustworthiness of Sanborn, Allen still did not set right such editorial arbitrariness as Sanborn's butchery of "The Service." Whether he asked Sanborn for permission to include in the Walden Edition the complete text of "The Service," which Sanborn had edited and Goodspeed had printed in 1902, or to consult the manuscript of "Martyrdom of John Brown" ["After the Death of John Brown"] one can only speculate. Allen's criticism of Bartholow Crawford's choice of texts for the Thoreau volume of the American Writers Series (1934) rings hollow in the context of his carrying over and compounding the corruptions of the Riverside Edition into the Walden Edition, which was to remain standard from 1906 to the present.[6]

With the inclusion in the present volume of the first authoritative text of "The Service," this collection of polemical writings becomes a microcosm of Thoreau's literary career: from "The Service," 1840, one of the best examples of Thoreau's early style and interests, it moves through "Life without Principle," published posthumously in 1863. To the middle period of Thoreau's writing career, the Princeton edition adds the hitherto unpublished "Reform and the Reformers," with its overtones of *Walden*. Every stage of an active writing career of twenty-two years is thus represented. And in this edition, for the first time since the Salt edition of 1890, these selections are accorded a volume to themselves.

[6] See "Editing Thoreau," *Saturday Review of Literature*, 13 (March 14, 1936), 9.

2. MANUSCRIPTS

Only one of the eleven selections in this volume is represented in full by the manuscript Thoreau intended for printer's copy.[7] When Margaret Fuller, as editor of *The Dial*, rejected "The Service" and returned the draft to Thoreau in 1840, she unwittingly insured its preservation. Only this selection of the eleven in this volume was initially rejected for publication. Nine were accepted (though publication of one, "Paradise (To Be) Regained," was delayed for a few months), and of the nine, printer's copy has been located for portions of only two: "A Plea for Captain John Brown" and "Martyrdom of John Brown." "Reform and the Reformers," here printed for the first time, is edited wholly from manuscript drafts that Thoreau never brought to printer's copy. The holograph material the editor and the staff have been able to discover for this edition has been for the most part preliminary drafts. For none of the selections are there known surviving proofsheets.

The amount of surviving holograph material varies widely among the selections. For "The Service" (1840), there are early fair-copy forms of many passages of Thoreau's printer's copy in volumes one, two, and three of the manuscript journal in the Morgan Library, the latter the so-called "lost journal" edited by Perry Miller as *Consciousness in Concord* (Boston, 1958) and covering the period from July 30, 1840, to January 22, 1841. Folder 2 of bMS AM 278.5 in the Houghton Library contains two sheets of a preliminary working draft, and folder 4D contains alter-

[7] For a full history, description, and analysis of Thoreau's manuscripts, see William L. Howarth, *The Literary Manuscripts of Henry David Thoreau* (Columbus: Ohio State University Press, 1973). Professor Howarth has located additional preliminary forms for passages of some of these essays.

nate versions of several paragraphs. For "Paradise (To Be) Regained" (1843), on the other hand, the editor has discovered no manuscript material whatsoever. For "Herald of Freedom" (1844), a revision in Thoreau's hand of the final paragraph of the selection as printed in *The Dial* is preserved in folder 11 at the Houghton Library, followed by three pages of new holograph material in which Thoreau has made a few corrections and deletions. The present editor has added the new material to the text of the selection, since there is internal evidence that this was Thoreau's intention. Two sheets of working notes for the three pages of added material are also preserved with the draft. For "Wendell Phillips Before Concord Lyceum," a working draft exists in MA 1303 in the Morgan Library, the latter portion of which is heavily revised.

"Resistance to Civil Government" (1849) is represented only by fourteen holograph fragments of varying lengths, most of them short, and differing considerably from the form in which they appeared in print in the *Aesthetic Papers*. This fact suggests that Thoreau may have put the selection through a number of drafts en route to publication, all of which are now lost. Six short passages are to be found in folder 14 in the Houghton collection, one in the long (78 pages) folder 18A, and one in folder 20. In the Huntington Library, in HM 13182, there is a marginal draft of a two-sentence passage, and in HM 924 there are drafts of five other passages. In other words, for what has come to be considered Thoreau's most cogent political statement, there not only exist no coherent and complete working drafts, but for the first printing of 960 lines, less than 44 lines have been found to exist in early holograph versions, and these are widely separated in the selection. No portion of the 1849 text of the essay appears in an earlier form in the manuscript journal. A genetic text of "Resistance to Civil Government," given the present knowledge of manuscript material, could not be produced. Moreover, holograph revisions of the first printing, which would establish as authorial the substantive alterations of the text (and title) that first appeared in the posthumous 1866 printing, have never been found.

The text of "Slavery in Massachusetts" (1854) Thoreau drew largely from his journal for April/May of 1851 and May/June of 1854. For approximately two-thirds of the selection—by rough count, 400 out of 660 printed lines—there are very close early drafts in the journal, some of which appear verbatim (except for slight alterations of the punctuation) in Garrison's printing of the lecture in *The Liberator*. No early versions of any portions of the text of "Slavery in Massachusetts" other than those versions in the journal have come to light. In preparing his text, Thoreau combined his responses to the Thomas Sims case of 1851 with those to the Anthony Burns case of 1854. The similarities in the two cases apparently made the assimilation easy. What he had written in anger of the treatment of Sims he found to be applicable to and interchangeable with his thoughts on the apprehension of Burns. "Slavery in Massachusetts" was thus an overflow of powerful feeling that fused at white heat without requiring long pondering and the repositioning of sections. The speed with which Thoreau prepared this lecture, and the lack of variation between the journals and *The Liberator*, make remote the possibility of his having prepared an intermediate version between the journal and printer's copy.

"A Plea for Captain John Brown" (1860) was composed also in response to an event which moved Thoreau deeply, driving him to record his responses in his journal. In the very long entries of October 19, 20, 21, and 22, 1859, Thoreau wrote the drafts of most of the paragraphs he later reorganized into the lecture he thrice delivered. It is clear that even as he composed the journal entries he was directing his remarks to an imaginary audience. In the entry for October 22, for instance, the second person is common: "You who pretend," "Though you may not approve," "Many of you have read," and so on. Sixty holograph sheets, written only on recto once comprised the lecture; of these, eleven have been preserved in HM 13202 and 13203 at the Huntington Library (pages 1, 3, 27, 31, 40, 46, 49, 50, 54, 57, and 60), one in the Thoreau Collection of the Clifton Waller Barrett Library of the University of Virginia (page 47), and an additional sheet (page 17) bound into a Manuscript Edition in private hands. Two other sheets (pages 18 and 60), preserved in HM 13203, are either parts of a previous working draft or individual sheets Thoreau decided to revise. What seems to have preserved these sheets from destruction was Thoreau's use of the verso of nearly all of them to chronicle data in minutely written lists under the captions "Calendar for March" and "General Phenomena for April," though this hypothesis does not explain Thoreau's retention of three of them on which there were only mathematical calculations, unless the calculations were in some way connected with the "Phenomena." Thoreau's cancelled entry beneath the title of this selection on page one of this holograph draft ("Sold for the benefit of Capt. Brown's Family") suggests that this may have been the draft Thoreau intended for printer's copy and sent to Redpath for

publication after his failure to interest any other publisher in putting out the lecture as a pamphlet. Of all
the selections in this volume, "A Plea for Captain John
Brown" is the only one for which there is more than
circumstantial evidence that Thoreau checked the
proofsheets. A fugitive from federal marshals, Redpath told Thoreau in a letter of February 6, 1860, that
he understood Thoreau's lecture had been sent to
him "for correction."[8]

Thoreau may have thought little of "Martyrdom
of John Brown" as a literary document, since he permitted Franklin B. Sanborn to see the record of the
Concord service through to publication. It is possible
that Thoreau read the proof for his translation from
Tacitus, since he refused to print the Emerson translation of the selection, which had been read at the
services. His draft of the translation from Tacitus is
the only portion of the record missing from MA 884
in the Morgan Library, printer's copy for the version
that appeared in James Redpath's *Echoes of Harper's
Ferry*. The substance of Thoreau's writing for this
occasion is contained in two paragraphs, the first of
which Thoreau revised from an entry in the manuscript journal for November 15, 1859. No holograph
version of the second paragraph has been found.

For "The Last Days of John Brown" (1860), prepared for delivery by R. J. Hinton at John Brown's
grave in North Elba, New York, on July 4, 1860,
Thoreau turned again to his manuscript journal for
November 15-17 and December 3-9, 1859. The most
restrained of the John Brown selections, it is comprised largely of post-execution reflections from the
December entries, with the paragraphs transposed but

[8] *The Correspondence of Henry David Thoreau*, Walter
Harding and Carl Bode, eds. (New York, 1958), p. 574.

the wording rarely altered. Only eleven sentences, including the three terminal ones, lack parallel versions in the journal entries; and the few substantive changes in wording in the first printing in *The Liberator* (July 27, 1860) suggest that the draft Thoreau handed to Hinton in Concord, to be read at the commemorative exercises, and to be used as printer's copy by Garrison, was the only draft of the selection Thoreau ever prepared.

For more than a decade, Thoreau accumulated the material out of which was to come the posthumously published "Life without Principle" (1863). At least a third of the printed text is represented by early versions in the manuscript journal, the first appearing in the entry for November 17, 1850, the last in the entry for November 16, 1858, the majority in 1851 and 1852. In a printing aggregating 875 lines, journal equivalents can be located for about 385. For three of the journal passages there are earlier drafts in folder 20 in the Houghton Library, where more than twenty passages ranging from three words to full paragraphs can be found. Folder 1 of the same collection contains three passages revised and used later in "Life without Principle"; folder 17F contains two. Nineteen sheets of material have been located, some very tentative, some near fair copy, but all presently or at one time bound into copies of the Manuscript Edition. Most are in institutional libraries, since privately held copies of the Manuscript Edition are difficult to locate. The editor has examined sixteen of them. What they reflect, and what the sequence of titles of the selection as lecture and printed essay suggests ("What Shall it Profit?"; "Life Misspent"; "The Higher Law" and "Life without Principle"), is that Thoreau revised parts of this selection many

with his line, but if he give you the dimensions of the Parthenon in feet and inches,
the figures will not embrace it like a
cord, but dangle from its entablature like
an elastic drapery.

His eye is the focus in which all the
rays, from whatever side, are collected;
for itself being within and central, the
entire circumference is revealed to it. Just
as we scan the whole concave of the
heavens at a glance, but can compass only
one side of the pebble at our feet. So
does his discretion give prevalence to his
valor. "Discretion is the wise man's soul,"
saith the poet. His prudence may safely
go many strides beyond the utmost rashness of the coward; for, while he observes
strictly the golden mean, he seems to
run through all extremes with impunity.
Like the sun, which, to the poor worldling,
now appears in the zenith, now in the
horizon, and again is faintly reflected from
the moon's disk, and has the credit
of describing an entire great circle, crossing
the equinoctial and solstitial colures,
without detriment to his steadfastness or
mediocrity. The golden mean, in ethics as
in physics, is the center of the system, and
that about which all revolve; and, though
a distant and plodding planet it be

"The Service," a manuscript page of Thoreau's printer's copy

say We and Our, as if they had never been assured of an individual existence. Our Indian policy, our coast defences, our national character. They are what are called public men, fashionable men, ambitious men, chaplains of the army or navy, men of property standing and respectability, for the most part, and in all cases created by society. Sometimes even they are embarked in "great causes," which have been stranded on the shores of society in a previous age, carrying them through with a kind of reflected and traditionary nobleness, certainly disinterestedness. The Conservative has many virtues which the Reformer has not, — ofttimes a singular and unexpected liberality and courtesy, a decided practicalness and reverence for fact, and with a little less irritability, or more indifference would be the more tolerable companion. He is the Steward of Society, and in this office at least is faithful and generous. He is a dutiful son but a tyrannical father, and does not foresee that

"Reform and the Reformers," a manuscript page
of Thoreau's final draft

A Plea

for

Capt. John Brown.

by

Henry D. Thoreau.

Read to the citizens of Concord Mass.
Sunday Evening Oct 30," 1859.
Sold for the benefit of Capt. Brown's Family.

I trust you will pardon me
for being here. I do not wish to force
my thoughts upon you, but I
feel forced myself. Little as I know
of Captain Brown, I would fain
do my part to correct the tone
and the statements of the newspapers,
and of my countrymen generally, respecting his character and actions.
It costs us nothing to be just. We
can at least express our sympathy with, and admiration of, him
and his companions, and that is
what I now propose to do.
First, as to his history.
I will endeavor to omit, as much as
possible, what you have already read.

"A Plea for Captain John Brown," a manuscript page of Thoreau's
reading draft and printer's copy

Martyrdom of John Brown.

EXERCISES
—— AT THE ——

TOWN, HALL, IN CONCORD,

On FRIDAY, December 2nd, 1859,

AT 2 O'CLOCK, P. M.

MUSIC.

PRAYER.

HYMN,
" Go to the grave in all thy glorious prime."

READING OF PERTINENT PASSAGES.

SELECTIONS FROM BROWN'S LAST WORDS.

SERVICE FOR THE DEATH OF A MARTYR.

DIRGE;

To-day beside Potomac's wave,
  Beneath Virginia's sky,
They slay the man who loved the slave,
  And dared for him to die.

The Pilgrim Fathers' earnest creed,
  Virginia's ancient faith,
Inspired this hero's noblest deed,
  And his reward is—Death !

Great Washington's indignant shade
  Forever urged him on,—
He heard from Monticello's glade
  The voice of Jefferson.

But chiefly on the Hebrew page
  He read Jehovah's law,
And this from youth to hoary age
  Obeyed with love and awe.

No selfish purpose armed his hand,
  No passion aimed his blow ;
How loyally he loved his land
  Impartial Time shall show.

But now the faithful martyr dies,
  His brave heart beats no more,
His soul ascends the equal skies,
  His earthly course is o'er.

For this we mourn, but not for him,
  Like him in God we trust ;
And though our eyes with tears are dim,
  We know that God is just.

Concord, Dec. 30, 1859.

John Brown broadside

times. The extensive binding of holograph sheets into copies of the Manuscript Edition probably doomed forever the possibility of genetic reconstruction of the manuscript.

"Reform and the Reformers," printed for the first time in this volume, was never finished by Thoreau. The process of repositioning paragraphs and shifting elements was still going on when Thoreau gave up his work on what was apparently to have been a lecture on the reform of reformers. The text printed here was edited from the holograph materials in folder 18B in the Houghton Library. Most of the 18B material—seventy percent or so—Thoreau refined from a notebook of jottings now preserved at the Houghton Library as folder 18A. One sheet of 18A material, keyed into 18B by Thoreau, is included in the present text. A large quantity of miscellaneous material in the 18A notebook Thoreau never worked into publishable form. Perhaps a fifth of the material in 18A is stricken with use marks, and another fifth cancelled, though Thoreau failed to mark most material that he carried over into 18B. That he considered at one time quarrying additional lectures from the 18A notebook is suggested by his transferal into the folder 14 manuscript of twenty-eight pages of material on the general subject of government, six short fragments of which he used in "Resistance to Civil Government." "Reform and the Reformers" was perhaps one revision removed from final form when Thoreau stopped work on it. The material on government in folder 14, however, was at least two removes from printer's copy, if we apply to it Thoreau's usual practices in revision —too far removed, at any rate, for editorial amalgamation; for this reason, it is not included in this volume.

3. THEORY OF COPY-TEXT
AND PRINCIPLES OF EMENDATION

In preparing the present volume, the editor has followed the editorial principles and procedures established by the Center for Editions of American Authors of the Modern Language Association of America. Since an outline of these principles and procedures is available in the Center's *Statement of Editorial Principles* (1967, 1972), and since fuller discussions may be found in the publications listed in the bibliography in the *Statement*, the present discussion will be concerned chiefly with the applicability of these principles and procedures to the editing of the antislavery and reform essays of Thoreau.

The aim of this edition, like that of the other editions supported by the Center for Editions of American Authors, is to produce texts as close as possible to the author's intention, texts that would have met with his approval. Intention is difficult to establish in some instances, particularly in the case of Thoreau, who considered many of these selections ephemeral and took few pains therefore to refine some of his texts. As a result, Thoreau's "intention" must at times be deduced by the editor on the basis of the "usual practice" criterion derived from close study of his personal and writing habits, particularly when fair-copy manuscript material cannot be recovered. But the crucial point is that the texts printed here are the author's, not the editor's. The aim of this volume is not to produce modernized texts, for Thoreau wrote in the idiom of his age. The aim is not to impose consistency in accidentals—in capitalization, punctuation, and the like—unless the inconsistencies are demonstrably the result of the carelessness or the unauthorized tampering of editor or printer. One of Thoreau's characteristics as a writer was his lack of concern for consistency in matters of this kind, after he had emancipated himself from the prescriptions of his Harvard instructors and had found his own idiom. Finally, it is not the aim of this edition to "improve" upon what Thoreau wrote; rather, it seeks to purge Thoreau's texts of the "improvements" of others, of Franklin B. Sanborn's dozens of well-meant alterations, for instance, in the text Thoreau intended for "The Service."

The editorial practices followed here are those that have proved themselves most satisfactory in restoring corrupt texts to the form the author would have approved. Fundamental to modern textual theory is that the author's intended printer's copy, or the subsequent form of the text closest to his printer's copy, is the form most reliable in accidentals, and most suitable, therefore, to serve as "copy-text." The first printing is less reliable in accidentals than printer's copy, even when the author has read proof, because even when an author makes substantive changes in the proof—changes affecting meaning–he rarely takes the time to correct carefully for accidentals. In the selections in this volume, even in those rare instances when Thoreau corrected the texts of a first printing in his personal copy, he paid little attention to accidentals. Meaning concerned him; what he considered the minutiae of punctuation, capitalization, etc., did not. This is the justification for W. W. Greg's insistence that the modern editor must distinguish "accidentals" from "substantives"; and Greg's theory is particularly applicable in the case of such a desultory proofreader as Thoreau.[9] Each resetting of the text from a previous printing, by this theory, compounds the corruptions in accidentals, moving the text farther and

[9] See "The Rationale of Copy-Text," *Studies in Bibliography*, 3 (1950), 19-36.

farther from the author's intention as it was once reflected in his printer's copy.

In choosing the copy-text for each of the eleven selections in the present volume, the editor has attempted to recover copies of every extant form in which each text survives. If printer's copy survives, as it does for "The Service" and for some portions of "A Plea for Captain John Brown," he has chosen it as his copy-text on the theory that printer's copy represents Thoreau's intention as to accidentals more closely than any other version. The printer's copy for most of the selections, however, was discarded by the printer who evidently considered the manuscript of no value after the type was set, and in these instances the editor has used as copy-text the next subsequent form closest to the author's hand. Printer's proof, as corrected by Thoreau, would be the next in authorial priority; but Thoreau had no opportunity to read proof for most of these selections, many of which appeared initially in newspapers or periodicals, and for none has proof been located. The copy-text for most of these selections, therefore, has been drawn from the first printed version that was set directly from the lost printer's copy. If no evidence can be educed to show that Thoreau intervened to revise or correct this first printed text, it must remain the sole authority. Later changes in the printed text may be emended into the copy-text, but only if it can be demonstrated that Thoreau—not a copyist, editor, or printer—made them. The exception is obvious errors that Thoreau missed and any editor should correct.

Since extensive substantive changes appear in the second printing (1866) of many of the selections in this volume, which substantive variants have authorial sanction and should be emended into the copy-texts is a crucial question. The present editor adopts a conservative policy of emendation. Though the issue of emendation of the *Yankee* substantives for each selection is discussed as a separate problem in the individual textual introduction for that selection, the extent of the problem warrants a brief survey here. *A Yankee* is the only posthumous collection to have a claim to authority; its historical importance derives from its having provided the texts on which most subsequent printings of the anti-slavery and reform papers were based.

The text of "Paradise (To Be) Regained," as it appeared initially in *The United States Magazine and Democratic Review*, was cut in *A Yankee* by about one-third. The sheer bulk of the deletions raises interesting editorial questions. First of all, Thoreau as a rule put his material through several drafts prior to publication, and wholesale revision after publication, therefore, was uncommon with him. No working drafts for this review, however, have been found. Second, the review was first rejected by J. L. O'Sullivan of *The Democratic Review*, whose suggestion that there be "addition & modification made with your concurrence" led Thoreau to remark to his mother that O'Sullivan wished him to "send them something else, or reform that."[10] The point is that to satisfy O'Sullivan and to get the review into print Thoreau may have made additions in the form of the long quotations from the Etzler volume, which he later deleted after having achieved his objective of publication. For ninety percent of the matter cut in the 1866 printing was material quoted by Thoreau from Etzler, the sort of material he could have added quickly before publication to appease O'Sullivan and could have stricken quickly and without detriment to con-

10 *Correspondence*, pp. 130, 132.

tinuity after the review appeared in print. But plausible as such evidence is, it is circumstantial, and the editor's policy of conservative emendation precludes assuming the deletions to have been authorial. Study of the deleted passages yields no certain clue to the identity of the hand that cut them.

Like the text of "Paradise (To Be) Regained," the text of "Herald of Freedom" as it appeared in *The Dial* of April 1844 is also heavily cut in the 1866 *Yankee*. Thoreau printed in *The Dial* six long quotations from editorials written by Nathaniel Rogers for issues of the *Herald of Freedom*, the first quotation being from the issue of July 14, 1838, the last two from the issue of March 15, 1844. Of the six quotations, the 1866 *Yankee* preserves only the second intact. It prints approximately one-half of the third. The remaining four were cut completely, along with much of Thoreau's scaffolding between the quotations. The final paragraph as it appeared in the 1866 text was completely revised.

The possibility that Thoreau himself made these heavy editorial deletions is slight. For, in addition to eliminating most of the matter quoted from Rogers, the 1866 editor attempted also to alter Thoreau's *Dial* text to make verb tenses and adverbs conform to the fact of Rogers' death subsequent to the *Dial* printing in 1844. The result was a mishmash of crudity and inconsistency that Thoreau, a stylistic perfectionist, would not have condoned.

The 1866 revision of the final paragraph, however, is authorial. Four pages of fair-copy holograph matter on Rogers, beginning with Thoreau's revision of the final paragraph of the *Dial* printing, are preserved in folder 11 at the Houghton Library. The final paragraph of the *Dial* copy-text for this review is therefore deleted in the present edition, and Thoreau's holo-

graph revision along with the subsequent holograph
material is made copy-text for the review from this
point. The fact that the material Thoreau apparently
intended to be printed following the revised paragraph was not included by the 1866 editor adds to the
evidence that it was not Thoreau who edited *A
Yankee*. The crudity of the revision of all but the final
paragraph supports the position that substantive
emendations of *Yankee* variants into the copy-texts
should be made only when the evidence for a particular emendation is unassailable.

In "Wendell Phillips Before Concord Lyceum,"
there is only one substantive change between *The
Liberator* version of 1845 (which provides the copy-
text) and the version in *A Yankee*—the pluralization
in the latter version of "conserver" (59.10). Since in
Thoreau's working copy for the selection the form is
plural, the present editor has emended the copy-text
without knowing whether the alteration in *A Yankee*
was the result of Thoreau's correcting the text of the
first printing or a lucky editorial surmise on the part
of the unidentified *Yankee* editor or compositor. Thoreau's probable intention is the issue, and the evidence that Thoreau intended the plural is judged by
the editor to outweigh the authority of the copy-text.

"Resistance to Civil Government" poses the problem of how to account for thirteen substantive variants in *A Yankee*. Nine are of the sort that could be
classified as compositorial errors resulting from misreading of the 1849 printed text, or as changes made
to accord with the stylistic taste of an unknown editor.
The remaining four substantive variants, however,
are not so simply accounted for. The 1849 title, "Resistance to Civil Government," is altered in 1866 to
"Civil Disobedience." From the end of one sentence,
twenty words are stricken. And in two cases, there

are significant additions. Six lines of poetry from George Peale's *The Battle of Alcazar* are inserted into the *Yankee* text at one point, and at another a sentence referring to Confucius. Extensive search of surviving Thoreau manuscripts has yielded no hard evidence that these posthumous variants are from Thoreau's hand. Though the case is not closed, editorial prudence presently dictates that it is safer to print the 1849 substantives for which Thoreau probably read proof than to emend on the basis of the negative evidence that it is unlikely that Thoreau's editor(s) would have made these changes without authority. If the editor was Franklin B. Sanborn—or if he was Ellery Channing—and neither can be definitely ruled out, the possibility that Thoreau's texts were altered is present. Channing altered many of the passages he quoted from Thoreau's journal in *Thoreau, the Poet-Naturalist* (1873); and Sanborn made numerous changes in Thoreau's printer's draft in publishing *The Service* (1902). Identification beyond doubt of the editor(s) of *A Yankee* would be a significant step in solving this problem.

Seven of the twenty-four substantive variants in the 1866 version of "Slavery in Massachusetts," on the contrary, appear to be authorial, since they are restorations of readings that appear in holograph forms antedating the publication in *The Liberator* in 1854. Though it cannot be proved beyond all doubt that someone other than Thoreau, having access to the manuscript journal, did not block out in the journal early versions of the first printing and emend that version on the basis of them, the likelihood that any person other than Thoreau would have gone to this very considerable trouble to locate the forms, collate, and restore the early readings, seems remote. Whether Thoreau was correcting printer's errors or the printer's deliberate alterations, or whether he had simply changed his mind, is immaterial.

In "A Plea for Captain John Brown" most of the eight substantive variants in the 1866 text are the sort that could have been made by a careless compositor, or by an editor seeking to "improve" the text. Two corrections in Thoreau's own hand in his personal copy of *Echoes of Harper's Ferry*, where the selection was first printed, suggest an intention on the part of Thoreau to revise the text, and his own corrections are of course incorporated into the text printed here. Since the corrections may also be found in early holograph forms that precede the first printing, they would be considered for emendation into the present text even though Thoreau had neglected to correct his personal copy.

The substantives in "The Last Days of John Brown" pose no problems. Only one substantive variant exists between the first printing in *The Liberator* (1860) and that in *A Yankee* (1866). The reading "ever" in *The Liberator*, which makes nonsense of the sentence in which it appears (at 148.35), was restored in *A Yankee* to "even," the reading of the manuscript journal (December 6, 1859). Nor is there a problem of substantive emendation in "Life without Principle," since the only two printings having possible authority were both posthumous—the *Atlantic Monthly* printing (1863), which Thoreau prepared in the last months of his life, and the *Yankee* printing of 1866. The only substantive variant in the 1866 version, "a window" for the 1863 reading "the window" (157.33) is dismissed as non-authorial for lack of evidence.

Editing eleven different selections, each with its unique history of composition, publication, and residual forms, has necessitated eleven separate textual introductions. The copy-text in each instance, however, has been chosen on the basis of the criteria suggested by W. W. Greg. In the case of unfinished, unpublished matter ("Reform and the Reformers"), the copy-text is the version preceding, but nearest to, what would have been printer's copy. In the case of selections for which printer's copy is extant and accessible (e.g., "The Service"), printer's copy provides the copy-text. Where printer's copy has not been recovered, as with most of the selections in this volume, the first printing becomes copy-text.

Consultations on difficult editorial questions have been extensive among representatives of the Center for Editions of American Authors, members of the executive committee of the Thoreau Edition, and the editor. In most instances unanimity has been achieved. In a few, the editor has resolved problems of copy-text and emendation without securing the accord of all. The former editor-in-chief of the Thoreau Edition argued cogently for the authority of the substantive variants in the 1866 printing of "Civil Disobedience," which the editor has finally decided to relegate to the textual notes, along with the title. The present editor-in-chief disagrees with the editor's decision to incorporate certain short, holograph post-copy-text revisions into the texts of "The Service" (at 11.3-11.7 and 11.28-12.4) and "Herald of Freedom" (at 56.12-57.32); to depart from the copy-text of "Reform and the Reformers" to follow a slightly altered version of nine lines in Houghton folder 18A (at 183.34-184.8); and to emend classes of accidentals in the printed copy-text of "Wendell Phillips Before Concord Lyceum" on the authority of Thoreau's working draft, MA 1303. Though admitting the cogency of all of the arguments, the editor has concluded that on balance the evidence supporting the substitutions outweighs that for discarding them.

The order of the eleven selections in the present edition accords with the chronology of Thoreau's preparation of them for publication. Though "The Service" did not appear in print *in toto* until 1902, Thoreau intended it to appear in *The Dial* in 1840; it therefore appears first in the volume. "Reform and the Reformers," the final selection, is the exception. Thoreau did not bring the manuscript of this selection to final form, and his intentions for publication are unknown.

4. CLASSES OF EMENDATIONS

Emendation of the copy-texts of the selections in this volume has been sparing, each case having been evaluated on the basis of the textual evidence available. The editor has assumed the burden of proving in the case of each moot copy-text reading that Thoreau would have wished the reading to be altered. All substantive emendations, from whatever source, are defended in the textual notes.

The editor has made other copy-text emendations in the class of accidentals when there is substantial evidence that Thoreau's usual practice is being contravened, or when for some other reason his probable intention is clearly being violated. A third class of emendations dealing with matters of typography and format is completely apart from Thoreau's intention. These classes of emendations may be further summarized as follows:

A. Emendations are made in the printer's styling of copy-texts from the first printings, since Thoreau obviously had no control over the setting of his texts.

Display capitals, unindented paragraphs, terminal punctuation of titles, non-authorial titles, and titles regularized by whatever method to conform with the format of a given magazine, newspaper, or book, are not reproduced in the present edition. Pagination of the copy-texts is of course disregarded and gathering symbols are dropped. Worn letters and marks of punctuation, if clearly legible, are silently restored.

B. Conventions in Thoreau's holograph drafts which seem not to reflect intention, but are scribal idiosyncrasies or the probable result of speed of composing or copying, are as a rule emended in the texts in this volume. Thoreau's linkage of two words by the crossing of a "t" in one of them—if clearly Thoreau intended the two-word form—is silently disregarded. If at times he wrote the form as one word, the attempt is made to determine his preference for the period from which the text comes. As a final check in moot instances, John Walker's *Critical Pronouncing Dictionary* (1823), Thoreau's known lexicon, and the *OED*, are consulted. Certain abbreviations are expanded: for instance, Thoreau's ampersand may be altered to "and," or "Capt." to "Captain." For all such cases, the table of emendations carries the record. Thoreau's "&." is allowed to stand since it carried a particular connotation and was common nineteenth-century practice, though the period is added (and noted) when Thoreau omitted it. Though it is a reasonable supposition that the printers supplied long forms for Thoreau's manuscript abbreviations in versions here used as copy-texts, the editor has been able to devise no satisfactory criteria for isolating these corruptions, and the copy-texts are therefore respected.

C. All typographical slips, errors of spelling, and obvious mistakes in punctuation and capitalization are corrected and recorded. "Mistake" is defined in this context as clear and probably inadvertent contravention of accepted nineteenth-century practice as established in such works as Walker's *Critical Pronouncing Dictionary*. Walker and the *OED* are consulted to verify all suspect copy-text spellings, and on the basis of the evidence individual decisions are made and recorded. When a question still exists, the form is searched for in the G. and C. Merriam dictionaries, in sequence, beginning with the edition of 1847 and ending (five editions later) with 1879. In the absence of any authority for emendation, the copytext form is permitted to stand.

The editor assumes that Thoreau would have wished to spell proper names correctly: "Gonzalo" is therefore emended into the text from "Gonzalve" in printer's copy; "Vallandigham" is substituted for "Vallandingham"; and so on. But current usage is not followed and no emendation is made in cases where Thoreau apparently preferred an archaic or obsolete spelling to the accepted one. Walker, for instance, rules "etherial" sub-standard. But the *OED* demonstrates that the form was still a possible variant of "ethereal"; hence no emendation of the copytext is made. The same reasoning justifies the editor's unwillingness to emend "boyantly" and "prophane." Though Walker frowns on "behove" as a vulgarization of "behoove," Thoreau clearly prefers the former, employing it possibly *because of* its stigma; and Thoreau's preference takes precedence over the lexicon. Forms unacceptable to Walker, and unsupported by historical usage or by a clear authorial preference (e.g., "now a days") are emended to the most commonly accepted form of the period. In questions of capitalization, initial words in sentences in holograph copy-texts are capitalized on the grounds that Thoreau's failure to do so was probably inadvertent; but where Thoreau had an obvious though unorthodox preference (e.g., "bibles"), his preference is respected.

D. In manuscript revisions of material not yet revised to fair copy, Thoreau on occasions made his changes without adapting what remained of the sentence to the alteration. At 11.29, for example, he cancelled "sweet but" from the element "a sweet but unheard," leaving the article "a" juxtaposed against the word "unheard." The editor's emendation to "an unheard" corrects Thoreau's oversight.

E. Thoreau's hyphenation can only be described as capricious. Only when Thoreau's practice overwhelmingly contradicts a particular copy-text form does the editor emend. For instance, "New-Englander" is emended to "New Englander" on the grounds that Thoreau omitted the hyphen in nine instances in texts in this volume. On the other hand, "half-way" is allowed to remain, despite "half score," "half brutish," "half timid," "half conscious," and "half-consciousness." Emendation of hyphens carries its risks when an author can write "down-hill" at one point and "up hill" three lines later, or "horse-power" and "horse power" on the same page. Such hyphenated forms as "to-day" and "to-morrow" are allowed to stand unaltered. The number of cases in this volume for which there is an equal count between the hyphenated and unhyphenated forms of a word runs into scores. Thoreau's hyphenation, moreover, is as random as a rule within individual texts as between texts whose composition was separated by periods of time. The editor standardizes the hyphenation in only one selection. Since no hyphenation of noun compounds appears in Thoreau's working copy of "Wendell Phillips Before Concord Lyceum," the editor removes the hyphens in all such forms in *The Liberator* copy-text, for which Thoreau did not read proof.

Thoreau's common practice of writing two words as one poses a related problem. The printer confronted with the decision to leave two words as one or to separate them found himself an unwitting editor, and a few emendations (supported by Walker and the *OED*) are made in this volume in the belief that the printer erred in reading Thoreau's intent. Overwhelming statistical evidence of Thoreau's usage provides the basis for such emendations. One group of forms, however, the editor exempts from all emendation—compounds of "any" and "every"—though the probability that printers on occasion forced their own preferences upon Thoreau's texts is inescapable. Thoreau had no settled preference between the two-word or single-word form. The following sampling of his usage from the 1840 "The Service" to the 1859 "A Plea for Captain John Brown" reflects his lack of consistency:

> "any thing" 77.1; 106.1; 115.13
> "anything" 112.7; 122.34
> "any where" 115.23
> "anywhere or at any time" 196.4
> "every where" 56.8
> "everywhere" 11.20
> "every thing" *with* "*something*" 74.9-12
> "everything" 27.32

Yet in certain other matters Thoreau can show surprising consistency. Spelled-out cardinal numbers made up of two elements are hyphenated unless they are multiples of one hundred, when Thoreau uses two separate words. Holograph as well as printed copy-texts reflect this pattern.

F. Thoreau's placement of apostrophes is too erratic to permit the establishment of norms of usage. Apostrophes omitted from contractions are therefore not supplied by emendation (e.g., "dont" at 134.6).

Apostrophes misplaced in contractions by twentieth-century standards are not shifted (e.g., "does'nt" and "did'nt"). When a possessive lacks an apostrophe in a holograph manuscript, on the other hand, the editor supplies it (e.g., "Apollo's" at 191.17) and records the emendation in the table of emendations.

G. Nor has it been possible to establish norms for the capitalization of common nouns on the basis of statistical tabulations for particular words. At 119.29 appears "Slavery"; at 120.23 "slavery." At 178.19 appears "government," and at 178.21 "Government." At 120.7 appears "Church," and at 120.32 "church." Though Thoreau capitalizes oftener than not, he had formulated no clear preference. One exception among these selections stands out. In his working draft for "Wendell Phillips Before Concord Lyceum" Thoreau used lower case uniformly for "state," "church," and "slavery." His consistency, in the opinion of the editor, lends superior authority to the working draft, and the random capitals in *The Liberator* copy-text are consequently emended.

H. Thoreau's marks of elision in his fair copy of different periods vary considerably in form. His printers, who seem occasionally to have substituted their own symbols of elision for Thoreau's, are also at variance. In his manuscripts for the selections in this volume, Thoreau used combinations of dots, dashes, asterisks, and crosses, and infrequently, a single long dash (e.g., 128.27). Since his different combinations seem not to have had differentiated functions, all marks of elision in the present texts are altered to the standard symbol of four dots (the period and three spaced dots), a symbol sufficiently current in Thoreau's day to appear frequently in the printed copy-texts for these selections. In the case of ligatures, Thoreau's holograph forms are assumed definitive; in the absence of a holograph form, the copy-text reading is followed. So "hypæthral" (171.24) remains un-expanded in the present text, while "praetor" at 175.30 in the same copy-text is expanded on the authority of a holograph pre-copy-text form.

I. Probable or certain distortion or wrenching of quotations from other authors is recorded in the textual notes. But rarely are the original author's readings restored by emendation, since it was demonstrably Thoreau's intention on occasion to alter his source to fit the exigencies of his own context. If, however, an examination of pre-copy-text forms in the journals, notebooks, or other manuscript forms discloses a probable authorial or non-authorial error in transcription, unintended by Thoreau, the original meaning is restored and the emendation noted. Wherever one set of quotation marks has been omitted, the editor supplies them. Wherever Thoreau has chosen to use single quotation marks instead of the usual double marks, however, they are allowed to remain. And Thoreau's practice of enclosing with quotation marks quoted passages clearly set off from his own text is not interfered with.

5. FORMS OF DOCUMENTATION

Information bearing upon the editorial problems of establishing the texts for these selections is recorded in the textual notes and tables positioned in this volume immediately following the textual introduction for each essay. All emendations are listed in tables, and those requiring explanation are discussed in textual notes. There are no silent emendations, except in those instances when all emendations of a particular sort (e.g., of manuscript ampersands) are collected at one point. When used in combination with the tables of variants, emendations, and manuscript alterations, the notes enable a reader to reconstruct the copy-text, and to recapture (in the case of manuscript copy-texts) the record of Thoreau's cancellations, interlineations, and changes of all kinds. Every alteration Thoreau made in the holograph drafts used as copy-texts in this volume is recorded in the tables.

The textual notes record the following classes of information, in addition to editorial emendations of the copy-text:

1. All pre-copy-text evidence for debatable emendations, and all evidence justifying decisions not to emend, the pre-copy-text evidence being accorded greater weight the closer it stands to fair copy.
2. Explanations of the editorial problems encountered in the attempt to establish an authoritative reading for any given passage, with the rationale for the final decision of the editor. Such explanations are intended to make it possible for informed re-evaluations of the evidence to be made.
3. The sources for Thoreau's quotations from other writers (if known) with a comment upon the probable accuracy of Thoreau's transcription of them. If the editor has been unable to identify Thoreau's precise source, he has cited a later edition as an aid to the reader. When an inexact transcription can be shown to have resulted from the carelessness of Thoreau or of the compositor, the correct version is substituted in the text, and the substitution recorded in the textual notes.

Following the textual notes for certain selections is a "Table of Alterations in Manuscript Copy-Texts." This table records all substantive revision Thoreau made in manuscripts that this edition adopts as copy-texts. Most accidental revision is not recorded, except for instances affecting Thoreau's meaning. The tables list both type (interlining, cancels, inserts, use marks) and medium (ink, pencil) of revision, specifying their exact appearance in the copy-text and thus reflecting the order of Thoreau's compositional process. For items marked *, see the textual notes.

Supplementing this table for most selections is a "Table of Textual Variants." Recorded in this table are any variants in the copy-text and in post-copy-text holograph or printed forms over which Thoreau might have exercised (or did exercise) control, or which might have resulted from the access of an editor to forms having authority. At the risk of seeming tedious, the editor also records in this table pre-copy-text variants from the manuscript journal or working drafts when they throw light upon a reading. Variants in accidentals not affecting meaning are as a rule excluded from the tables since the aggregate of such variants runs into thousands of items. Since the line between those accidentals that affect meaning and those that do not is extremely difficult to draw (the deletion or inclusion of a comma can often have a substantive impact upon a sentence), the present editor has taken the risk of erring in the direction of fullness of entry rather than of niggardliness.

The following example illustrates the form of entry used in the tables of textual variants, supplied for all selections except those with holograph copy-texts. Abbreviations designate separate forms of the various texts; full identification can be made by referring to section six of this introduction, "Symbols, Abbreviations, Collations," pages 253-260.

*59.10 conservers] MA 1303 Y; conserver L-WP

The Arabic numerals on the left margin designate the page and line (page 59, line 15) in this volume on which the entry to the left of the bracket appears.

The line count is always literal; line scales—accurate only for pages set in standard type—appear on the endpapers and dust jacket. Since L-WP is in this case the copy-text for the selection ("Wendell Phillips Before Concord Lyceum") and since the reading in the copy-text ("conserver") is different from the reading in the present volume ("conservers"), the entry shows that the editor has emended his copy-text and has recorded the emendation and the reason therefor in the textual notes and table of emendations. The several locations of this reading and the variant forms in the different texts appear to the right of the bracket. What has happened in this instance, as the historical record shows, is that Thoreau first used the form "conservers" in his working copy, MA 1303, and that this form was printed by the editor(s) of *A Yankee* (1866). But the printer of *The Liberator* version missed the terminal "s," possibly because the letter was indistinctly formed in Thoreau's printer's copy, possibly because of carelessness. The *Yankee* editor or printer probably supplied the plural to bring the number of the word into accord with that of the subject ("descendants"). The present editor emends to restore the form used by Thoreau in his working draft, having no evidence that the 1866 reading is authoritative, though it may have been. That Thoreau could have intended to alter the plausible form of MA 1303 for the implausible one of the copy-text, the editor deems unlikely.

Following each table of textual variants is a table of "Emendations in the Copy-text." Every alteration of the copy-text in the present edition, except for those specified in section four of this introduction, is recorded in this table. To the left of the bracket is the emended form as it appears in this edition; to the right, the rejected copy-text form. Substantive emendations marked * are explained in the textual notes.

Two lists of words follow each table of emendations. The first records all words divided at the end of the line in the copy-text that could possibly be hyphenated compounds rather than single words. The form of the word in the listing is that of this edition, arrived at by comparison with Thoreau's usage elsewhere in the selection and in the manuscripts of the period, and by consultation of Walker's *Critical Pronouncing Dictionary*, Thoreau's lexicon. The second list records all words hyphenated in the text of this volume that would have been hyphenated no matter where they fell in the line. Words divided at the end of the line and not listed should be read as one word.

The seal of the Center for Editions of American Authors on this volume means that one of a panel of textual experts serving the Center has approved the text and the textual apparatus of this volume, and that it has been proof-read at least five times by three different individuals, including the present editor, in galley and page proof.

6. SYMBOLS, ABBREVIATIONS, COLLATIONS

Below are listed the major documents used in establishing the texts of the reform papers in the present volume. The symbols are those used to refer to these documents in the textual introductions, the textual notes, the tables of textual variants and emendations, and the tables of alterations in manuscript copy-texts, and are here alphabetized for convenience of reference. Copy-texts for all or portions of selections are designated by asterisks. All collations of printed copies from the same impression are noted, and locations of copies given. Such collations, intended to reveal variants within an impression, were done by carefully superimposing photographs of identically paginated pages from different copies upon each other over the illuminated glass surface of a photoviewer adapted for the purpose. All variations, even those resulting from the wearing of type, were by this means easily detected. Two examinations of each pair of pages were made, with the position of the pages in the second examination being reversed. As an additional check, in several instances machine collations were made using the Hinman collator.

* AM: first printing of "Life without Principle" in *The Atlantic Monthly*, 12 (October, 1863), 484-95, copy in the library of the University of Minnesota, Duluth, no call number, signature "J Mitchell" on the title page. Collated with copy in the Wilson Library of the University of Minnesota, Minneapolis, call number 050 At63. No variants discovered.

* AP: first printing of "Resistance to Civil Government" in the *Aesthetic Papers*, Elizabeth Peabody, ed. (Boston, 1849), pp. 189-211, copy in the library of Walter Harding, Geneseo, New York, numbered 2976. Collated with copy in the Wilson Library of the University of Minnesota, Minneapolis, call number Y 810.5 Ae89, and with the facsimile edition produced by Joseph Jones (Gainesville, Florida, 1957) in the library of the University of Minnesota, Duluth, numbered 1594496. Harding copy also machine collated with Wilson Library copy. No variants discovered.

B: fragments of the text of "The Service" printed in *Concord Lectures in Philosophy*, Raymond L. Bridgman, ed. (1883).

Corre-spond-ence: *The Correspondence of Henry David Thoreau*, Walter Harding and Carl Bode, eds. (New York, 1958).

* CB: page 47 of the lecture draft and printer's copy for a portion of "A Plea for Captain John Brown" in the Thoreau Collection of the Clifton Waller Barrett Library of the University of Virginia.

* D: first printing of "Herald of Freedom" in *The Dial*, 4 (April, 1844), 507-12, copy in the library of Walter Harding, Geneseo, New York, numbered 5092. Collated with copy in the Wilson Library of the University of Minnesota, Minneapolis, call number 050 0541. No variants discovered.

* DR: first printing of "Paradise (To Be) Regained" in the *United States Magazine and Democratic Review*, 13 (November, 1843), 451-63, copy in the library of Walter Harding, Geneseo, New York, numbered 5946. Collated with the copy in the Wilson Library of the University of Minnesota, Minneapolis, call number PR 050 D39. No variants discovered.

E: J. A. Etzler, *The Paradise Within the Reach of All Men, Without Labor, by Powers of Nature and Machinery*, Second English Edition (London: J. Cleave, 1842), copy in the Kress Library of Business and Economics, Harvard University, numbered 144425, call number MS JC3 N44. The object of Thoreau's review, "Paradise (To Be) Regained."

* Folder 1
to Folder
21, inc.: designations of holograph material in the Houghton Library of Harvard University, preserved under number bMS AM 278.5. Folder 18B is copy-text for the major portion of "Reform and the Reformers," folder 18A for the remaining portion. Folder 4D provides the copy-text for a portion of "The Service," folder 11 for a portion of "Herald of Freedom."

H: *Herald of Freedom*, edited by Nathaniel P. Rogers (1838-1845), issued weekly. Reviewed by Thoreau in "Herald of Freedom."

* HM
13202;
HM
13203: designations of holograph material in the Henry E. Huntington Library, San Marino, California, in which are preserved pp. 1, 3, 27, 31, 40, 46, 49, 50, 54, 57, and 60 of Thoreau's lecture draft and probable printer's copy for "A Plea for Captain John Brown," copy-text for those portions of the lecture.

* L-LD: first printing of "The Last Days of John Brown" in *The Liberator*, 30, no. 30 (July 27, 1860), copy on microfilm from the New York Public Library, in the Wilson Library of the University of Minnesota, Minneapolis, call number NR 8, Film 52, Reel 9. Collated with copy in the Cornell University Library, Ithaca, New York, call number Rare E 441 A3 L69. No variants discovered.

* L-SIM: first printing of "Slavery in Massachusetts" in *The Liberator*, 24, no. 29 (July 21, 1854), copy on microfilm from the New York Public Library, in the Wilson Library of the University of Minnesota, Minneapolis, call number NR 8, Film 52, Reel 8. Collated with copy in the library of Walter Harding, Geneseo, New York, numbered 5969. No variants discovered.

* L-WP: first printing of "Wendell Phillips Before Concord Lyceum" in *The Liberator*, 15, no. 13 (March 28, 1845), copy on microfilm from the New York Public Library, in the microfilm collection of the Wilson Library of the University of Minnesota, Minneapolis, call number NR 8, Film 52, Reel 6. Collated with copy in the library of Walter Harding, Geneseo, New York, numbered 6051. No variants discovered.

* MA 607: Thoreau's intended printer's copy of "The Service," rejected by Margaret Fuller for publication in *The Dial*. Preserved under this number in the Pierpont Morgan Library.

* MA 884: printer's copy of a portion of "Martyrdom of John Brown," preserved under this number in the Pierpont Morgan Library.

MA 1303: Thoreau's working draft of "Wendell Phillips Before Concord Lyceum," preserved under this number in the Pierpont Morgan Library.

MA 2556: early fair-copy form of a portion of "Life without Principle" preserved under this number in the Pierpont Morgan Library.

* MF: page 17 of the lecture draft and probable printer's copy of "A Plea for Captain John Brown" in volume one of the Manuscript Edition (# 586) of Thoreau's works owned by Mr. Malcolm Ferguson of West Concord, Massachusetts.

MJ: the thirty-nine volumes of Thoreau's manuscript journal preserved in the Pierpont
Morgan Library under number MA 1302.
1-39.

NS: the version of a portion of "Slavery in
Massachusetts" reprinted from *The Liberator* in *The National Anti-Slavery Standard*, 15 (August 12, 1854), copy on microfilm from the New York Public Library,
owned by the editor. Collation with L-SIM
disclosed many variants.

PE: Princeton Edition, the present volume of
THE WRITINGS OF HENRY D. THOREAU. All
page-line numbers unless otherwise noted
refer to this volume.

* R-AP: first printing of "A Plea for Captain John
Brown" in *Echoes of Harper's Ferry*, James
Redpath, ed. (Boston: Thayer and Eldridge,
1860), pp. 17-42, Thoreau's personal copy
in the Pierpont Morgan Library, volume
number 16911, call number E-3 90 D. Copy-
text for that portion of the lecture not represented by recaptured sheets of the lecture draft. Copies checked for corrections
Thoreau made in his personal volume include:
    1) copy in the Michigan State Library,
East Lansing, call number Film 1583
M. 165 Reel 165
    2) copy in the Indiana University Li-
brary, Bloomington, call number E
451 R28
    3) copy in the Iowa State University Li-
brary, Ames, call number E 451 R31

4) copy in the Midwest Inter-Library Center, Chicago, call number MF 187, Reel 165

Collation with the copy in the Wilson Library, University of Minnesota, Minneapolis, call number 973.68 R249-2, disclosed no variants.

* R-MJB: first printing of "Martyrdom of John Brown" in *Echoes of Harper's Ferry*, James Redpath, ed. (Boston: Thayer and Eldridge, 1860), pp. 439-45, Thoreau's personal copy in the Pierpont Morgan Library, volume number 16911, call number E-3 90 D. For collation see R-AP above. Copy-text for the portion of this selection translated by Thoreau from Tacitus.

S: *The Service*, Franklin B. Sanborn, ed. (Boston: Charles E. Goodspeed, 1902), first printing of the manuscript rejected by Margaret Fuller in 1840, copy in the library of the University of Minnesota, Duluth, call number 818 T 391 Ser, copy number in the impression #182. Collated with copy in the Wilson Library of the University of Minnesota, Minneapolis, call number Z81 T39 OS, copy number in the impression #431. No variants discovered.

SEP: *Statement of Editorial Principles. A Working Manual for Editing Nineteenth Century American Texts* (Modern Language Association of America, July 1967).

T: version of "Slavery in Massachusetts" reprinted from *The Liberator* in *The New-York Daily Tribune* (August 2, 1854), copy number RP 16 in The Thoreau Edition collection, Geneseo, New York. Collation with L-SIM disclosed many variants.

W: *Critical Pronouncing Dictionary and Expositor of the English Language* compiled by John Walker (New York, 1823), copy in the Wilson Library of the University of Minnesota, Minneapolis, call number 423 W15, volume number 175853. Thoreau's lexicon.

Y: *A Yankee in Canada, with Anti-Slavery and Reform Papers* (Boston: Ticknor and Fields, 1866), copy in the Library of Walter Harding, Geneseo, New York, numbered 720. Collated with the following:

    1) copy in the New York State Library, Albany, call number 818.31 ZA

    2) copy in the Wilson Library of the University of Minnesota, Minneapolis, numbered 620108, call number 81 T39 OY

    3) copy of the 1878 impression, numbered 450590 in the Buffalo Public Library, Buffalo, New York, call number 824.1 T488 Y (2)

    4) copy of the 1881 impression in the library of Walter Harding, Geneseo, New York, numbered 6429

    5) copy of the 1891 impression in the Duluth Public Library, Duluth, Minnesota, call number 818 T39 Y.

Aside from considerable plate wear in the late impressions, no variants were discovered.

The Service

Textual Introduction

THOREAU worked up this essay in the spring and early summer of 1840, culling heavily from the "Lost Journal," volume three of the thirty-nine bound holograph volumes in the Pierpont Morgan Library, though he took scattered snippets from volumes one and two of the journals as well. The first journal entry to find its way into the completed manuscript is dated December 12, 1837. The scattered residual working drafts bear evidence that bringing the essay into focus was not easy; and at least one critic of the day rendered the judgment that Thoreau had failed. But Thoreau finished the essay in "July–1840," so dating it in pencil on the final page of his manuscript draft, and sent it to Margaret Fuller with the confident expectation that she would accept it for publication in *The Dial*. Emerson acted as midwife: "He is trying to give you a piece of prose out of his 'Brave Man,' an essay which he read to Caroline."

But Miss Fuller was unmoved. She rejected the manuscript in a letter dated "1st Dec. [1840]" in spite of Emerson's apparent dissatisfaction with her decision, admitting in her letter of rejection to Thoreau that "It is true as Mr. E. says, that essays not to be compared with this have found their way into the Dial."[1] To Miss Fuller's invitation in her letter

[1] Emerson's letter may be found in *The Letters of Ralph Waldo Emerson*, Ralph L. Rusk, ed. (New York, 1939), II, p. 315. Margaret Fuller's letter of rejection is preserved in the Morgan Library with the rejected manuscript, MA 607. Her frank comment ("But then the thoughts seem to me so out of their natural order, that I cannot read it through without

that he resubmit the essay—"Yet I hope you will give it me again, and if you see no force in my objections disregard them"—Thoreau apparently turned a deaf ear. Franklin B. Sanborn observed that the manuscript "seems never to have been returned to Thoreau," but was sent to Emerson and remained in his hands until after Thoreau's death, and perhaps even until Emerson's death in 1882, whence it came to Sanborn along with certain portfolios of Emerson's.[2] It seems reasonable to trust Sanborn's account of the provenience of the manuscript; he had possession of it in 1882 because he read excerpts from it at the Concord School of Philosophy in the summer of that year, and he still had it in his possession when he published it in 1902 in Boston in a limited edition of 500 copies. How Margaret Fuller's letter of rejection, which obviously went to Thoreau himself, came to be appended to the holograph manuscript is not clear. One can surmise that Emerson asked to see both manuscript and letter upon their return to Thoreau, and neglected to return them. Whatever the circumstances, Mr. J. P. Morgan acquired both by private treaty through the dealer George S. Hellman in 1909, according to the Morgan Library records preserved with the manuscript.

If the copy Thoreau sent to Miss Fuller was clean, however, it may after its rejection have come directly back to Thoreau. For two paragraphs in the manuscript (beginning in PE at 11.3 and 11.28, respectively) are revised in ink and pencil; Thoreau was dissatisfied with them either before he submitted the manuscript or after it was returned to him. He recopied the two paragraphs, very nearly as revised on the

---

pain.") was hardly the sort that would induce Thoreau to subject his essay to such a critic a second time.

[2] "Introductory Note," *The Service* (Boston, 1902), p. x.

manuscript, as a part of four pages of scattered paragraphs from "The Service" now preserved in the Houghton Library in folder D of bMS AM 278.5. If Thoreau's revisions followed the rejection of his manuscript by Miss Fuller, then it might be argued that under the duress of rejection he set to work on the manuscript again, hoping perhaps to make it acceptable to her; and that his original manuscript should serve as copy-text for the whole of "The Service." But this position is weakened, the present editor feels, by the incoherence of the substance of the paragraphs themselves. Whether Thoreau revised these paragraphs before or after the rejection, he clearly had not shaped them to his satisfaction in his original manuscript; and on the grounds that he would have preferred coherence to incoherence, the present editor has used the revised versions of these two paragraphs as his copy-text for those portions of the essay. Copy-text for the remainder of the essay is the manuscript submitted to Miss Fuller, now preserved as MA 607 in the Pierpont Morgan Library.

The first portion of "The Service" to appear in print was a short 600-word excerpt abstracted from the manuscript by Sanborn, and published in *Concord Lectures in Philosophy*, Raymond L. Bridgman, ed. (Cambridge, Mass., 1883), pages 124-25. The passage reflects the heavy editorial hand of Sanborn, who made twelve substantive changes in wording and forty-four in accidentals in the two pages. Since Bridgman asserts that his texts were "revised by the several lecturers," one can only conclude that Sanborn's corruptions were not the result of lackadaisical transcription, but of design. Scudder's text in the 1883 Riverside Edition (x, 35-37) was based upon the Bridgman fragment, and preserves all of Sanborn's corruptions. The Walden and Manuscript editions of 1906 (IV, 277-79) follow the corrupt text of the Riverside.

Nor is Sanborn's complete edition (Boston, 1902) any less corrupt. Collation with MA 607 discloses more than 150 variants in substantives and accidentals, nearly all explicable in terms of Sanborn's compulsion to "improve" upon the Thoreau text. Kenneth Cameron's *The Transcendentalists and Minerva* (Hartford, 1958) reproduces MA 607 in facsimile, but follows the manuscript reproduction with the corrupt printed text of the 1902 Sanborn edition. Thoreau's intentions for the text of "The Service," to this point, have been poorly served. Perhaps it was hurt pride resulting from Margaret Fuller's rejection that discouraged Thoreau from moving ahead with the publication of the essay; perhaps he decided against printing it after using passages from it in the first draft (HM 935) of "Sir Walter Raleigh," which he seems to have prepared in the summer of 1841. Whatever his reason, the consequence was that the essay lay in manuscript for sixty years before publication, and even then the published text was corrupt.

Abbreviations used in the textual notes and tables for "The Service" are identified in section 6 of the General Introduction, "Symbols, Abbreviations, Collations," pages 253 to 260. The textual tables record all of Thoreau's alterations in the holograph copy-texts (MA 607 and folder 4D); all substantive variants between the copy-texts and the first complete printing (S); and all of the present editor's emendations, substantive or accidental, of the copy-texts. Items marked * in the tables are discussed in the textual notes.

Textual Notes

3. title: Thoreau italicized his title in MA 607, following it with a period. The title here is emended to Roman type, and the period removed. A period following the sub-title is also deleted. The Latin motto may be found also in HM 13182 in an early form, where Virgil is identified as the author. The translation is probably Thoreau's. The source is the *Aeneid*, XI, 1, 309.

3.21-22 "But there . . . wish.": Sanborn identified this quotation (S, p. 29): "From Aeschylus, 'Seven against [*sic*] Thebes,' verse 588 (Paley's edition)." The words are those of the scout to Eteocles. In the translation of Herbert Weir Smyth (Cambridge, 1946), p. 371, the passage is rendered: "Blazon was there none upon its orb—for his resolve is not to seem the bravest, but to be. . . ."

4.4 His . . . measurable: Interlined by Thoreau in pencil. The reading in S is without authority: "His greatness is not measurable; not such a greatness as when we. . . ." It represents Sanborn's attempt to amalgamate the interlineation with the succeeding sentence, though Thoreau in MA 607 clearly intended the two sentences to be distinct.

4.27-28 "Discretion . . . soul,": The source of the quotation is unidentified.

5.18-19 "The house roof . . . know it.": The source of the quotation is unidentified.

7.1 angulosity: Though MA 607 clearly reads "angulosity," S prints "angularity." The word is not clear in MJ (July 4, 1840); the printed *Journal* (1906) has "angularity." W lists "angularity" and "angulous" but not "angulosity."

7.3 "made Fortune . . . Fortitude,": The quotation is transcribed from MJ (December 1839).

7.13-14 "Tumble . . . yet.": The poem is transcribed from MJ (December 1839).

8.7 "things terrestrial: S, p. 29, locates the quotation in Plutarch's "Morals," in "the old version of Dryden's day, since edited by Professor Goodwin, with an Introduction by Emerson." The "old version" to which Sanborn alludes is presumably that of Philemon Holland (1603).

The passage quoted by Thoreau is taken from Plutarch's answer to "Question 78" of "The Roman Questions."

9.1-4 Each . . . be.: The poem is accepted by Carl Bode as Thoreau's, and is included in the *Collected Poems of Henry Thoreau* (Baltimore, 1964), p. 119. An early draft of this poem may be found in folder 2 in the Houghton Library, and an intermediate draft in folder 4D.

9.6 more: S; omitted in MA 607, but present in MJ (December 1839). Since Thoreau was here transcribing a long section from his journal essentially without change, his omission from his printer's copy of this needed word was presumably inadvertent.

10.3 rare: Though this word in MA 607 is unclear and could perhaps be read "sane," PE follows S on authority of the form "but rarely" in MJ ("July and August 1840").

10.19-27 "Plato thinks: Sanborn (S, p. 30) conjectured that this quotation was "apparently taken from the old version of Plutarch's 'Morals.' " The quotation is indeed from the *Moralia*, specifically from "Of Superstition," but if by "the old version" Sanborn meant the translation of Philemon Holland (1603) he was mistaken. Thoreau apparently transcribed the quotation verbatim from a holograph note now preserved in folder 4D in the Houghton Library.

10.31-11.1 The sound . . . creation: A variant form of this passage may be found in folder 4D marked "2" for transposition. It reads: "A bugle heard in the stillness of the night sends forth its voice to the farthest stars and marshals them in new order and harmony. The notes seem to flash out in the horizon like heat lightning, quickening the pulse of creation." The version in MA 607 is apparently the later form.

11.3 To the sensitive soul: Thoreau had much difficulty with the phrasing of this and the succeeding two sentences. After cancellations and interlineations in MA 607, the passage was left in the following incoherent state:

To the sensitive soul, the Universe has her own fixed measure, which is its measure also; and is expressed in the regularity of its pulse is inseparable from a healthy body, so is its healthiness dependent on the regularity of its rythm. In all sounds the soul recognizes its own rythm and seeks to express its sympathy by a correspondent movement of the limbs. When the body marches to the measure of the soul, then is true courage and invincible strength.

Though there is no certainty that the variant version of this passage in folder 4D postdates the completion of MA 607, there is some plausibility in thinking so, since another paragraph on the verso of the same leaf in 4D is demonstrably a rendering of a version Thoreau heavily emended in the MA 607 draft. The version in PE is that of folder 4D.

11.10 all: A following insertion in MA 607 appears to be less a revision of the phrasing than a note evincing an intention to emend or add to the thought later. The insertion is omitted in PE.

11.28 A man's life: The holograph form of this paragraph in folder 4D postdates the version in MA 607. All substantive emendations made by Thoreau in this passage in MA 607 he incorporated later into the folder 4D version. The revised form in folder 4D is followed at this point in accidentals also, and all deviations from MA 607 are recorded in the textual notes and the table of textual variants.

11.34 melody is no longer heard,: So in folder 4D and S. Revising from MJ (June 30, 1840) Thoreau first wrote in MA 607 "melody runs into such depth and wildness as no longer to be heard," by cancellation emending to the shorter, clearer version. Sanborn's substitution of "is" for "as" correcting an obvious inadvertence of Thoreau is followed in PE. Thoreau himself made the change in folder 4D.

12.title: A period following the title in MA 607 has been deleted. The source of the quoted motto is *Antony and Cleopatra*, IV, xiii, 87.

13.1 nowadays: S. Thoreau's version in MA 607 of "now a days" is unacceptable both to W and *OED*. The form used in PE is that prescribed by W and permitted by *OED*.

13.32-36 —returns . . . Surrounds—: S, p. 30, locates

these lines in "Milton's lament on his blindness in 'Paradise Lost.'" The lines are from Book III, lines 41ff. Thoreau probably regularized Milton's "ev'n" in line 42.

14.16. "Sit not down: Sanborn speculated (S, p. 30) that Thoreau took this quotation "Possibly from Jeremy Taylor, but more likely from Sir Thomas Browne." His second surmise is correct; the quotation is from "Part The First" of Browne's *Christian Morals*, "published from the original and correct manuscript of the author; by John Jeffery, D. D., Archdeacon of Norwich" (1716). Thoreau has possibly added a phrase; the version of *Christian Morals*, C. H. Herford, ed. (London, 1940) reads:

> Sit not down in the popular Forms and common Level of Virtues. Offer not only Peace-Offerings but Holocausts unto God: where all is due make no reserve, and cut not a Cummin-seed with the Almighty: (p. 234).

14.34-36 "before . . . close.": Thoreau transcribed these lines from MJ (December 16, 1837). He was later to use them in *A Week*, at the conclusion of "Monday," following a prose passage which he drew from the final paragraph of "The Service." The source is *Paradise Lost*, II, 535-37.

15.1 behoves: Under the listing for "behoove" W enters a note that the word is "sometimes improperly written *behove*." But Thoreau's preference for the shorter form is clear (cf. 88.5).

15.31 life. And: Thoreau's questionable capitalization of "And" led S to render these two sentences as one, and to substitute a comma for the period of MA 607. Though a possible reading results, it is here judged to be without authority.

16.6 canvass: This is the probable spelling in MA 607 at this point, though the second "s" is cramped at the end of the line. It is clearly Thoreau's spelling at 16.29 and 17.20. W prescribes this form.

16.22-24 Every stroke . . . marble;: In MA 608 (p. 80), an early commonplace book at the Morgan Library, Thoreau phrased the thought as follows: "He is the true artist whose life is his material—every stroke of the chisel must enter his own flesh and blood—and not grate dully on marble."

16.34   of nature,:   Thoreau may have intended to personify "nature" by capitalization at this point; but since this is the only instance in MA 607 of his possible intent to capitalize "nature" in mid-line, PE normalizes the form.

17.23-25   Methinks . . . soul: In the margin of MA 607, Margaret Fuller responded with "bella." Despite Sanborn's implication in the introductory note to his edition that he found pencillings in the manuscript, "evidently by Miss Fuller, saying of particular sentences, 'Good,' 'bella,' etc.," this comment on the terminal paragraph of MA 607 is the only pencilled remark by Miss Fuller presently remaining. Vertical lines pencilled in the left margin may be Miss Fuller's; there is no clue to their origin.

Table of Alterations
in Manuscript Copy-Texts

*	4.4	His . . . measurable.] *interlined above in pencil* MA 607
*	9.2	this] *interlined in ink above cancelled* sad MA 607
	9.18-19	To secure . . . out.] *inserted in ink in right margin* MA 607
	9.26-27	things thus] *interlined in pencil above parenthesized* woods and walls MA 607
*	11.3-7	To the . . . strength] folder 4D; *heavily revised in pencil* MA 607
	11.8	The coward] *followed by pencilled parenthesis* MA 607
*	11.10	all] *followed by pencilled line to* suspects (*possibly* respects) only—*interlined below* MA 607
	11.14	feeble . . . slender] *written in ink over erasures* MA 607
	11.18	brave] courageous *interlined in pencil above cancelled* brave folder 2
	11.23	and subtle] *interlined in pencil with a caret* MA 607
	11.28	An] *altered in pencil from* a *followed by parenthesized* sweet but MA 607
	11.29	seems] folder 4D; may *interlined in ink above cancelled* shall *followed by* seem MA 607
	11.30	will] *followed by* only *cancelled in ink* MA 607
	11.31	measure] *followed by* or *cancelled in ink* MA 607
	11.31	which only] *interlined in ink* MA 607
	11.31	ear] *followed by* detect *interlined in ink above cancelled* hurry him into a thousand symphonies and concordant variations. MA 607
	11.34	deepened] folder 4D; deeper *interlined in ink with a caret* MA 607
	11.34	melody] *followed by* runs into such depth and wildness *cancelled in ink* MA 607

11.34   longer] *followed by* to be *cancelled in ink*
               MA 607

12.2   circumstances,] folder 4D; *interlined in ink*
               above cancelled times MA 607

12.3   volume] *followed by* sweetness and
               cancelled in ink MA 607

12.4   and] folder 4D; *followed by* itself *cancelled*
               in ink MA 607

13.7   Falsehood] *written in ink over erasure*
               MA 607

13.18-19   or . . . scabbards] *inserted in left margin*
               in ink with a line leading to caret in right
               margin MA 607

14.5   the pledge] *interlined in ink with a caret*
               MA 607

14.7   instead] *followed by* that they make
               cancelled in pencil MA 607

14.7   of causing] *interlined in pencil with a caret*
               MA 607

15.31   death to life] *written in ink over erasure*
               MA 607

* 16.34   of nature,] *interlined in ink with a caret*
               MA 607

17.27   evening.] *followed by holograph signature*
               and July–1840 *in pencil.*

Table of Textual Variants

6.23   pole] MA 607; polar S
* 7.1   angulosity] MA 607; angularity S
8.25   flexile] MA 607; flexible S
8.33   mellower] MA 607; mellow S
9.26-27   things thus] MA 607; woods and walls
               cancelled MA 607 MJ (December, 1839)
10.10   sublime] MA 607; *omitted* S
* 10.31-11.1   The sound . . . creation.] MA 607; *variant*
               passage folder 4D
11.3-7   To the . . . strength.] 4D; *variant passage*
               MA 607 S
11.19   brave] MA 607; courageous folder 2

Table of Emendations

* 16.34   nature] S; *possibly* Nature MA 607
  17.18   Gonzalo] S; Gonzalve MA 607
  17.27   evening.] *followed by Thoreau's signature and date* MA 607

End-of-Line Hyphenation

THE compounds or possible compounds in list A, below, are hyphenated at the end of the line in "The Service" copy-texts. The editor has resolved each to the form recorded in this list, in accord with the principles discussed in the General Introduction, page 246. A curiosity of "The Service" copy-texts is that they contain no hyphenated forms except at line ends and in one quotation. All end-of-line hyphenations in this edition should be transcribed without the hyphen in order to duplicate the copy-text forms.

LIST A

3.14	sunrise	13.6	withdrawing
6.4	cannot	13.16	whirlwind
7.9	yourself	16.33	landscapes
7.16	without	17.23	methinks
8.3-4	eyelids		

Paradise (To Be) Regained

Textual Introduction

COLLECTIVE search yields no holograph form of this review of J. A. Etzler's book, *The Paradise Within the Reach of All Men, Without Labor, by Powers of Nature and Machinery*, Second English Edition (London: J. Cleave, 1842). No proof sheets have been found, and even Emerson's copy of the book (sent by Alcott from England, and loaned to Thoreau for review) seems to have disappeared. Although much of Thoreau's journal for the Staten Island period survives, it contains no working drafts for this particular essay. The editor seeking to establish an authoritative text is limited to two printed forms: that appearing in the *United States Magazine and Democratic Review*, 13 (Nov., 1843), 451-63, hereafter designated the *Democratic Review*, and that collected in *A Yankee in Canada, with Anti-Slavery and Reform Papers* (Boston, 1866), pages 182-205.

Thoreau wrote this review at the suggestion of Emerson, who hoped to print it in *The Dial* (*Correspondence*, page 85). But Thoreau submitted it instead to J. L. O'Sullivan of the *Democratic Review*, who initially rejected it (*Correspondence*, page 130; letter of 28 July 1843), at the same time asking to see Thoreau's copy of Etzler's book. Thoreau's letter of reply is apparently not extant, but Thomas Blanding has discovered in the Huntington Library (HM 13193) a pencilled preliminary draft in which Thoreau disclaims knowledge of the book's whereabouts, admits to his own dissatisfaction with the review, but asserts nevertheless his disinclination to alter its "general trend." His "extracts," he told O'Sullivan, were "rather too favorable, beside being improved by the liberties I have taken"—and the liberties he had taken with Etzler's text number in the hundreds. In his letter of rejection, O'Sullivan had prescribed his terms for printing the review: "if you would not object I think it very likely that some addition & modification made with your concurrence would put your review of it into the shape to suit my peculiar notion on the subject." At issue was Thoreau's ridicule of Utopian communities, of which O'Sullivan was a staunch defender.

Thoreau's aversion to the intervention of editors is well known; yet he seems to have desired so strongly to place the review with O'Sullivan that he may have made token revisions under duress. The record is not complete. In any event, he wrote to his mother from Staten Island on August 6, 1843, reporting the incident without rancor: "They were very polite, and earnest that I should send them something else, or reform that" (*Correspondence*, page 132). Five weeks later, on September 14, 1843, Thoreau wrote to Emerson that "O'Sullivan is printing the manuscript I sent him some time ago, having objected only to my want of sympathy with the Communities" (*Correspondence*, page 139). Yet on October 1 he told his mother (*Correspondence*, page 142) that O'Sullivan was still holding up publication of the essay "that I may include in it a notice of another book by the same author, which they have found, and are going to send me." But the editor has found no record that any other book by Etzler was sent, or even that any other was written. Moreover, the review was published in the November number, which would have given Thoreau little time to read another uncongenial Etzler book, write his comments on it, and incorporate them into the initial version of his review. The "want of sympathy with the Communities," however, which

had triggered the delay in publication, is still conspicuous in the version O'Sullivan accepted and published: Thoreau wrote, for example, "In this matter
of reforming the world, we have little faith in corporations. . . ." (42.9-11). The fact that extended passages in the review drip with irony may augur that
Thoreau won his battle with O'Sullivan, without
having to tone down or excise offensive passages. In
any case, Bartholow Crawford was sufficiently satisfied with the first printing of "Paradise (To Be) Regained" to choose it as his text for the Thoreau volume
of the American Writers Series, though Francis H.
Allen believed the choice to be a mistake.[1]

In accordance with the editorial policies of the
Center for Editions of American Authors, the choice
of copy-text for this edition is the version first printed
by J. L. O'Sullivan in the *Democratic Review*. Certain
additional observations on the posthumously published second printing in *A Yankee* seem warranted,
however (see page 237 above), since this printing
deviates significantly from the first, and since editorial responsibility for the alterations cannot be
assigned.

The text of this review in *A Yankee* is remarkable,
first of all, for the sheer number and bulk of the substantive changes from the periodical version. No
other essay reprinted in that volume is subjected to
such massive cutting; approximately one-third of the
1843 text is pruned from the 1866 version. The
reduction is effected for the most part by the trunca-
tion of long passages quoted from Etzler, though there
are several alterations also in the matter written by
Thoreau. In addition, certain of the Etzler remnants
retained in 1866 are edited, apparently by someone
who had access to the Etzler text or to some form of

[1] *Thoreau's Editors / History and Reminiscence*, Thoreau
Society Booklet Number Seven (1950), p. 10.

the essay other than the 1843 printing. Deletions from the Etzler text are authoritatively indicated by symbols in the 1866 version where the 1843 version shows none. Material pieced together by Thoreau from widely separated portions of Etzler's book and printed in 1843 as contiguous and sequential is divided by the 1866 editor into separate paragraphs. Certain editorial changes in 1866 in the Etzler material do not have Etzler's authority—the introduction of italics, for example, where the 1843 printing uses Roman type. And of course the entire review reflects the imposition in 1866 of the Ticknor and Fields house style.

Collation of the long quoted excerpts from Etzler's *A Paradise* with Thoreau's rendering of them in the *Democratic Review* reveals that Thoreau silently and extensively altered nearly all of them. In transcribing Etzler's first paragraph into his 1843 review, for instance, Thoreau made approximately thirty-five separate alterations of the text in a passage of slightly more than 300 words.[2] He cancelled fourteen words, in many cases substituting others; he added one phrase of five words not in Etzler's text; he transposed words, pluralized singulars, and extensively changed the punctuation. The 1866 printing perpetuates the corruption of Etzler's text; all of the substantive changes in the truncated Etzler excerpts are retained. Since it was demonstrably not Thoreau's intention to render Etzler faithfully, no purifying of Etzler's text is undertaken in this edition.

The explanation as to why the editor(s) of *A Yankee* should have deleted so extensively material Thoreau quoted from Etzler in the 1843 printing can only be conjectured. Perhaps the publisher, James T. Fields, sought to reduce the size of the volume to save

[2] For a fuller description of Thoreau's handling of Etzler's text, see Wendell Glick, "Thoreau's Use of his Sources," *The New England Quarterly*, 44, no. 1 (March 1971), 101-09.

space and cost. Perhaps Sophia Thoreau and/or Ellery Channing saw little reason to include so much material from another hand in a volume of Thoreau's works, in particular from an author with whose ideas Thoreau had had scant sympathy. Perhaps Emerson, who cannot be ruled out as editor, and who was in close contact with Thoreau as he wrote the essay, had information on Thoreau's wishes that can no longer be recovered. In order to secure a reluctant editor's approval of the review in 1843, Thoreau may have included more matter from Etzler than he wished, and Emerson may have been aware of the circumstances.

None of these conjectures, however, would account for the several cases in the 1866 printing of the improved accuracy in the handling of quoted Etzler material, unless a copy of the Etzler volume was available to the 1866 editors. And if a copy was available to them, why they should have made restitution to Etzler for Thoreau's mishandling of his text in a few cases and not in all is unclear. More likely is the possibility that Thoreau may have left a marked copy of the 1843 printing. Since the deleted passages themselves, however, provide no clue to the identity of the person or persons who did the cutting, this editor has not emended them into the present text.

Abbreviations used in the textual notes and tables for "Paradise (To Be) Regained" are identified in section 6 of the General Introduction, "Symbols, Abbreviations, Collations," pages 253-260. Elisions in Y of matter cut from the 1843 printing appear in the present text at 25.2-26.6, 27.1-11, 28.1-13, 28.25-29.36, 31.7-19, 31.29-32.20, 33.36-34.3, 34.5-35.3, 37.25-33, 38.28-34, 39.1-18, 39.25-32, 44.4-19. They are recorded in the table of variants, and descriptions of typical alterations by Thoreau of the Etzler text are included in the notes.

Textual Notes

19.13 "Fellow Men!: This long quotation from E, p. 5, is Etzler's opening paragraph following his preface. It is not merely quoted by Thoreau; it is revised.

20.28 and ague: Y adds the conjunction, a plausible emendation since in four other instances in the series the conjunction is included.

22.12 hyena: The spelling followed is that of W. At this point and at 46.5 DR has "hyæna" with the ligature, a form Thoreau used in none of the early holograph manuscripts examined by this editor. At 40.15 DR has the present form.

23.17 True,: The reading in Y. DR prints "Here," which in the context is confusing.

28.12 3,000,000,000,000: Printer's end-of-line hyphenation of cardinal numeral in DR ("3,000-000,000,000") emended to Thoreau's original form.

31.1 sunshine,: Capitalization of this word in DR does not accord with lower case usage at 45.18, 46.31, or 47.4. Cf. also "sunlit" at 3.13 in MA 607, copy-text of "The Service."

33.33 pages: Y. DR has "page" which is inappropriate in the context.

35.26 "The dwellings: This paragraph, ending at 36.15, was made up by Thoreau from three widely separated passages in E on pp. 35, 32, and 38, in that order. Thoreau gives no hint in DR that the matter was not sequential in his source. Yet in Y, the paragraph is broken down into three paragraph units that correspond exactly to the separate locales in Etzler. How the editor of Y could have known where to make the separations is not clear, unless Thoreau left a marked copy of the DR text.

The new paragraph beginning at 36.16 was drawn from p. 33 of E. Thoreau gives no hint in DR that it was not a part of a contiguous passage.

At 35.32 (heat,–) Thoreau silently deleted from his source (E, p. 32) two complete sentences and the first word of a third.

36.36 "tie up the rudder: Thoreau almost certainly took this phrase from "Section 1, Part The First" of Sir

Thomas Browne's *Christian Morals.* In the version edited by C. H. Herford (London, 1940), the passage reads:

> In this virtuous Voyage of thy Life hull not about like the Ark, without the use of Rudder, Mast, or Sail, and bound for no Port. Let not Disappointment cause Despondency, nor difficulty despair. Think not that you are Sailing from *Lima* to *Manillia*, when you may fasten up the Rudder, and sleep before the Wind; but expect rough Seas, Flaws, and contrary Blasts. . . .

The copy-text form of "Manilla" is not listed by W, but the form is accepted in the G. and C. Merriam *American Dictionary* (1847).

37.9 "The twenty-five: The quotation following is a composite of passages united by Thoreau without hint of their original lack of contiguity. In sequence, they are drawn from E, pp. 39, 38, 37 *passim.* Thoreau took broad liberties in adapting these passages from E to his purposes in DR, and the DR text was again substantively altered before publication in Y.

37.22 Any member: For this sentence, Thoreau regressed one page in Etzler's text (to p. 38), substituting the words "Any member" for Etzler's "He." DR gives no hint that a break of one page exists in the text between "exertion" and "Any member." Y supplies an ellipsis, despite its misleading implication that "Any member" begins a subsequent sentence rather than a much earlier one.

37.38 "One or two: The matter of this paragraph is made up by Thoreau from portions of two successive paragraphs in E, p. 37. Y italicizes the quotation beginning at 38.3 ("any"), though without authority from Etzler. But Y also marks with an ellipsis the point where material from Etzler was deleted, though DR does not.

40.34-35 "The whole world,": Thoreau constructed this sentence by combining parts of two very widely separated sentences in E: "The . . . paradise," (E, p. 49) is merged with "within . . . machinery." (E, p. 19).

41.16-17 no income but our outgoes: Though Y alters the passage to "no income, but outgoes" the version in DR seems justified by the context. Cf. "our virtue" (41.15) and "our money" (41.16).

41.28 "It will now: This paragraph is an eclectic one constructed of excerpts from (in this order) E, p. 49, p. 53, p. 50, with significant alterations.

43.29 : The line of iambic trimeter is from Euripides' *Orestes*, line 420, and was probably taken from the journal for June 14, 1840 (1, 139). Professors Joseph Schork and Robert Sonkowsky of the Department of Classics of the University of Minnesota note that "Thoreau has slightly misquoted the line in that it is badly punctuated in a way which conceals the fact that the subject of the verb is supplied by the context of line 419, i.e., Loxias. It would be more faithful to Euripides to use a Greek colon so that the line would look as follows: 'Μέλλει· τὸ θεῖον δ'ἐστι τοιοῦτον φύοει.' Menelaus in line 419 says, 'And does Loxias protect you in these evils?' In the line quoted by Thoreau, Orestes is replying, 'He delays (is always on the verge of) [doing so]: such is the nature of the divine (literally: the divine is such by nature).'"

46.16 Sarma?: So in Y, correcting the misspelling ("Sunma") in DR. The quotation from Sarma, according to Professor Ethel Seybold, is item #24 in a group of entries in the *Library of Congress Literary Notebook*, p. 8. It appears also in *The Dial*, 3 (July, 1842) as number eighty-four in a group of selections called "Extracts from the Heetopades of Veeshnoo Sarma." In his introduction to *The Dial* "Extracts," Thoreau asserts that he has taken the sentence from Charles Wilkins' translation of the *Heetopades* or *The Amicable Instructions of Veeshnoo Sarma.*

46.35 clarity,: So in Y, and in Raleigh's *History of the World*, Chapter 1, Section xi. The form in DR ("elasity") is possible, but the assumption of the editor is that the compositor misread Thoreau's copy. W does not list "elasity."

47.2-3 the light of light,": So in Y. DR encloses the phrase in quotation marks, leaving unresolved the question as to where the major quotation ends.

Table of Textual Variants

THE following table records all substantive variants in DR and Y, including the long passages quoted from E. The many hundreds of variants between DR and E reflecting Thoreau's promiscuous handling of the text of the book he was reviewing are excluded. An asterisk signifies a textual note.

20.25	the pestilent] DR; this ~ Y
* 20.28	and ague] Y; ague DR
20.34	paradise;] DR; a ~ Y
21.1	Hygeian] DR; Hygeia Y
21.21	thorough-bred] DR; throughbred Y
21.26	the tempests;] DR; tempests; Y
21.29	gases;] DR; gas; Y
22.24	relation with] DR; ~ to Y
22.25	nature;] DR; nature even; Y
* 23.17	True,] Y; Here, DR
23.33	a-head.] DR; ahead. Y
25.2	"We know,"] *deleted in* Y *to* 26.6 We do
27.1	If you] *deleted in* Y *to* 27.11 Men
27.31	ship.] DR; chip. Y
28.1	The following] *deleted in* Y *to* 28.13 This power
28.22	whenever] DR; wherever Y
28.24	"However] *deleted in* Y *to* 29.42 Verily
31.7	"How to] *deleted in* Y *to* 31.19 So much
31.20	So much] DR; no ¶ ~ ~ Y
31.30	"But as] *deleted in* Y *to* 32.20 we may
32.40	wasted,] DR E; wanted Y
33.8-9	(Etzler's Mechanical System).] DR; *omitted* Y
* 33.33	pages] Y; page DR
33.33	27."] DR; 27. Y
33.34	though] *deleted in* Y *to* 34.2 author.
34.4	"Any wilderness,] *deleted in* Y *to* 35.3 Who knows
36.18	a victim] DR; the ~ Y
* 37.22	exertion.] DR; ~ . . . Y
37.25	he may,] *deleted in* Y *to* 37.37 "One
* 38.3	Any] DR E; *any* Y

38.9	These last sentences] DR; This last sentence Y
38.12	the deep] DR; this ∼ Y
38.30	The channels] *deleted in Y to* 38.38 The walks
39.1	while the] *deleted in Y to* 39.21 "At night
39.30	"Such is] *deleted in Y to* 39.38 Thus is
40.28	like] DR; liked Y
* 41.16	no income but our outgoes;] DR; no income, but outgoes; Y
44.3	"There was] *deleted in Y to* 44.21 Mr. Etzler
45.3	execution.] DR; accomplishment. Y
* 46.16	Sarma?] Y; Sunma? DR
46.22	the waves,] DR; waves, Y
* 46.35	clarity,] Y; elasity, DR
* 47.3	∧ the light of light,"] Y; "∼ ∼ ∼ ∼," DR
47.24	almshouses,] DR; almshouse, Y
47.28	greater] Y; gearter DR

Table of Emendations

19.title	*Period following title deleted*
* 20.28	and ague,] Y; ague DR
* 22.12	hyena] Y; hyæna DR
* 23.17	True,] Y; Here, DR
* 28.12	3,000,000,000,000] 3,000-000,000,000 DR
28.38	men."] ∼ . ∧ DR
* 31.1	sunshine] Sunshine DR Y
* 33.33	pages] Y; page DR
35.2	constitution] constitntion DR
35.36	is to be] Y; is to DR
36.11	breaking."] ∼ . ∧ DR
37.37	afford."] ∼ . ∧ DR
39.21	delights."] ∼ . ∧ DR
* 43.29	*Early form of circumflex (⌒) substituted for late form (∼)*
46.5	hyenas,] Y; hyænas, DR
* 46.16	Sarma?] Y; Sunma? DR
* 46.35	clarity,] Y; elasity, DR
* 47.3	∧ the light of light,"] Y; "∼ ∼ ∼ ∼," DR
47.28	greater] Y; gearter DR

End-of-Line Hyphenation

THE compounds or possible compounds in list A, below, are hyphenated at the end of the line in the "Paradise (To Be) Regained" copy-text. The editor has resolved each to the form recorded in this list, in accord with the principles discussed in the General Introduction, page 246. List B records only those compounds hyphenated at the end of the line in this edition that should be transcribed with the hyphen in order to duplicate the copy-text forms.

LIST A

20.31	counteracted	33.12	millwrights
24.27	water-power	39.6	gas-light (from E)
24.35	sailing-vessel	41.11	something
28.7	sea-water	44.13	hap-hazard
29.39	every-where		(from E)
	(from E)	45.18	sunshine

LIST B

34.22	wooden-stuff	46.27	horse-power

Herald of Freedom

Textual Introduction

Herald of Freedom, the anti-slavery news-paper about which Thoreau's review of the same name was written, was a weekly founded in Concord, New Hampshire, on February 20, 1835, by "an association of gentlemen" (Albe Cady, George Storrs, George Kent, and Amos Wood), with Joseph Horace Kimball as editor. From the beginning it was beset with difficulties. In addition to the financial problems that plagued all the New England anti-slavery journals, the *Herald of Freedom* suffered from the outset from the indisposition of the editor, who, though only twenty-two when he took over the paper, was already showing symptoms of consumption. Kimball was at the helm for only a short eighteen months before fleeing to the West Indies in the futile hope of regaining his health, though his name remained on the masthead. On March 24, 1838, he resigned because of "severe and increasing ill health," with the explanation to his subscribers that "Since last June we have been able to go to the office but once." On April 11 he died, and the issue of the *Herald of Freedom* for April 14, 1838, printed his obituary. He was twenty-five. If Thoreau read the paper while it was published under Kimball's editorship and under that of the interim committee that issued it during Kimball's illness and following his death, he gave no sign. During most of the period he was a student in college, and probably had other things to occupy his time.[1]

[1] These and following data relating to the *Herald of Freedom* are drawn from the newspaper itself on the dates mentioned.

The name of "N. P. Rogers" appeared on the mast-head with the issue of June 30, 1838. It is not clear whether Thoreau began his reading of the *Herald* with the first issue for which Rogers was responsible. But when he wrote his review of Rogers and of the *Herald of Freedom* almost six years later, publishing it in *The Dial* of April, 1844, he drew the first of the six long passages he quoted out of the third issue Rogers published, dated July 14, 1838. He drew the second passage from Rogers' editorial of August 18, 1838, the third from that of February 10, 1843, the fourth from the issue of May 26, 1843, and the final two from the issue of March 15, 1844. In his foot-note on page one of his review, Thoreau referred to the March 15 issue only. Though too much can be made of these dates, they seem to suggest that Tho-reau's reading of the *Herald*, though sporadic, spanned nearly the whole period of Rogers' editorship. Thoreau tells his readers in the first sentence of "Herald of Freedom" that he had "occasionally, for several years, met with a number of this spirited journal." Where he found copies of the paper poses no problem. Sub-scription lists were published regularly by Rogers; and occasional subscriptions were purchased by resi-dents of Concord, Massachusetts. The Concord Fe-male Anti-Slavery Society subscribed from Septem-ber, 1843, through July, 1845; and the women of the Thoreau household were among its most active mem-bers.

Ironically, Rogers' tenure as editor hardly outlasted the date of Thoreau's laudatory review, which came out in the April 1844 issue of *The Dial*. Rogers' issue of December 6, 1844, was his last before William Lloyd Garrison and Stephen Foster, embittered by Rogers' candor and outspokenness, wrested the paper from him and terminated its publication in a series of legalistic manipulations through the New Hampshire Anti-Slavery Society, launching concurrently in *The Liberator* a bombardment of charges against Rogers that estranged him from many of his friends and added to the burden of his declining health. On March 14, 1845, after an interval of more than three months, Rogers succeeded in reestablishing the paper, issuing it weekly through the first six months of 1846, all the while becoming increasingly weak and despondent. On August 6, 1846, his name appeared on the masthead for the last time; and on October 16, 1846, he died. The final, October 23, 1846, issue of the *Herald of Freedom*, "new series," published by friends during the final few months, carried a long obituary notice captioned, "N. P. Rogers is dead." His age was fifty-two. Much of the remainder of the final issue was given over to obituary notices copied from other newspapers. Horace Greeley's *New-York Daily Tribune* praised Rogers for his *Letters from the Old Man of the Mountain*. The dimensions of Rogers that struck the *Tribune* writer most favorably were many of the same that appealed to Thoreau.

Rogers' death, of which Thoreau was probably very promptly aware, may have revived his interest in the man and his work. At some time after October 16, 1846, Thoreau scribbled two pages of notes on Rogers, and on the basis of the notes, wrote four pages of fair-copy material, much of it quoted from a Rogers editorial in the *Herald of Freedom* of September 2, 1842. Internal evidence indicates that he intended to append the new material to the "Herald of Freedom" text. This material, now preserved in folder 11 at the Houghton Library, is the only holograph matter relating to "Herald of Freedom" that has been found.

Only the first three printings of the review have

any claim to authority, and one of these, the second, can be very quickly dismissed so far as its candidacy for copy-text is concerned. The first printing appeared in *The Dial*, 4 (April, 1844), pages 507-12, signed "H. D. T." The second appeared in *Herald of Freedom*, 10 (May 10, 1844), placed there by Rogers himself upon being sent a copy of the *Dial* text by an unidentified correspondent.[2] Rogers remarked in a covering comment that preceded the text of Thoreau's review that he was reprinting it from *The Dial*, and since he also expressed complete puzzlement over who Thoreau might be, the possibility that Thoreau himself might have sent Rogers corrected copy of the six pages from *The Dial* is remote. Collation of the Rogers printing with the text of *The Dial* reveals that Rogers did indeed use this version as the basis for his text in *Herald of Freedom*, reprinting with only a dozen or so compositor's slips and editorial changes in accidentals, faithfully reproducing even most of Thoreau's misquotations. And Thoreau had been conspicuously free in his rendering of Rogers' texts.

The third text of "Herald of Freedom" having possible claim to authority is that of the 1866 *A Yankee in Canada, with Anti-Slavery and Reform Papers*. Since the textual principles of W. W. Greg dictate that a copy from the *Dial* printing of "Herald of Freedom" should be chosen as the copy-text, though the later *Yankee* text contains significant substantive alterations that could possibly have had authorial sanction, an analysis of the evidence in support of the claims of each text seems warranted.

Thoreau exercised more control than was usual

---

[2] For a discussion of the circumstances, see Wendell P. Glick, "Thoreau and the 'Herald of Freedom,'" *The New England Quarterly*, 22, no. 2 (June 1949), 193-204.

for him over the publication of "Herald of Freedom" in *The Dial*. After Margaret Fuller relinquished her editorship of the periodical with the winter issue of 1841, Emerson took over the task, and Thoreau was soon associated with him in putting the journal together. For the spring issue of 1843, Thoreau assumed the major responsibility. He had every opportunity with Emerson as editor to refine his own contributions and see them through to publication; and they must represent his intentions at the time of publication. Thoreau's personal copy of *The Dial*, moreover, is extant in the library of Southern Illinois University, bearing his marginal corrections. For the "Herald of Freedom" there are no marginalia at all. The evidence supporting *The Dial* version of this essay for copy-text is therefore considerable—a key question being, however, whether Thoreau's intentions for this review underwent a later change.

Collation of *The Dial* text with that of the 1866 *Yankee* seems at first to suggest that Thoreau's intentions underwent a very considerable change. As in the case of "Paradise (To Be) Regained," the 1866 version of "Herald of Freedom" is heavily elided; for the most part the material stricken consists of quotations and portions of quotations from Rogers that run to great length in *The Dial* printing. In a few instances Thoreau's wording is altered in the interest ostensibly of effecting continuity in the elided text. But the alterations in the 1866 printing go far beyond the simple deletion of quoted material. Someone, aware of Rogers' death in 1846, attempted to rewrite the text, altering tenses and supplying new adverbs to accommodate each sentence to this new fact. The result is a muddle of inconsistencies. That Thoreau would wish such a text as the 1866 one with its gaucheries to represent his final intention for this review is not, to this editor, conceivable. Stylistic crudity is not Thoreau's trademark.

Comparison of the first sentence of the 1844 and 1866 versions makes clear what the 1866 version is attempting, and just as clear also that shifting the writer's point of view from 1844 to post-1846 will not be easy. First, the opening sentence from the *Dial* text of 1844:

> We have occasionally, for several years, met with a number of this spirited journal, edited, as abolitionists need not be informed, by Nathaniel P. Rogers, once a counsellor at law in Plymouth, still further up the Merrimack, but now, in his riper years, come down the hills thus far, to be the Herald of Freedom to those parts.

No problem of internal consistency arises. Not so, however, in the first sentence of the text in the 1866 *Yankee*:

> We had occasionally, for several years, met with a number of this spirited journal, edited, as abolitionists need not be informed, by Nathaniel P. Rogers, once a counsellor at law in Plymouth, still farther up the Merrimac, but now, in his riper years, come down the hills thus far, to be the Herald of Freedom to these parts.

If "We have" is to become "We had" in consideration of Rogers' death in 1846 and a lapse of time, can "but now, in his riper years," be permitted to stand? "Now" in the first version is 1844 and Rogers is alive; "now" in the second version is post-1846 and Rogers is dead. He is not in "his riper years." Such crudities persist from the beginning of the review to 50.28 where the biographical comments on Rogers terminate and a more impersonal analysis of Rogers' style begins.

The principal classes of variants between the 1844 and 1866 texts are four:

1. Alterations in verbs, pronouns, and adverbs in the introductory portion of the review (49.1 to 50.28) which produce stylistic inconsistencies on a scale uncharacteristic of Thoreau;
2. Alterations which contravene Thoreau's normal spelling preferences, e.g., "Merrimack" at 49.5 (1844) to "Merrimac" (1866), and which suggest unauthorized editorial meddling;
3. The deletion in 1866 of much of the material quoted from Rogers, though a major emphasis of the review is upon the effectiveness of Rogers' prose style;
4. The revision in the 1866 version of the final paragraph of the review, which surviving holograph matter in folder 11 demonstrates to have been authorial.

This editor believes that the surviving holograph matter on Rogers at the Houghton Library clearly has a bearing upon Thoreau's final intention for this review. Of the six pages, two are filled with scribbled notes written on recto and verso of one 7½″ x 9½″ sheet of faded blue, lined, wove paper. They include truncated quotations from Rogers that were expanded in the text of the draft on the remaining four pages. Though there is some cancellation and interlineation on these four pages, the care with which Thoreau wrote seems to suggest that he was thinking of printer's copy. The paper of the draft is the same as that used for the notes. The four pages, however, consist of but one 9½″ x 15″ sheet folded once to make two recto and two verso sides.

That the text of the four pages was written after Rogers' death is clear. Thoreau laments Rogers' death in an ambiguous passage that implies that the death was recent: "But since our voyage Rogers has died, and now there is no one in New England to express the indignation or contempt which may still be felt at any cant or inhumanity."

To what "voyage" is Thoreau alluding? The answer must be that he is thinking either of his trip to the Catskills with Ellery Channing in the summer of 1844, or to the Maine Woods "voyage" with George Thatcher in August of 1846. Franklin B. Sanborn has asserted that John and Henry Thoreau called on Rogers at Plymouth during their canoe trip on the Merrimack, a probable extrapolation from Thoreau's observations in the Houghton notes, but he almost certainly erred, because in Rogers' response to the publication of "Herald of Freedom" (*Herald of Freedom*, 10, no. 12 [May 10, 1844]), Rogers professed that he had never before heard Thoreau's name. Both script and paper, moreover, testify to ca. 1848 as the time of the composition of these four pages. They were apparently written when the memory of Rogers was still green.[3]

That Thoreau intended the fair-copy draft in folder 11 to become part of any reprinting of "Herald of Freedom" is suggested by the fact that the first paragraph of the draft is a revision of the final paragraph of the 1844 text. The 1866 editor(s), moreover, had access to the revised form, which they substituted for the first printed version, disdaining, however, to include the remaining material in the draft that follows the revised paragraph without interruption. Though Thoreau was at this time assembling material for *A Week on the Concord and Merrimack Rivers* and may have considered making the "Herald of Freedom" as

[3] See Sanborn's *The Life of Henry David Thoreau* (Boston, 1917), p. 228.

revised a part of that volume, he did not do so. If he ever thought of the review with his additions and revisions as part of a longer work, he changed his mind. Since this editor can discover no proof that Thoreau revised his 1844 text with such an intention, but since there is proof that Thoreau altered the final paragraph of the 1844 printing and added the new material, both revision and addendum are made a part of the copy-text for the present edition. Had Thoreau himself reissued the review, this editor believes he would have incorporated his own revisions into the the new version.

In the notes and tables that follow are recorded all substantive and accidental changes in the copy-text that affect meaning. All sources of transcriptions from Rogers' editorials are identified, but only gross liberties taken in transcription are discussed in these notes. The table of textual variations records all substantive variations between Thoreau's text and his sources. Only one passage taken by Thoreau from Rogers is emended to bring it into accord with its source. The disparities in most instances are so marked that it is assumed that Thoreau intended them. Significant revisions are listed in the table of alterations, page 298.

The text of this essay in the Riverside Edition (volume 10, 70-75) is based on the 1866 impression (Y) and is therefore without authority. The Walden and Manuscript editions (volume 4, 306-10), based on the Riverside, are likewise non-authorial. Abbreviations used in the textual notes and tables for "Herald of Freedom" are identified in section 6 of the General Introduction, "Symbols, Abbreviations, Collations," pages 253-260.

Textual Notes

49.1 have: So in D. But in Y, the tense has been changed to past, in accordance with the fact of Rogers' death. For a statement of the problems generated by this change, see the textual introduction above (pp. 291ff.).

49.24-26 We . . . author.: Y omits this sentence, opening the paragraph with "Mr. Rogers" of the succeeding sentence.

51.8-40 We cannot do better . . . *Wait and see.*: This passage from D, including the long quotation from Rogers' editorial, "The Discussion" (*Herald of Freedom*, 4, no. 20 [July 14, 1838]), was deleted in Y, which bridges the hiatus with the substitute sentence: "Some extracts will show in what sense he was a poet as well as a reformer." The ellipsis at 51.39 (Thoreau used a long dash) indicates an elision of 14 lines from Rogers' text.

52.4 To none: This quotation is from Rogers' editorial "The Convention—THE CONVENTION" in *Herald of Freedom*, 4, no. 25 (August 18, 1838), *passim.* Errors in the spelling of place-names ("Kearsarge" [52.8] and "Ammonoosuck" [52.22]) are corrected.

52.12 lay: Rogers should have used the present form, "lie." Thoreau added the comma between "lay" and "scattered," sharply altering Rogers' meaning.

52.34 Ho, then: The long quotation from Rogers consists of two extracts from the editorial "The New-England Convention" in *Herald of Freedom*, 9, no. 14 (May 26, 1843). The first extract terminates at 53.42.

53.28 "And green Vermont,: Beginning with these words, Y deletes to 56.6, the beginning of the final paragraph that Thoreau revised in folder 11.

53.40 minstrelsy*: In the footnote supplied by Thoreau, The Hutchinsons, a family singing group, are identified. Rogers had referred to them at length in a passage Thoreau deleted.

54.17 "Denied a chance: Thoreau drew this excerpt from near the center of a 4,000-word Rogers editorial, "Massachusetts Annual Meeting," *Herald of Freedom*, 8, no. 51 (February 10, 1843). Immediately preceding the excerpt Rogers had written the sentence, "Our movement seems to give opportunity to all the odd folks." The pro-

noun "they" of Thoreau's quotation (54.17) referred originally to "odd folks" rather than directly to "the Folsoms
and Lamsons," who had a reputation for disruption at
anti-slavery meetings.

54.38 "Webster is: This passage was excerpted from
"Daniel Webster on Christian Institutions," *Herald of
Freedom*, 10, no. 4 (March 15, 1844).

55.20 "I saw account,":   For this quotation Thoreau
combined four extracts from Rogers' editorial "Bursting
of the Paixhan Gun," *Herald of Freedom*, 10, no. 4 (March
15, 1844).

55.37 rites: D has "right." Since Rogers' version
seems more appropriate in context, Thoreau's mistrans-
cription at this point is deemed an inadvertence.

56.6 Such timely,:   This paragraph is Thoreau's
holograph revision in folder 11 of the final two paragraphs
in D. It is also the exact form of the final paragraph of
Y.

56.11 But since: The source of the text from this
point to the end is Thoreau's autograph manuscript in
bMS AM 278.5 in the Houghton Library (folder 11).

56.16 "Why do you: Thoreau's source for this incident is unknown. A search of the files of the *Herald of
Freedom* does not disclose it.

57.3 "Swamscot is: Thoreau transcribed this passage
from Rogers' editorial, "At Home Again," *Herald of Freedom*, 8, no. 28 (Sept. 2, 1842). Thoreau changed "laying"
to "lying" (57.16), "lay" to "lie" (57.20) and made six
changes in accidentals.

Table of Alterations
in Manuscript Copy-Text

56.11   Rogers] *interlined in ink above cancelled*
         he folder 11
56.12   express] *followed by* adequately the
         contempt and (or *interlined above and*
         cancelled) cancelled in ink folder 11
56.12   the] *added in ink* folder 11
56.13   or contempt] *interlined in ink with a caret*
         folder 11
56.31   of] *followed by* the reformer and *cancelled*
         in ink folder 11
56.34   the] *added in ink* folder 11
57.2   anywhere] *interlined in ink with a caret*
         folder 11
57.14   the] *added in ink* folder 11
57.29   His style . . . overlooked.] *interlined in ink*
         followed by
         He was born and bred far up this stream,
         under the shadow of the higher hills. "Few
         places," says he, "of so little note, strike
         the eye of the traveller so pleasantly as the
         town of Plymouth in Grafton County. A
         beautiful expanse of interval opens on the
         eye like a lake among the hills and woods,
         and the pretty river Pemigewasset, re-
         freshed with its recent tributary, Baker's
         river, from the foot of Moose hillock, and
         bordered along its crooked sides with rows
         of maple, meanders widely from upland to
         upland through the meadows, and realizes
         to the mind some of the sequestered spots
         in the valleys of the Swiss cantons." To this
         scenery his memory continually reverted,
         even to the graceful elm—"in night from
         our old *home* on the banks of the Pemige-
         wasset. We have seen larger, but never one
         of such perfect symmetry and beauty. It
         stood just across that cold stream, near the
         bridge   *cancelled in ink*   folder 11

Table of Textual Variants

THE following table records every disparity affecting meaning, whether accidental or substantive, between the text of this edition and the copy-texts ("D") from *The Dial*, 4, no. 4 (April, 1844), pp. 507-12 and folder 11 of bMS AM 278.5 in the Houghton Library. Folder 11 provides the copy-text from 56.6 to the end of the selection. The table records also the variants in the first book version ("Y"), *A Yankee in Canada* (1866), pp. 206-10. Thoreau's mistranscriptions of matter quoted from Rogers ("H" with date) are also recorded if the effect is to alter the meaning. In one special case a quotation is emended to conform with Rogers' version in the *Herald of Freedom*.

* 49.1	have] D; had Y
49.3	need not be] D; need not to be Y
49.5	further] D; farther Y
49.7	those] D; these Y
49.7	have] D; had Y
* 49.24-26	We . . . author.] D; *omitted* Y
49.27	to occupy] D; to have occupied Y
50.4	The present editor is] D; This editor was Y
50.9	is] D; was Y
50.10	has] D; had Y
50.11	takes] D; took Y
50.12	may] D; might Y
50.12	shall] D; should Y
50.13	keeps] D; kept Y
50.15	asserts] D; asserted Y
50.17	is, beside,] D; was ∧ ~ ∧ Y
50.19	are] D; were Y
50.21	are] D; were Y
50.22	looks] D; looked Y
50.23	is] D; was Y
50.28	But] D; ⊄ ~ Y
* 51.8-40	We cannot . . . . *see.*"] D; *omitted in* Y. *Sentence substituted*: "Some extracts will show in what sense he was a poet as well as a reformer."

51.39   own." . . . "But] *twelve lines from* H (July 14, 1838) *omitted in* D *and* Y

52.1   He thus] D; *no* ⊄ ~ ~ Y

52.5   spirits." . . . "From] *eleven lines from* H (August 18, 1838) *deleted from* D *and* Y

52.7   sea." . . . "From] *twelve lines from* H (August 18, 1838) *omitted from* D *and* Y

* 52.12   lay,] D; ~ ∧ H (August 18, 1838)

52.16   Lawrence. ⊄] D Y; *no* ⊄ H (August 18, 1838)

52.23   Connecticut." . . .] *eighteen lines from* H (August 18, 1838) *omitted from* D *and* Y

52.30   the] D; a Y

53.3   that] D H (May 26, 1843); the Y

* 53.28   "And green Vermont,] D; *deleted to* 56.6 Y

* 53.40   minstrelsy*] D; ~ ∧ H (May 26, 1843)

53.41-42   stage-coach." . . .] *thirty-six lines of* H (May 26, 1843) *omitted from* D

54.3   enough] D; ~ behind H (May 26, 1843)

54.8   straits] D; straights H (May 26, 1843)

* 54.17   ⊄ "Denied] D; *no* ⊄ ∧ ~ H (February 10, 1843)

* 54.38   ⊄ "Webster] D; *no* ⊄ ∧ ~ H (March 15, 1844)

54.39   They had better] D; They better H (March 15, 1844)

* 55.20   ⊄ "I saw] D; *no* ⊄ ∧ ~ ~ H (March 15, 1844)

55.26   funeral. . . ."] *Six lines following in* H (March 15, 1844) *omitted from* D

* 55.37   rites] H (March 15, 1844); right D

55.37   sepulture. . . ."] *The following twenty-six lines in* H (March 15, 1844) *omitted in* D

55.41-56.1   waiters. . . ."] *Ten following lines in* H (March 15, 1844) *omitted from* D

56.2   life,] D; life time, H (March 15, 1844)

* 56.6   Such timely] folder 11 Y; We deem such D

56.9   are the] folder 11 Y; the D

56.9   gifts which] folder 11 Y; gifts D

56.10   make.] folder 11 Y; *continues* and should be glad to see the scraps from which we have quoted, and the others which we have not seen, collected into a volume. It might, perchance, penetrate into some quarters

which the unpopular cause of freedom has
not reached. (*paragraph*) Long may we
hear the voice of this Herald. (*paragraph*)
H. D. T. D

57.16	lying] laying H (September 2, 1842)
57.20	lie] lay H (September 2, 1842)

Emendations of the Copy-Texts

49. title	*Period following title deleted*
49.1	We] WE D
51.14	"Bandy] ——— "Bandy D
51.39	." . . . "] "———" D
* 52.4	"To] ———"To D
52.5	." . . ."] ."———" D *Also at* 52.7
52.8	Kearsarge,] Kearsage D
52.22	Ammonoosuck] Ammonosuck D
52.23	Connecticut." . . .] ~ ." ——— D
52.24	"We] ——— "We D
53.41	stage-coach." . . .] ~ . ———" D
54.1	"Let] ——— "Let D
55.26	." . . ."]". . . ." D *Also at* 55.33, 56.1
55.35	unburied] unburried D
* 55.37	rites] right D
57.12	Every thing] Every-thing folder 11
57.13	Flakes,] Flakes,' folder 11

End-of-Line Hyphenation

THE compounds or possible compounds in list A, below, are hyphenated at the end of the line in the "Herald of Freedom" copy-texts. The editor has resolved each to the form recorded in this list, in accord with the principles discussed in the General Introduction, page 246. In doubtful cases occurring within quotations, the original forms in H are reprinted. List B records only those compounds hyphenated at the end of the line in this edition that should be transcribed with the hyphen in order to duplicate the copy-text forms.

LIST A		LIST B	
51.12	understandings	53.28	anti-slavery
51.33	pro-slavery	53.36	winter-killed
53.4	seaward	53.38	bloody-footed
53.19	everglade	53.41	stage-coach
53.28	anti-slavery	54.11	anti-slavery
54.15	anti-slavery	54.31	pro-slavery
55.4	Comeouters		
57.12	Every thing		
57.25	sea-flow		

Wendell Phillips Before Concord Lyceum

Textual Introduction

WENDELL PHILLIPS is recorded in the official minutes of the Concord Lyceum as having spoken six times before that forum between 1838 and 1860, the years of Thoreau's active involvement as a lyceum member. On the first three occasions (December 21, 1842, January 18, 1844, and March 11, 1845), Phillips spoke on the subject of "Slavery," in each instance fomenting a debate within the lyceum between liberal and conservative factions over the propriety of using the lyceum platform to air controversial "social questions." Hon. John Keyes, a conservative curator, attempted vainly to block the first lecture by Phillips, and on March 5, 1845, resigned his office rather than invite Phillips for a third time. Thereafter, "liberal" curators were elected, among them Thoreau, who staunchly supported the faction contending that the discussion of such issues as slavery was not only appropriate, but desirable. The final resolution of the controversy came with a vote by the membership on November 12, 1845, to give the curators full authority to engage whatever speakers they chose: "When the Curators secure a Lecturer . . . their decision is final without and [any] further interference from the Lyceum."[1]

Thoreau's letter to *The Liberator* extolling Phillips' third speech was probably not a spontaneous over-

---

[1] The records of the Concord Lyceum for this period (1838-1845) are reproduced in *The Transcendental Climate*, Kenneth Cameron, ed. (Hartford: Transcendental Books, n. d.), III, 688-700.

flow of enthusiasm for that speech only. Internal evidence from a surviving working draft suggests that the letter did not come easily. Thoreau probably wrote a first draft as a response to the first or second speech of Phillips, revising the draft later on the original sheets, once in ink and once in pencil, before preparing a fair-copy draft to send to Garrison shortly after Phillips' third appearance. It is possible even that Thoreau had his letter ready, or nearly so, in anticipation of the third speech. He dated the letter to *The Liberator* March 12, 1845, the day following Phillips' third address; and it was in print in the issue of March 28.

Thoreau's working draft is preserved in a holograph volume containing chiefly early draft portions of *A Week on the Concord and Merrimack Rivers*. The volume is bound, with brown spine and mottled boards, and is designated MA 1303 in the Pierpont Morgan Library, call number R-V 12 F. It is written in ink, on unlined sheets measuring $7\frac{3}{4}$" x $12\frac{5}{8}$", with interlineations in both pencil and ink, and paginated in pencil by Thoreau on recto using odd numbers only to page 241. Some sheets are scissored out. The working draft of "Wendell Phillips Before Concord Lyceum" appears without pagination on what would be page 203 if the numbering were sequential, concluding on what would have been page 209 recto, following a passage dealing with boating and interspersed with observations on writers and reviewers. His failure to paginate the Phillips material suggests that Thoreau may have considered it an intrusion upon the other matter of the volume.

The draft provides a preliminary form for every paragraph of the letter except the final one. In general, the first part of the draft approaches fair copy and lends itself to close collation with the printed versions. Cancellations and interlineations are frequent, but the uncancelled matter is so close to the printed forms that it is a fair conjecture that Thoreau may have moved directly to printer's copy from the first portion of the draft, and perhaps for the whole of it. As the draft proceeds, however, it becomes more and more remote from the final form. Large sections of matter are cancelled with the characteristic waved lines, matter that is not reinstated in any form in the printed versions. Some of the late matter underwent multiple revisions on these sheets before the decision was finally made to eliminate it or to include it. In the process of reworking some passages, Thoreau seems to have concluded that they did not serve his purpose. Some few late passages are so thoroughly written over as to be indecipherable. Several of the segments, moreover, are not in the sequence in which they were finally to appear.

Two extant versions of this letter possess demonstrable authority: the version in MA 1303, which in many respects does not represent Thoreau's final intention, and the first printed version in *The Liberator*, 15, no. 13 (March 28, 1845), set from a manuscript that Garrison destroyed forthwith if he followed his usual practice. The first book printing (in *A Yankee in Canada, with Anti-Slavery and Reform Papers* [Boston, 1866], pages 274-77) was based on the text from *The Liberator*. Collation of the *Liberator* and *Yankee* versions reveals only one change in substantives, the necessary pluralization of a noun in the *Yankee* version to make it accord with its plural complement. In accidentals, on the other hand, variants are numerous.

In accordance with the editorial policy of the Center for Editions of American Authors, the *Liberator* version of this letter becomes copy-text for this edition.

Two classes of accidentals in the copy-text are emended, however, since they are in conflict with the working draft and with Thoreau's known practice for this period. Thoreau almost never clearly capitalized the common nouns "state," "church," and "slavery" in his working draft; preoccupied with all three as personified evils, Garrison (and his printer, Knapp) consistently capitalized all three in the columns of *The Liberator*. Lower case is restored in this edition.

In addition, in his working draft Thoreau never hyphenates compounds made up of two nouns. Though it is remotely possible that he may have intended to supply hyphens in his finished draft or that he may have done so, the first portion of the working draft is so close to final form in most particulars that it acquires some authority over accidentals; and the absence of hyphenation in *all* compounds of nouns must be considered significant. Hyphenations of compounds of nouns in the copy-text are removed in this edition, therefore, on the grounds that to remove them all brings the text of this letter closer to Thoreau's intention.

The accidentals in this text take on a more than normal significance, since Thoreau's haste to move to printer's copy from the second half of the MA 1303 working draft may account for the tortured syntax of a few of his sentences. Some misplaced commas and periods have substantive impact. The sentence beginning at 60.20, for example, which in both *The Liberator* and *A Yankee* included the subsequent sentence as well, is so misshapen as to border on incomprehensibility. The working copy is less cumbered by commas than either of the printed versions and has greater appeal therefore to the twentieth-century ear. But since Thoreau did in fact strew extra commas at times in final copy, reducing sentences to lock-step, the occasional deletion in this edition of commas from the copy-text has been done sparingly with the authority of the working draft, and then only when necessary to bring coherence out of incoherence. For example, the first sentence of the letter in Thoreau's working draft has no commas at all; the only internal punctuation is a semi-colon after "Phillips." In *The Liberator* the sentence reads:

> We have now, for the third winter, had our spirits refreshed, and our faith in the destiny of the Commonwealth strengthened, by the presence and the eloquence of Wendell Phillips; and we wish to tender to him our thanks and our sympathy.

Editorial preference for the holograph version has not been allowed to obscure the strong possibility that the commas are Thoreau's, and they are allowed to remain.

Abbreviations used in the textual notes and tables for "Wendell Phillips Before Concord Lyceum" are identified in section 6 of the General Introduction, "Symbols, Abbreviations, Collations," pages 253 to 260.

Textual Notes

59.title: Thoreau's working copy bears no title, and since he wrote this selection as a letter to the editor of *The Liberator*, he may not initially have supplied one. The copy-text, which omits the article ("the"), is here followed rather than the smoother version of Y which supplies it.

59.10   conservers: L-WP prints the singular, Y the plural. MA 1303 uses the plural form. The plural is the expected form, since the word is the complement of the subject of the sentence ("descendants"). The singular of L-WP is a probable printer's misreading of an ill-formed terminal "s" in Thoreau's printer's copy.

59.13-14   by coming . . . lecture room,:   The version in MA 1303 differs from that printed in L-WP and Y. It reads "by bringing all their sons and all their cousins to the lecture room—." Thoreau may have felt that the early version gave the impression of flippancy.

60.6   American Society: Between these two words in MA 1303, Thoreau injected what appears to be "Anti"; presumably he initially intended to revise to "American Anti-Slavery Society" and later changed his mind, neglecting to cancel the prefix.

60.12-14   and, . . . audience.:   Thoreau wrote initially in MA 1303: "and secures the genuine respect of his audience aside from their admiration of his rhetoric." This is left uncancelled but does not appear in the printed version.

60.20   No one: The syntax of this and the succeeding sentence in PE, which in Y, L-WP, and MA 1303 are one, is tortured. The matter from which Thoreau formed the sentence for publication in L-WP appears at two widely separated points in MA 1303. The only large break in the MA 1303 text—a skip of perhaps two lines—occurs immediately following the first part of the sentence which ends with "pieces," (60.28) and a cancellation. Thoreau's attempt to amalgamate the two widely separated sections by cancelling the concluding words of the first (eight words following "pieces,"), inserting a comma after "pieces," and adding on the long cumbersome passage dealing with Frederick Douglass, was not successful. The sentence in PE is arbitrarily broken with a period after "Frederick ———" (60.30). At 60.23 "who" in the copy-text is emended to "which."

From this point on in MA 1303, Thoreau's transpositions and cancellations become so common and his emendations so extensive that no word by word collation of MA 1303 with L-WP and Y is possible, though significant variations are recorded in these notes.

60.28-29   till there shall not remain: MA 1303 reads: "while there remains" and is not emended.

61.16   slavery,:   MA 1303 follows with "or reform the church—" which is neither cancelled nor included in L-WP and Y.

61.25   trivial ends.:   MA 1303 reads "untrivial ends." But Thoreau's initial casting of this clause was positive; "not" (62.14) is careted in.

62.5   like an electuary: In MA 1303 this phrase follows "of all parties." An "X" following "parties" apparently indicates Thoreau's intention to reposition it.

Table of Textual Variants

THE following table records all variant readings affecting meaning between the copy-text, L-WP, and Y. Also noted are significant variants in MA 1303. An asterisk (*) indicates a textual note.

Emendations of the Copy-Text

* 59. title	*Period following title deleted*
59.4-5	commonwealth] MA 1303; Commonwealth L-WP
59.8-9	fellow citizens] MA 1303; ~ – ~ L-WP
* 59.10	conservers] MA 1303 Y; conserver L-WP
59.20	state] MA 1303; State L-WP; *also at* 59.27, 60.1, 62.9
59.21	church] MA 1303; Church L-WP; *also at* 59.27, 59.34, 62.9
59.27	slavery] MA 1303; Slavery L-WP; *also at* 61.4
* 60.21	which] who MA 1303 L-WP
60.31	———. To] ———; to L-WP

End-of-Line Hyphenation

THE following word is the only compound or possible compound hyphenated at the end of the line in the copy-text. It is resolved as hyphenated in accord with Thoreau's usage in his working draft. Every hyphenation at the end of the line in this edition should be transcribed as one word.

62.18   Red-cross

Resistance to Civil Government

Textual Introduction

CHARACTERISTICALLY, this essay had its origin as a lecture that developed over a period of years, coming into focus for Thoreau only after his night in jail in late July 1846. According to Bronson Alcott, the lecture was delivered before the Concord Lyceum on January 26, 1848, though Thoreau continued to work on the text.[1] Three weeks later it was either repeated or a second installment of it delivered from the same podium. A hiatus in the minutes of the Concord Lyceum for the fall of 1847 and the spring of 1848 obliterates the official record, but Thoreau corroborates Alcott in a letter to Emerson dated February 23, 1848:

> Lectures begin to multiply on my desk. I have one on Friendship which is new—and the materials of some others. I read one last week to the Lyceum on The Rights and Duties of the Individual in relation to Government—much to Mr. Alcott's satisfaction.[2]

Thoreau could not have been alluding to the January 26 lecture on the same subject if his recollection of the time interval was accurate. In his journal for February 13, 1848, about mid-way between the dates of the two lectures, Alcott commented that Thoreau at that time was still working on the lecture.[3] The text of the second lecture, therefore, was probably either

[1] *The Journals of Bronson Alcott*, Odell Shepard, ed. (Boston: Little, Brown & Co., 1938), p. 201.

[2] *Correspondence*, p. 208.

[3] Thomas Blanding discovered this information in Alcott's holograph journal at the Houghton Library, as reported in *The Thoreau Society Bulletin*, 109 (Fall 1969).

a revision, or extension, or both, of the first. And Thoreau may have continued thereafter to refine the text. In a footnote in the first printing (PE 88.n) he remarked that the extracts from Webster in the latter part of the essay had been added "since the lecture was read," though he does not say on which occasion.

Elizabeth Peabody heard of the lecture—perhaps from her sister, Sophia Hawthorne—and requested in the spring of 1849 that Thoreau submit a manuscript of it for publication in her projected periodical, *Aesthetic Papers*. Thoreau agreed to do so on April 5 (*Correspondence*, page 242), though complaining, "I have so much writing to do at present, with the printers in the rear of me, that I have almost no time left." Throughout the month of April he was busy with the galley proofs of *A Week* that were coming in batches from James Munroe & Co. "Resistance to Civil Government" appeared in print, however, on May 14, 1849, as "ART. X" immediately following "Abuse of Representative Government" by S. H. Perkins, Esq. Since Thoreau's lead time before publication had been only five weeks, and he had been forced to prepare his manuscript during a ten-day period when he was particularly busy, the possibility must not be discounted that the printer's copy he dispatched to Miss Peabody was not in every respect as he would have liked it to be.

The second printing of the essay was in the posthumous *A Yankee in Canada, with Anti-Slavery and Reform Papers* (Boston, 1866), pages 123-51. Collation of the 1849 text with that of the second printing discloses thirteen substantive variants, four of them very pronounced: the deletion in *A Yankee* of a portion of a sentence (following "themselves" PE 63.29); the addition of six inexactly rendered lines from

George Peele's *The Battle of Alcazar* (following "conformity." PE 86.10); the addition of a sentence on
Confucius (following "individual." PE 89.25); and
the altering of the title "Resistance to Civil Government" to "Civil Disobedience." The text at scattered
points in 1866 retained what were apparently signs
of haste: several awkward sentences (cf. 88.1ff.)
could profitably have been reworked.

Since no holograph fair-copy forms have been discovered, disagreement has been widespread among
editors as to the authority of the posthumous printing
in *A Yankee*. Bartholow Crawford chose for the American Writers Series *Thoreau* (New York, 1934) title
and text of the 1849 printing. Carl Bode in *The
Portable Thoreau* (New York, 1947) printed title and
text of the 1866 version, dating the essay "1849,"
however, in his "Table of Contents." Owen Thomas
chose as his "authoritative" text for the Norton Critical Edition (New York, 1966) the 1849 version, but
substituted the 1866 title for the original one. In
substantives, Scudder in the Riverside Edition (1883)
followed the 1866 text; and the Walden and Manuscript editions of 1906 were based on the Riverside.
Walter Harding printed the 1866 version in *The
Variorum Walden and the Variorum Civil Disobedience* "on the assumption that it was based on a corrected copy made by Thoreau" (New York, 1968,
page 341).

The disappearance of all authoritative holograph
forms of the essay as well as the proofsheets enhances
the importance of the residual prepublication fragments. But of these also there is a dearth. Since Thoreau put the essay through two or more preliminary
forms, one would expect to discover surviving working drafts. Yet extensive search has uncovered fragments only, and of these a very limited number. No

material later used in "Resistance to Civil Government" appears in the *Journal* for the period from July 1846, when Thoreau was jailed for non-payment of his taxes, and May of 1849 when the essay appeared. Preliminary forms for six short passages are preserved in folder 14 of bMS AM 278.5 in the Houghton Library, and for two others in folders 18A and 20 of the same collection. A preliminary form for one short passage is to be found in HM 13182 and forms for five others in HM 924 in the Huntington Library, one of the latter being a quotation from Webster. Verbal overtones of "Resistance to Civil Government" can perhaps be discerned here and there in passages from the scattered unpublished manuscripts in the major collections. But the early forms are too limited and too tentative, in most cases, to provide a significant check on either the accidentals or substantives in the printed versions. None of the extant preliminary drafts throws any light upon the critical substantive alterations of the 1849 version in the 1866 printing.

Firm evidence of the circumstances of the revision and publication of the 1866 version is scant. That Thoreau before his death did contemplate reissuing the essay, however, is supported circumstantially by an unsigned editorial in the Boston *Commonwealth* for March 13, 1863, a copy of which is transcribed on pages 83-84 of the two-volume scrapbook compiled by Alfred W. Hosmer and labeled "Henry David Thoreau / Reviews, Criticisms, Etc." now preserved in the Concord Free Public Library. The writer of the editorial describes plans for collecting and publishing Thoreau's works, based on "a list, prepared by himself shortly before his death." On the list of various essays appears the following: "In Æsthetic Papers. Resistance to Civil Government." If the list is genuine,

Thoreau "shortly before his death" had made no plans for altering his title. Whatever the circumstances were, editorial policy of the Center for Editions of American Authors dictates that the *Aesthetic Papers* version provide the copy-text for this edition. But since no marked copy of the first printing that Thoreau might have left has been found, the decision as to whether to emend the copy-text with some or all of the 1866 substantive variants must rest, at present, upon internal evidence.

The accidentals yield few clues. Comparison of the accidentals in the first printing with those of the second provides slight basis for any comfortable deductions. The second printing in *A Yankee* is far more consistent as to capitalization, punctuation, and so on, but its relative consistency is in itself disconcerting, for consistency in accidentals is not one of Thoreau's virtues and probably reflects unauthorized editorial or compositorial intervention. The first printing uses the nonvocative "Oh," which in *A Yankee* is altered to "O"; and in the first printing there are two instances of "Aye," which in *A Yankee* are altered to "Ay." It is not possible, however, to argue that Thoreau's preferences on such matters altered between 1849 and the end of his life; he apparently considered such distinctions trivial. Variants in capitalization and punctuation (particularly as to the use of the comma-dash combination) are very numerous between the first and second printings, but it is clear that they reflect the Ticknor and Fields house style and the desire of an editor or compositor for consistency rather than the practice of Thoreau. In *A Yankee* four sentences from the first printing are divided into a total of eight—at PE 64.4 (It is excellent), PE 67.13 (If one were), PE 69.22 (There are nine hundred), and at PE 70.10 (I hear of a convention). The changes perhaps make the sentences as they appear in *A Yankee* more tidy to the twentieth-century reader, but nothing marks them as Thoreau's. Though Thoreau was a life-long refiner of sentences, one cannot argue that the 1866 sentences reflect the kind of revision he would likely do at the end of his life. As a matter of fact, the revisions are clearly the sort an editor might make in an attempt to "improve" the syntax. The preference of an unknown editor might just as easily explain the transposition at PE 78.16: "they dread the consequences of disobedience to it to their property and families" in 1849 became "they dread the consequences to their property and families of disobedience to it." in 1866. At PE 83.32 the alteration of "most" in 1849 to "many" in 1866 ("This may be to judge my neighbors harshly; for I believe that most of them are not aware that they have such an institution as the jail in their village.") may have been Thoreau's attempt at a more accurate estimate of the sentiment of his neighbors; but it may just as well have been the posthumous attempt of the presumptive editor, Sophia, who probably after her brother's death retained a sharp recollection of Thoreau's jailing and the community response to it. Or, it may simply have been the 1866 printer's misreading.

Nothing conclusive so far as their authenticity is concerned can be deduced from the above variants. The case for the authority of the 1866 substantive variants rests finally with the four very pronounced changes noted earlier: the deletion in *A Yankee* of a portion of a sentence at PE 63.30; the addition of six lines from Peele at PE 86.10; the addition of a sentence on Confucius at PE 89.25; and the altering of the title. All sound like changes Thoreau *might* have made.

The deletion of a portion of a sentence at PE 63.29

could have been made by Thoreau: that is to say, there is nothing in the change that would preclude Thoreau's having made it. But nothing in the sentence itself is so characteristic of Thoreau that it can be argued Thoreau *must have made* the elision. Speaking of the "American government," Thoreau wrote in 1849: "It is a sort of wooden gun to the people themselves; and, if ever they should use it in earnest as a real one against each other, it will surely split." In the 1866 version, the sentence ends with a period at "themselves." The context with its trailing pronoun ("But it is not the less necessary for this;") might argue, incidentally, for the superiority of the uncut version. But superiority aside, why could not a literal-minded Ticknor and Fields reader have reasoned that wooden guns do not split, and have stricken the second clause? Or why might not Sophia or the publisher have felt that the 1849 reading was unfortunately suggestive of the Civil War?

The six lines from Peele added in the 1866 version at PE 86.10 one naturally is tempted to accord authority, if not on the basis of positive evidence, at least on the negative evidence that it is unlikely that the editor of *A Yankee*, probably a close friend of Thoreau (Channing perhaps, or Emerson, or Sophia) would have been so brazen as to add matter in such an amount. Moreover, Thoreau demonstrably read Peele, naming him in the section on "old English poets" in his journal (volume one [1906], 465-66), though no holograph transcription of the selection from Peele appears there or has been discovered by the editor in the commonplace books. Even discovery of a copy of the lines in Thoreau's hand, however, would still prove nothing so far as his inclusion of the passage in the essay is concerned, unless with the transcription there were contiguous portions of the essay, also in his hand. The decision of the present editor has been to print what Thoreau unquestionably wrote once, not what he may have written later.

The sentence on Confucius added to the text of *A Yankee* (following "individual" at PE 89.25) is plausibly Thoreau's since he had used a quotation from Confucius earlier in the essay (at PE 78.33); but the sentence is rejected as a part of the text in this edition on the grounds that plausibility is not enough to justify adopting a sentence which, even though it may be Thoreau's, may not have been intended for insertion here.

Finally, what does the shift of title between 1849 and 1866 suggest? Intensive search by this editor and by many other scholars has yielded (1) no evidence that the title of the 1866 printing was Thoreau's; (2) no evidence that it was not; (3) no evidence that the term "Civil Disobedience" had appeared in print before 1866, or that Thoreau himself ever used the term anywhere in his writing. The *OED*, the DAE, and the *Dictionary of Americanisms* do not have an entry for the term. Neither "Resistance to Civil Government" nor "Civil Disobedience" can be proved to be Thoreau's title from surviving holograph forms, but Elizabeth Peabody in printing the work of a living author and acquaintance in 1849 would probably have been less susceptible to supplying a title of her own than an unknown editor of a posthumously published volume would have been.

It is unfortunate that though the records of the Concord Lyceum were as a rule kept with care by the successive secretaries during the twenty-two years of Thoreau's active participation—from April 11, 1838, when he delivered his first lecture ("On Society") until February 8, 1860, when he delivered

his twenty-second and last ("Wild Apples")—no de-
tailed minutes were recorded for the fall of 1847 and
the spring of 1848, when Thoreau delivered the lecture he referred to as "The Rights and Duties of the
Individual in Relation to Government."[4] The succinct
title, "Civil Disobedience" has become established in
the American literary canon. But though its appropri-
ateness has been remarked by scholars, it is the opinion of this editor that the 1849 title of the copy-text is
the more defensible choice for this edition.

Abbreviations used in the textual notes and tables
for "Resistance to Civil Government" are identified in
section 6 of the General Introduction, "Symbols, Abbreviations, Collations," pages 253 to 260.

[4] See his letter to Emerson of February 23, 1848, in *Correspondence*, p. 208.

Textual Notes

63.title RESISTANCE TO CIVIL GOVERNMENT: The full title in AP was "ART. X.—RESISTANCE TO CIVIL GOVERNMENT." It was first altered to "Civil Disobedience" without comment in Y, though an asterisk followed the new title referring to the following footnote: "*Æsthetic Papers, No. 1. Boston, 1849." PE supplies the indentation of the first paragraph.

63.1-2 "That government is best: The common attribution of this quotation to Jefferson is probably in error. In a letter dated December 9, 1969, Julian P. Boyd, editor of *The Papers of Thomas Jefferson*, commented in response to this editor's inquiry: "Although I have been on the lookout for it ever since this edition was started twenty-five years ago, I have never found the sentence . . . in Jefferson's writings." In a memo dated May 30, 1962, dealing with the question of the origin of the quotation, Professor Boyd cites the essay of Raymond Adams, "Thoreau's Sources for 'Resistance to Civil Government,'" *Studies in Philology*, 42 (July 1945), 642n:

> The motto, "That government is best which governs least," has been attributed to Thomas Jefferson; but to Thoreau it was literally a motto, the motto which appeared regularly on the cover and the title page of *The United States Magazine and Democratic Review*, where the sentence is "The best government is that which governs least."

Lee A. Pederson in "Thoreau's Source Of The Motto In 'Civil Disobedience'" (*Thoreau Society Bulletin*, no. 67), has pointed out that the sentence "The best government is that which governs least." appeared in "The Democratic Principle—The Importance of Its Assertion and Application to Our Political System and Literature," *The United States Magazine and Democratic Review*, 1, no. 1 (October 1837), 6.

It is an editorial surmise that the statement Thoreau encloses in quotes in the following sentence (63.5)— "That government is best which governs not at all"—is Thoreau's succinct extension of the motto, set off with quotes to call attention to the parallelism.

63.29 themselves: Y concludes the sentence at this point, deleting the remainder: "and, if ever they should use it in earnest as a real one against each other, it will surely split."

64.4-5 It . . . allow;: Thoreau apparently tempered his criticism of the United States Government with a late injection of such commendatory statements. This comment does not appear in a prior form of the passage in folder 14. At "allow;" Y divides the sentence into two.

64.10 accomplished;: In folder 14 Thoreau had written "accomplished since, which is not a little," continuing with the sentence as it appeared in AP and Y.

66.3-6 "Not a drum: The quatrain is quoted from "Burial of Sir John Moore at Corunna" by Charles Wolfe (1791-1823). Two apparent errors in transcription in AP were corrected in Y: "nor a funeral" in AP (line 1) became "not a funeral"; and "ramparts" in AP (line 2) became "rampart." See Harold A. Small, *The Field of His Fame* (Berkeley, 1953), p. 7.

66.28-29 "stop . . . away,": *Hamlet*, v, i, 236-37.

66.31 "I am too: The source is *King John*, v, ii, 79-82. In folder 14 Thoreau omitted hyphenation of "high-born" and "serving-man," which both AP and Y correctly restore.

66.35-36 fellow-men appears: So in AP and Y. Folder 14 reads "fellow men seems."

67.33-34 "Duty of Submission to Civil Government,": The exact title was "The Duty of Submission to Civil Government Explained"—Chapter III of Book VI of *The Principles of Moral and Political Philosophy*. The location of Thoreau's personal copies of Paley's volume is not known, though he owned both an English edition (London, n.d.) and an American one (Philadelphia, 1836), according to the listing in *Thoreau's Library*, Walter Harding, ed., (Charlottesville, 1957), p. 77. If it may be assumed that he quoted here from the American edition which he had used as a textbook at Harvard, the passage Thoreau cited read as follows:

"[Paley's quotes] that so long as the interest of the whole society requires it, that is, so long as the established government cannot be resisted or changed without publick inconveniency, it is the will of God (which *will* universally determines our duty) that the established government be obeyed,"—and no longer.

This principle being admitted, the justice of every particular case of resistance is reduced to a computation of the quantity of the danger and grievance on the one side, and of the probability and expense of redressing it on the other.

Thoreau regularized the spelling of "publick," altered the punctuation, deleted the parenthetical element, and signalled his merging of the paragraphs with a misleading long dash (at 68.4), altered in PE to." . . .

68.23-24   "A drab: Thoreau's transcription of these lines from "Actus v" of Cyril Tourneur's *The Revenger's Tragaedie* is probably inexact, though his source for the lines is not known. The text in *A Select Collection of Old English Plays*, W. Carew Heglitt, ed., Fourth Edition (London, 1875), pp. 86-87 reads:

A drab of state, a cloth-o'-silver slut,
To have her train borne up, and her soul trail i' th' dirt!

The unmodernized text in *The Plays and Poems of Cyril Tourneur*, John Churton Collins, ed., 2 vols. (London, 1878), II, p. 123 reads:

A drab of State, a cloath, a siluery slut!
To haue her traine borne up, and her soule traile
i' th' durt—Great!—

69.18   well-disposed: The hyphen is added to accord with Thoreau's settled practice. Cf. 65.18, 75.14. W has no listing for the form, though comparable forms are spelled as one word, e.g., "wellborn," "wellbred," "welldone."

72.3   The broadest: Thoreau begins a new paragraph at this point in an early version of this passage (folder 18A), and eliminates the paragraph break in a subsequent version (folder 20), finally restoring it in AP.

77.36   "Show me: The Biblical quotations in this passage are from Matthew 22: 19 and 21, and are inexactly transcribed in both AP and Y. Thoreau's hyphenation of "tribute-money" is not supported by the King James Version, nor is Thoreau's rendering of verse 21. The original reads: "Render therefore unto Caesar the things that are Caesar's; and unto God the things that are God's."

78.33-36 "If a state: Thoreau drew this quotation from his commonplace book now in the Berg Collection, p. 134, where "subjects" (78.34) originally read "a subject." The translation is probably Thoreau's, from *"Les Quatre Livres Il Philosophie Morale Et Politique* . . . tr. du Chinois Par M. G. Panthier (Paris, 1841)." This is his attribution, though the many transcriptions from Confucius in the commonplace book are in English. Though the sentence is from *The Analects*, Book VIII, Chapter xiii, Thoreau's English rendering is not to be found in any of the standard translations.

84.7 "My Prisons.": The reference is to the title of the autobiography of Silvio Pellico (1788-1854).

86.10 conformity.: At this point Y introduces the following lines from *The Battle of Alcazar*, II, ii, by George Peele:

"We must affect our country as our parents;
And if at any time we alienate
Our love or industry from doing it honor,
We must respect effects and teach the soul
Matter of conscience and religion,
And not desire of rule or benefit."

The quotation marks are a part of the Y text.

87.30-35 "I have: The quotation is from Webster's speech on "The Admission of Texas," delivered December 22, 1845. The text of the passage as recorded in *The Writings and Speeches of Daniel Webster*, National Edition, 18 vols. (Boston, 1903), IX, p. 57 reads:

Sir, I have never made an effort, and never propose to make an effort; I have never countenanced an effort, and never mean to countenance an effort, to disturb the arrangements, as originally made, by which the various States came into the Union.

A search of Webster's works does not reveal the source of the quotation beginning at 87.36. It is possible that Thoreau was recalling from memory a line from Webster's seventh of March speech (1850), "The Constitution and the Union" (*op. cit.*, X, pp. 57-98).

88.1 Notwithstanding: Horace Scudder's emendation of this tortured sentence (Riverside Edition, X, p.

167) is accepted as the simplest emendation of the versions in AP and Y that will give the sentence minimal lucidity. Scudder supplies the dash following the comma after "slavery,—" (88.6). W labels "behoves" as substandard (88.5), but it is clearly Thoreau's preferred form (cf. 15.1 and 105.20), and is listed in the *OED*.

88.11 "The manner: Thoreau quoted from Webster's speech of August 12, 1848, "Exclusion of Slavery from the Territories" (*op. cit.*, x, p. 38), silently deleting six words from the end of the second sentence. The passage reads:

> The manner in which the governments of those states where slavery exists are to regulate it, is for their own consideration, under their responsibility to their constituents, to the general laws of propriety, humanity, and justice, and to God. Associations formed elsewhere, springing from a feeling of humanity, or any other cause, have nothing whatever to do with it, nor right to interfere with it. They have never received any encouragement from me, and they never will.

88.11 governments: AP has "government," which is almost certainly an error in transcribing from Webster. Y restores the plural.

89.25 individual.: Y at this point added the following sentence: "Even the Chinese philosopher was wise enough to regard the individual as the basis of the empire."

Table of Textual Variants

THE following table records all variant read-ings affecting meaning between the copy-text AP, and Y. An asterisk (*) indicates a textual note. Also noted are significant variants in early drafts.

* 63. title	ART. X. ——— RESISTANCE TO CIVIL GOVERN-MENT AP; CIVIL DISOBEDIENCE.* Y; *Footnote in Y citing AP*
* 63.29-30	and, . . . split.] *Deleted in* Y
* 64.4-5	It . . . allow.] AP Y; *omitted* folder 14
* 64.5	allow; yet] AP; ∼ . Yet Y
* 64.10	accomplished;] AP Y; ∼ since, which is not a little, folder 14
64.22	punished with] AP Y; ∼ along ∼ folder 14
64.28	government.] Y; goverment. AP
* 66.3	not a funeral] Y; nor ∼ ∼ AP
66.4	rampart] Y; ramparts AP
66.26	treated by it as enemies.] AP; treated as enemies by it. Y
66.31	high-born] AP Y; ∼ ∧ ∼ folder 14
66.33	serving-man] AP Y; ∼ ∧ ∼ folder 14
66.35	fellow-men] AP Y; ∼ ∧ ∼ folder 14
67.17	them: all] AP; ∼ . All Y
69.23	man; but] AP; ∼ . But Y
70.15	come to, shall] AP; ∼ ∼? Shall Y
* 72.3	The broadest] folder 18 AP Y; *no* ❡ folder 20
74.10	he cannot] Y; be ∼ AP
75.18	action?] AP; ∼ . Y
78.17	consequences of disobedience to it to their property and families.] AP; consequences to their property and families of disobedi-ence to it. Y
79.13	"Pay it,"] AP; "Pay," Y
83.13	the tax,] AP; that ∼, Y
83.32	most] AP; many Y
* 86.10	conformity.] AP; *added in* Y: "We must affect our country as our parents;

And if at any time we alienate
Our love or industry from doing it honor,
We must respect effects and teach the
    soul
Matter of conscience and religion,
And not desire of rule or benefit."

* 88.11   governments] Y; government AP
* 89.25   individual.] AP; *added in* Y: Even the
            Chinese philosopher was wise enough to
            regard the individual as the basis of the
            empire.

Emendations of the Copy-Text

* 63. title   ART. X. ——— *preceding title and period*
               following title deleted
  64.28   government.] goverment. AP
  66.3   not] nor AP
  66.4   rampart] ramparts AP
  68.4   longer." . . .] ~." ——— AP
* 69.18   well-disposed] ~ ∧ ~ AP
  74.10   he] be AP
  88.6   slavery,–] ~, ∧ AP
  88.11-12   governments] government AP

End-of-Line Hyphenation

THE compounds or possible compounds in list A, below, are hyphenated at the end of the line in the copy-text (AP) of "Resistance to Civil Government." The editor has resolved each to the form recorded in this list, in accord with the principles discussed in the General Introduction, page 246. List B records only those compounds hyphenated at the end of the line in this edition that should be transcribed with the hyphen in order to duplicate the copy-text forms.

LIST A

69.16	to-day	79.18	schoolmaster
69.26	backgammon	80.29	half-witted
70.11	elsewhere	83.24	Chinamen
75.28	newspapers	86.7	tax-gatherer
78.21	tax-bill	86.28	imagination-free

LIST B

66.19	office-holders	83.15	gray-headed
69.22	ninety-nine	84.11	fellow-countrymen
81.26	room-mate	88.31	much-vexed

Slavery in Massachusetts

Textual Introduction

DELIVERED initially as a lecture at the "anti-slavery celebration" at Framingham on July 4, 1854, this selection was first printed by William Lloyd Garrison in *The Liberator* for July 21, 1854. A check of *The Liberator* from June 23, 1854, through August 18, 1854, reveals (1) that although the names of most of the principal speakers were announced in advance, as early as June 23, 1854, Thoreau's was not; (2) that Thoreau did not read the entire text of his speech: "Henry Thoreau, of Concord, read portions of a racy and ably written address, the whole of which will be published in the *Liberator*";[1] (3) that there is no mention of the speech in *The Liberator* following its publication on July 21, and none of Garrison's correspondents mentioned it in their letters, notwithstanding that there were comments upon some of the other speeches; (4) that Thoreau's name does not appear in the list of 197 persons who made contributions to the society at the Framingham meeting. Thoreau's address was apparently less regarded by readers and subscribers of *The Liberator* than the more flamboyant addresses of Garrison, Phillips, and Charles Remond.

Horace Greeley reprinted Thoreau's address in the *New-York Daily Tribune* of August 2, 1854, without paragraphing, and with no comment. Collation reveals his source to have been *The Liberator*. *The National Anti-Slavery Standard* followed on August 12 (15, no. 8). Under the caption, "Words That

[1] "The Meeting at Framingham," *The Liberator*, 24, no. 27 (July 7, 1854).

Burn," the *Standard* editor reprinted from *The Liberator* most of the text exclusive of the first three paragraphs, terming as "little better than profanity" the
"imputations" that Thoreau was a "mere satellite and
imitator" of Emerson, and apologizing for having
initially overlooked the speech. In the issue of September 9, 1854 (15, no. 16), as if to make further
amends, *The Standard* printed a favorable review of
Walden, attributed to the *Christian Register*, and
alluded again to Thoreau's Framingham address.

Thoreau himself makes only oblique references to
the lecture. His journal entry for July 4 is a terse
"8 A.M.–To Framingham." In a personal letter to
H. G. O. Blake from Concord on August 8, 1854, he
expressed disillusionment with his recent (and occasional) forays into activism (the Framingham
speech, presumably, included): "Methinks I have
spent a rather unprofitable summer thus far. I have
been too much with the world, as the poet might say.
. . . I find it, as ever, very unprofitable to have much
to do with men" (*Correspondence*, page 330). He
seems to have preserved no holograph copy of the
address, and printer's copy has not been found. To
Sarah E. Webb, who wrote to him requesting a copy
(*Correspondence*, page 337), he replied from Concord on September 15: "The address . . . appeared in
the Liberator, from which it was copied into the
Tribune, &, with omissions, into the Anti-Slavery
Standard. I am sorry that I have not a copy to send
you."

Thoreau's observation to Sarah Webb that *The
Liberator* was Greeley's source for the *Tribune* text
is supported by collation. But anomalies nonetheless
arise. Some of the substantive alterations of the
1854 *Liberator* version that appeared in the 1866
Yankee were made in the 1854 *Tribune* version as
well: for example, "store-house" (107.31) in *The*

Liberator became "stone house" in the *Tribune* and in the 1866 *Yankee*; and the form is confirmed by the manuscript journal entry for June 16, 1854, from which Thoreau took the passage. Did the context suggest the correct reading to the *Tribune* editor or compositor ("No prudent man will build a stone house under these circumstances, or engage in any peaceful enterprise which it requires a long time to accomplish.")? Or did Thoreau supply Greeley with a corrected copy of the *Liberator* text? Since almost all of the more than 200 variants in the *Tribune* text can be accounted for as printer's corruptions, however, the evidence that Thoreau in any way influenced the *Tribune* version is slight. Thoreau's word to Sarah E. Webb that it was copied from *The Liberator* puts it an additional remove, therefore, from its author's hand. It seems likely that Garrison requested and received Thoreau's holograph text at Framingham after Thoreau delivered his lecture, and discarded it after the printing. Garrison's remarks in *The Liberator* about the "celebration" at Framingham reveal no clues as to the fate of the manuscript.

The only other possibly authoritative text is that appearing in the 1866 *Yankee*. Twenty-four clear substantive variants from the 1854 *Liberator* text emerge in the *Yankee* version. Most appear to be printer's misreadings of the 1854 text, from which the book version was probably set. The blunt, worn type of *The Liberator* and/or compositorial carelessness could account for such variants as these:

1854	1866
have	leave
ever	even
dispensing	dispersing
worst	worse
secured	scented

But misreading cannot explain another group of variants. Such sequences of readings as the following, in which the 1866 printing restores a journal form not appearing in the *Liberator* copy-text, could only have been the work of someone thoroughly familiar with the genesis of the text:

Journal	Liberator	Tribune	Standard	Yankee
sensible	reasonable	reasonable	reasonable	sensible
& obey the successful candidate	*omitted*	*omitted*	*omitted*	and obey the successful candidate
all merely	all other merely	all other merely	all other merely	all merely
with	in	with	in	with
stone house	store house	stone house	store-house	stone house
which it	which	which	which	which it
requires	requires	requires	requires	requires
will	may	will	may	will

Though it is arguable that a few of these restorations might have been the result of fortuitous editorial surmise, all of them patently are not. On the grounds that it is unlikely that any editor preparing the 1866 copy would have gone back over four years of the journal to identify widely separated forms, collate them closely with the *Liberator* text, and make alterations where variants were discovered, the restorations in 1866 of journal readings are assumed in this edition to be authorial, and are emended into the copy-text. Where a substantive 1866 variant exists in the journal, the 1866 reading is confirmed in nine cases, the 1854 *Liberator* reading in three. The best explanation seems to be that Thoreau left the 1866 editors a corrected copy of the *Liberator* text.

If he did so, he probably paid no attention to the accidentals of the first printing. His copy consistently reflects his lack of concern for such matters. Someone connected with the 1866 printing, however, attempted to regularize his usage and eliminate inconsistency. Receiving attention were the mix of lower case and capitalization for such common nouns as "state" and "slavery" and "slaveholder"; the combination of lower case with caps in such proper nouns as "Yellowstone river" (91.21) and "Court street" (107.14); and the erratic hyphenation, for example, "down-hill" at 104.1 but "up hill" at 104.4. The 1866 editor did not find to his taste the use of "Court House" without hyphenation in one instance (92.8) and with hyphenation at another (105.6). With no sense of impropriety, Thoreau could spell "country," referring to the United States, in lower case in one sentence (108.9), and capitalize "State" in the next.

Thoreau's haste in preparing this lecture accounts to some degree perhaps for his greater than normal inconsistency in the use of accidentals. Many of the journal entries that found their way essentially unchanged into the lecture were hardly two weeks old. One may conjecture that the reason Thoreau's appearance at Framingham was not announced in *The Liberator* in advance was that he himself had made no plans to speak there until a few days before the event. Moreover, he may have had no idea when he left Concord on July 4, 1854, that the draft he carried in his pocket would be in print within the month. But whatever the reason for the inconsistencies, by far the larger portion of them are Thoreau's; and they are permitted to remain in the present edition.

Abbreviations used in the textual notes and tables for "Slavery in Massachusetts" are identified in section 6 of the General Introduction, "Symbols, Abbreviations, Collations," pages 253 to 260.

Textual Notes

91. title SLAVERY IN MASSACHUSETTS: A period following the title in L-SIM is deleted, along with the following sub-title: "AN ADDRESS, *Delivered at the Anti-Slavery
Celebration at Framingham, July 4th, 1854*, BY HENRY
D. THOREAU, OF CONCORD, (Mass.)." Y relegates the sub-
title to a footnote.

92.1 Law: Followed in Y by "of 1850" which may
be authorial. Since no comparable form is to be found
in MJ, however, the copy-text is not emended.

93.28 a recent law: The statute from which Thoreau quotes is not identified.

95.21 million: An emendation from "millions" in
L-SIM and Y. MJ has "million" (April 1851), and a deliberate change to the more cumbersome form by Thoreau seems unlikely in light of his usual practice. Scudder
in the Riverside Edition emended to "million."

95.24 could but get one: MJ (April 26, 1851) Y;
L-SIM has "could get but one." Since the form in Y is a
restoration of a journal form, it is judged authorial.

96.23 ever: Y has "even," a possible reading since
Thoreau's terminal "n" and "r" are often indistinguishable.

97.2 sensible: An emendation from MJ (April 1851)
and Y. L-SIM, T and S have "reasonable."

99.1 Boxboro: T's "Roxboro" is probably a compositor's error. "Boxboro" typified the small town to Thoreau
(see MJ, November 26, 1860).

99.14 It is evident: Though the punctuation followed
in this sentence is that of L-SIM, the question arises as
to whether it represents Thoreau's intention. Did he wish
the sentence to read: "in this Commonwealth, at least,"
or "in this Commonwealth, at least two parties"? No form
for this paragraph is to be found in MJ.

103.28 and obey the successful candidate,: MJ
(June 17, 1854) and Y. Omitted in L-SIM, T, and NS.
The emendation is judged to be authorial.

105.24 the accusers and their judges.: So in L-SIM
and NS. T alters the text of L-SIM to the form later used
by Y: "their accusers and judges." There is no corroborative form in MJ.

106.9　all merely:　The form of MJ (June 16, 1854) and Y. The reading in L-SIM, T, and NS is "all other merely." The restoration of the form of MJ in Y is judged to be authorial.

107.13　with:　L-SIM and NS print "in." Y in emending to "with" restores the form of MJ (June 16, 1854) and of T.

107.31　stone house:　A restoration (L-SIM prints "store-house") of the form in MJ (June 16, 1854), followed also in T and Y.

107.33　which it requires:　The reading in Y, supported by that of MJ (June 16, 1854). L-SIM, T, and NS print "which requires."

108.12　I scented:　So in Y, supported by the reading "I scent" in MJ (June 16, 1854) and the context. L-SIM, T, and NS print "I secured."

108.25　will:　MJ (June 16, 1854), T, and Y. L-SIM prints "may."

108.33　*Nymphœa Douglassii.*:　The allusion here may be to Frederick Douglass, the Black abolitionist, though the intent is not clear. Thoreau correctly identifies the white Concord water-lily in MJ (June 16, 1854) as *Nymphœa Odorata.* If the allusion were to Senator Stephen Douglas, the reference to "compromise" would be clear, but the spelling of "Douglas" erroneous.

Table of Textual Variants

THE following table lists all variations affecting meaning in L-SIM, T, and Y. Variations in the fragmentary text of NS are listed in a few significant instances, though there is no evidence that Thoreau directly affected it. Variants in MJ are listed only when they have a bearing upon editorial emendations of the copy-text. An asterisk (*) indicates a textual note.

	91.6	not of] L-SIM Y; not T
	91.23	have] L-SIM T; leave Y
*	92.1	Law] L-SIM T; Law of 1850 Y
	92.29	that] MJ (May 29, 1854) L-SIM T; that that Y
	93.32	fugitive] L-SIM Y; fugitives T
	95.17	cannons] L-SIM Y; cannon T
*	95.21	million] MJ (April 1851); millions L-SIM T Y
*	95.24	could but get one] MJ (April 26, 1851) Y; could get but one L-SIM T
	95.27	fire; that] L-SIM; ~ : ~ T; ~ . That Y
*	96.23	ever] L-SIM T; even Y
*	97.2	sensible] MJ (April 1851) Y; reasonable L-SIM T
	97.21	case; the] L-SIM T; ~ . The Y
	98.2	not!] L-SIM T; ~? Y
	98.26	has discerned] L-SIM T; can discern Y
*	99.1	Boxboro] L-SIM Y; Roxboro T
	99.28	on] L-SIM Y; upon T
	99.29	on] L-SIM Y; upon T
	100.4	from the] L-SIM Y; ~ a T
	100.10	dispensing] L-SIM T; dispersing Y; MJ (April 1851) *illegible*
	100.22	worst] L-SIM T; worse Y
*	103.28	and obey the successful candidate,] Y; & ~ ~ ~ ~ MJ (June 17, 1854); *omitted* L-SIM T
	103.31	out of] L-SIM T; out Y
	103.33	down hill] L-SIM T NS; down a hill Y

104.12	merely] L-SIM Y; *omitted* T
* 105.24	the accusers and their judges] L-SIM NS; their accusers and judges T Y
106.1	any thing] L-SIM; anything T Y
* 106.9	all merely] MJ (June 16, 1854) Y; ∼ other ∼ L-SIM T
106.22	I had lived] L-SIM T; I lived Y
107.3	worth less,] L-SIM Y; worthless, MJ (June 16, 1854) T
107.4	worth less.] MJ (June 16, 1854) L-SIM Y; worthless. T
107.7	pursuits, &c.,] MJ (June 16, 1854) L-SIM T NS; pursuits, Y
* 107.13	with] MJ (June 16, 1854) T Y; in L-SIM NS
* 107.31	stone house] MJ (June 16, 1854) T Y; store-house L-SIM NS
* 107.33	which it] MJ (June 16, 1854) Y; which L-SIM T NS
* 108.12	I scented] Y; I secured L-SIM T; again I scent MJ (June 16, 1854)
* 108.25	will] MJ (June 16, 1854) T Y; may L-SIM NS

Emendations of the Copy-Text

* 91. title	*Sub-title in L-SIM deleted* ("An Address, *Delivered at the Anti-Slavery Celebration at Framingham, July 4th, 1854,* by Henry D. Thoreau, of Concord, [Mass.]")
* 95.21	million] millions L-SIM
* 95.24	could but get one] could get but one L-SIM
* 97.2	sensible] reasonable L-SIM
* 103.28	and obey the successful candidate,] *omitted* L-SIM
* 106.9	all merely] ∼ other ∼ L-SIM
* 107.13	with my] in ∼ L-SIM
* 107.31	stone house] store-house L-SIM
* 107.33	which it] which L-SIM
* 108.12	scented] secured L-SIM
* 108.25	will smell] may ∼ L-SIM

End-of-Line Hyphenation

THE compounds or possible compounds in List A, below, are hyphenated at the end of the line in the copy-text (L-SIM) of "Slavery in Massachusetts." The editor has resolved each to the form recorded in this list, in accord with the principles discussed in the General Introduction, page 246. List B records only those compounds hyphenated at the end of the line in this edition that should be transcribed with the hyphen in order to duplicate the copy-text forms.

LIST A

92.23-4	Commander-in-Chief	98.23	whoever
		100.27	themselves
95.1	seventy-nine	104.5	backsliders

LIST B

107.25	newly-bought	109.12	sweet-scented

A Plea for Captain John Brown

Textual Introduction

THE text of "A Plea for Captain John Brown" developed as a lecture. It exists in whole or in part in three forms over which Thoreau unquestionably exercised a measure of control. Fifteen numbered pages of holograph material have been located in the Huntington and Barrett collections and in private hands; thirteen of these fifteen pages appear to be from Thoreau's final reading draft (which also served as printer's copy). For page 60 (the last page of the original draft) there is both a preliminary and a final form; and page 18 (recto), containing portions of two sentences only, appears to be an early version for which no holograph revision has been found. What may have preserved these fifteen pages from destruction was Thoreau's having covered the verso side of each sheet with journal indexes, calendars for March and April, and miscellaneous lists. Forty-seven fair-copy pages of the total of sixty have not been located.

The second authorial form of "A Plea" is the first printed version in James Redpath's anthology of the John Brown affair, *Echoes of Harper's Ferry* (Boston: Thayer and Eldridge, 1860), pages 17-42. Thoreau's personal copy of this volume is now preserved in the Morgan Library, numbered 16911, call number E-3 90 D. The text in this copy bears four pencilled changes in Thoreau's hand.

The third form, the posthumous *A Yankee in Canada, with Anti-Slavery and Reform Papers* (Boston, 1866), prints the corrections made by Thoreau in the Morgan copy of *Echoes of Harper's Ferry*. But it makes three other substantive changes for which authority is doubtful, two of which could very easily have been printer's errors. And the dozens of uncharacteristic accidental variants in *A Yankee* certainly did not issue from Thoreau's hand.

The problem of choice of copy-text from among these three forms hinges on whether the surviving holograph pages were printer's copy for Redpath. Since it is this editor's conclusion that they probably were, they become copy-text for the scattered portions of the essay they cover. A copy from *Echoes of Harper's Ferry*, the first printing, becomes copy-text for the remainder.

Impelled by a sense of the rightness of Brown's actions at Harper's Ferry and the desire to aid Brown's family, Thoreau assembled the text of "A Plea" in haste between October 18, 1859, when Brown was captured by Colonel Washington and the United States militia, and October 30, 1859, when the lecture was delivered in the Concord Town Hall. For his material, Thoreau drew heavily from his journal for the two-week period. On October 31, he wrote to H. G. O. Blake offering to repeat the lecture in Worcester; and on the same day he received a wire from Charles W. Slack in Boston requesting that he deliver the lecture there, substituting for Frederick Douglass (*Correspondence*, pages 563-564). Thoreau accepted Slack's invitation and delivered the lecture the following day (November 1) at the Tremont Temple in Boston; and it was reported or summarized in the Boston *Traveler*, the Boston *Journal*, the *Boston Atlas and Daily Bee*, the *New-York Daily Tribune*, and *The Liberator*. On November 3 he delivered the lecture a third time in Washburn Hall in Worcester, having altered a statement on page 57 of his reading text (PE 137.21-22) from "on the 2nd of December Brown will be hung." to "this morning, perchance, Capt. Brown was hung." But at the time he prepared his text, his hopes of selling the publication rights were dashed; and he cancelled therefore on page one of his reading copy, "Sold for the benefit of Capt. Brown's Family," substituting in pencil, "(Also as the 5th Lecture of the Fraternity Course in Boston, Nov 1st)" followed by the entry "A[t] Worcester Nov 3rd." At some time very shortly thereafter he sent printer's copy to Redpath. In an attempt to capitalize upon the moment, Redpath was moving toward publication with great haste, and probably asked Thoreau for quick delivery of his manuscript. It seems probable that, having a fair-copy reading draft available, and no further requests for lectures, Thoreau sent his reading draft as printer's copy without taking the time to transcribe it.

Thoreau was far from pleased with the reports of his lecture in the newspapers. What apparently disturbed him most of all was the abridgement of his text. In a letter to Calvin Greene, dated "Concord Nov. 24. '59" (*Correspondence*, page 566), he responded to a request for copies of certain of his lectures in these words:

> The lectures which you refer to were reported in the newspapers, *after a fashion*, the last one in some half dozen of them, and if I possessed one, or all, of those reports I would send them to you, bad as they are. The best, or at least the longest one of the Brown Lecture was in the Boston "Atlas & Bee" of Nov 2nd. Maybe the whole. There were others in the Traveller—the Journal &c of the same date.
>
> I am glad to know that you are interested to see my things. & I wish that I had them in a printed form to send to you. I exerted myself considerably to get the last discourse printed & sold for the benefit of Brown's family—but the publishers are afraid of pamphlets & it is now too late.

Redpath's task in preparing the materials for publication of *Echoes of Harper's Ferry* could only have been formidable, since in addition to dealing with more than forty authors, his assistance to John Brown prior to the Harper's Ferry incident had drawn upon him the harassment of federal authorities from whom he was forced to hide. He apparently attempted, nonetheless, to publish texts that would be faithful to their authors' intentions. In a letter of February 6, 1860, he observed to Thoreau (*Correspondence*, page 574): "I directed your Lecture to be sent to you for correction; which—I am told—has been done." And he asserted in the "Preface" to *Echoes* (page 5): "The papers of which it consists have been revised by their authors, at my request; or they are printed, with their consent, from properly corrected editions." But there is some doubt that Redpath's statement in the "Preface" accurately describes the handling of "A Plea." Collation of the twelve fair-copy manuscript pages with the first printing in *Echoes* reveals no evidence of revision by Thoreau. Nor is there corroborative evidence of any kind of Thoreau's receipt of or return of the manuscript. The claim for editorial conscientiousness begins and ends with Redpath's own testimony. Redpath admitted in the same letter, moreover, that there were "very numerous faults of language" in the book, and promised to "heed the hint," (presumably Thoreau's) "to take more time in fixing another original volume."

Yet the "faults of language" seem less grievous than they might have been, considering the speed with which Redpath, while dodging the authorities, rushed *Echoes* into print. By February 6 when Redpath wrote his letter to Thoreau, he was able to tell Thoreau that "The 33d thousand has been printed"—though it had been but a scant three months since Thoreau had read his "Plea" for the first time, and a scant two since he had read his "Martyrdom of John Brown," also printed in the *Echoes*. Redpath added, moreover, that the book "contains many corrections *not* in the edition I sent you." If this statement was accurate, editorial changes were being made in the course of the run. A check of eight copies of *Echoes* discloses no variants whatever in the text of "A Plea"; though eight copies are not conclusive, there is some reason to question the extent of the "corrections" Redpath speaks of. Redpath in his letter may have been throwing a sop to an irate author who had protested the handling of his text. Variants in accidentals between the *Echoes* text and the twelve fair-copy holograph pages run to a total of about forty-five, or four to a page. There are two substantive variants. If these pages are typical, the text of "A Plea" as printed in *Echoes* would have had about 225 variants in accidentals and ten in substantives from the printer's copy Thoreau provided—a number that Redpath may have considered moderate under the circumstances, but Thoreau would have thought indefensible.

Abbreviations used in the textual notes and tables for "A Plea For Captain John Brown" are identified in section 6 of the General Introduction, "Symbols, Abbreviations, Collations," pages 253 to 260.

Textual Notes

111. title   A Plea For Captain John Brown*:   Thus
the title in HM 13203 except for lower case "for" and
abbreviation of "Captain" as "Capt." Since in the surviving
sheets of printer's copy, the abbreviation is more often
expanded than not (e.g., at PE 111.3, 138.35), the long
form is emended into the title in the present edition.
R-AP follows HM 13203 in the Table of Contents, altering the title at the head of the selection, however, to
"LECTURE BY HENRY D. THOREAU*" which was probably
supplied by Redpath without Thoreau's authorization. In
HM 13203 Thoreau followed the title with a period, here
deleted, and the following: "by Henry D. Thoreau. Read
to the citizens of Concord Mass. Sunday evening Oct.
30,th [?] 1859. Sold for the benefit of Capt. Brown's
Family. [cancelled in pencil] (Also as the 5th Lecture of
the Fraternity Course in Boston, Nov 1st) A[t] Worcester
Nov 3d [interlined in pencil]." How Thoreau would have
handled this material had he copied it over is moot: this
editor has supplied the asterisk following the title and
gathered the material in a footnote, following R-AP.

114.5   as one has recently written,:   Almost surely,
the "one" of whom Thoreau was speaking was James
Redpath, who included a similar passage in *The Public
Life of John Brown* (Boston, 1860), pp. 113-14. Redpath
had visited Brown's camp in Kansas in 1856 and had
heard Brown make the remark that Thoreau records in
this paragraph. Thoreau's rendering varies slightly from
Redpath's.

114.11   principle. . . .:   R-AP, the copy-text at this
point, prints a period followed by three asterisks. Thoreau
probably used crosses in his draft.

116.35   Vallandigham: So corrected by Thoreau in
the Morgan copy of R-AP, which printed "Vallandingham."
In many newspaper reports of the Brown incident, the
congressman's name was misspelled with two "n's."

117.1-2   "it was among: James Redpath (in *The
Public Life of John Brown* [Boston, 1860], p. 285) records
the sentence from Vallandigham as: "Certainly it was one
of the best planned and best executed conspiracies that
ever failed."

118.24 "pluck,"—: The remark of Governor Wise was widely printed. It was from his speech upon his return from Harper's Ferry to Richmond, reported in *The Richmond Whig* of October 1859. Thoreau's source was probably the summary in the *New-York Daily Tribune*, 19, no. 5772 (October 22, 1859), 7, where the governor is quoted as having observed: "He is the gamest man I ever saw." Thoreau has altered the governor's "I" to "he" —direct discourse to indirect—without removing the quotation marks. The speech was also printed in abridged form in *The Liberator*, 29, no. 44 (November 4, 1859) and in the *New York Herald* of October 25, 1859 (Whole Number 8450), 4. The *Liberator* text would have been too late for Thoreau's use.

121.19 are: So in MJ (October 19, 1859). R-AP, the copy-text at this point, prints "were." Since past tense is out of harmony with the context, the editor assumes that either Thoreau made a mistake in transcribing from MJ, or the printer misread his copy.

122.30 Even the *Liberator*: Thoreau probably drew these words from the issue of October 21, 1859 (29, no. 42). "C. K. W." in reporting on Thoreau's lecture at the Fraternity Course in Boston charged that Thoreau had "distorted" Garrison's initial comment upon John Brown. See *The Liberator*, 29, no. 44 (November 4, 1859).

122.31 insane . . . effort.": Thoreau's four dashes in HM 13202 (p. 27), presumably signifying elision, are standardized. His source is not known.

123.24-25 "under the auspices: James Redpath in *The Public Life of John Brown* (Boston, 1860), p. 281, renders this statement exactly as Thoreau has it. It was taken from the widely printed "Conversation" between John Brown and four interrogators including Governor Wise and Senator Mason of Virginia. Thoreau remarked that he read it in the *New York Herald* of October 21, 1859, Whole Number 8846, p. 1 (see 127.24).

124.7 "It was always conceded: The quotation is from the editorial, "Who Is Brown, The Leader?" in the *New York Herald*, Whole Number 8444 (October 19, 1859), p. 10. Thoreau added the comma after "inoffensive."

124.16 the politician asserts: Thoreau may have been using the word "politician" collectⁱvely; a number of politicians, particularly among the "moral suasionists," issued statements similar to this following the raid on Harper's Ferry.

124.29-30 "on the principle of revenge.": Richard D. Webb in *The Life and Letters of Captain John Brown* (London, 1861), p. 129, notes that a "gentleman" who conversed with Brown in Chicago wrote: "There is one thing he charged me to do when I last saw him. It is this:—'Do not allow any one to say I acted from revenge. I claim no man has a right to revenge himself.' "

127.21 Sharps' rifles: Thoreau was unsure of the spelling of this term. In HM 13202 (p. 49) the spelling is "Sharpe's," as in both R and Y at 127.21, 127.22, 133.22, and 133.25. Yet in MJ (July 28, 1856) Thoreau wrote "Sharp's." Sharps' rifles were manufactured at Hartford, Connecticut, by the firearms company founded by Christian Sharps (1811-1874). None of the writers who chronicled John Brown's life (Richard Hinton, James Redpath, F. B. Sanborn, Richard Webb) spelled the name accurately, most using Thoreau's usual misspelling, "Sharpe's rifles."

127.32 "Any questions: James Redpath in *The Public Life of John Brown* (Boston, 1860), p. 278, renders the quotation exactly as Thoreau quoted it. The source was probably the *New York Herald* of October 21, 1859, Whole Number 8446, p. 1; the *New-York Daily Tribune* did not print the "Conversation."

128.10 "They are: This heavily edited passage is from Governor Wise's report to the people of Virginia upon his return to Richmond from Harper's Ferry. Thoreau has not only elided heavily at the points indicated, but has made other minor changes. See note to 118.24.

128.16 Wise): Never having encountered another case of Thoreau's placement of a comma as R-AP prints it ["Wise,)"], the editor has deleted it.

128.26 Stevens, and Coppoc,: Thoreau is consistent in his misspelling of the names of these followers of Brown. In MJ (October 22, 1859), HM 13202 (p. 40), R-AP, and Y the spelling is "Stephens," and "Coppic." Thoreau's error is understandable; the spelling in newspaper reports varied among "Stevens" and "Stephens," and "Coppic," "Coppoc," "Coppock." Scudder corrected the spelling in the Riverside Edition (x, 221), and subsequent editors have followed him.

128.31 "it is vain: The Vallandigham statement, as James Redpath reported it in *The Public Life of John Brown* (Boston, 1860), p. 285, read as follows:

> It is in vain to underrate either the man or the conspiracy. . . . He is the farthest possible remove from the ordinary ruffian, fanatic, or madman."

Two deleted sentences speak to Brown's qualifications as a "consummate partisan commander." Y's substitution of "removed" for "remove" (128.33) is not justified by the Vallandigham text.

128.35 "All is quiet: The line between "journals" and "newspapers" was not distinct for Thoreau. But among other "journals" Thoreau probably had in mind the *New York Herald*, which announced editorially on October 20, 1859 (Whole Number 8445, p. 3), that "Peace and quiet are restored at Harper's Ferry."

131.4-5 Vigilant Committee: R-AP uses lower case for both words. Emendation is justified by the capitalization at 131.2, 131.6, and 131.21.

132.17 proceeding: So in R-AP and Y. HM 13202 (p. 47) has "proceeding by" which possibly reflects a change of Thoreau's thought in mid-sentence and a failure to cancel.

133.33 laid: So in R-AP, though Thoreau clearly wrote "lay" in HM 13202 (p. 50). The emendation is made on the authority of W and the *OED*.

135.15 "Unless above himself: These lines were emended by Thoreau in his copy of *Echoes*. Redpath had printed:

> "Unless above himself he doth erect himself,
> How poor a thing is man!"

Y followed Thoreau's emendation. The quotation is from Samuel Daniel's "To the Lady Margaret, Countess of Cumberland," lines 95-96.

137.34 "No man: Thoreau took this and the succeeding quotations at 138.2, 138.7, 138.9, 138.16 and 138.20 from the "Conversation" of John Brown, Senator Mason, and Congressman Vallandigham of Ohio. Since Thoreau observes at 127.24 that the *New York Herald* reported the conversation *"verbatim,"* it would seem probable that his quotations are from this source. See note to 123.24.

As was his custom, Thoreau made some unnoted elisions, changes of wording, and changes in punctuation, if it was indeed the *Herald* version from which he quoted.

138.28 I foresee: Thus begins the final sheet of HM 13202 (p. 60) which exists in two forms, one a preliminary form of the other. At the top of the preliminary version of p. 60 appears a version of a portion of the first paragraph of missing sheet no. 58 of Thoreau's printer's copy (137.31-36), cancelled with the characteristic heavy waved line:

> And you have read today* his speech to the court that sentenced him; clear as a cloudless sky; true as the voice of nature is.

Since Thoreau transferred the latter half of this cancelled sentence (clear . . . is.) to sheet 58, which he had previously written, amalgamating it with a paragraph from MJ (October 21, 1859), two drafts of sheet 58 at one time existed.

Holograph Alterations in Manuscript and Printed Copy-Texts

Table of Textual Variants

THE following table records all variant readings affecting meaning in HM 13202 and HM 13203, R-AP, and Y. Two forms from MJ are also noted. An asterisk indicates a textual note.

120.16   these; —a] R-AP; these. A Y
* 121.19   are] MJ (October 19, 1859) Y; were R-AP
* 122.31   insane . . . effort] ~ ————— ~ HM 13202
              (p. 27); ~ ——— ~ R-AP
124.35   or] HM 13202 (p. 31) Y; nor R-AP
126.19   sane] R-AP MJ (October 21, 1859); same Y
126.23   insane.] R-AP; ~ ? Y
128.27   firm. . . ."] R-AP; ~ , ———". HM 13202
              (p. 40)
* 128.33   remove] HM 13202 (p. 40) R-AP; removed
              Y
132.1   apparently] R-AP *possibly* apparently
              HM 13202 (p. 46)
* 132.17   proceeding] R-AP Y; ~ by CB (p. 47)
* 133.33   laid] R-AP Y; lay HM 13202 (p. 50)
134.11   vail] HM 13202 (p. 50) R-AP; veil Y
136.6   these men] HM 13202 (p. 54) R-AP;
              this man Y
136.15   captivity. And] HM 13202 (p. 54); ~ ;
              and R-AP Y
137.13   thing.] R-AP; thing. ——— HM 13202
              (p. 57)
137.24   Angel of Light.] *probable caps* HM 13202
              (p. 57); angel of light R-AP

Emendations of the Copy-Text

* 111.title   A Plea For Captain John Brown*] A Plea
              for Capt. John Brown. HM 13203 (p. 1);
              record of lectures at this point in HM 13203
              (p. 1) *relegated to footnote*
* 114.11   principle. . . .] principle. * * * R-AP
* 116.35   Vallandigham] Vallandingham R-AP; *also
              at* 128.30
* 121.19   are] were R-AP
122.20   and] & HM 13203 (p. 27); *also at* 122.27
              (2 cases), 122.31, 122.32, 128.26, 131.30,
              133.32, 133.33, 136.16
* 122.30   *Liberator*] Liberator HM 13202 (p. 27)

* 122.31	insane . . . effort."] ———— HM 13202 (p. 27)
123.29	&.] & ₍ R-AP
126.35	Gessler] Gesler R-AP
* 127.21	Sharps'] Sharpe's R-AP. *Also at* 127.22, 133.22, 133.25
* 128.16	Wise)] ∼ ,) R-AP
128.18	him. . . . Colonel] ∼ . + + + − Col. HM 13202 (p. 40)
* 128.26	Stevens, and Coppoc,] Stephens, & Coppic, HM 13202 (p. 40)
128.27	firm. . . ."] ∼ , ———". HM 13202 (p. 40)
128.32	. . . .] . + + + − HM 13202 (p. 40)
* 131.4-5	Vigilant Committee] vigilant committee R-AP
* 132.17	proceeding] ∼ by CB (p. 47)
* 133.33	laid] lay HM 13202 (p. 50)
* 135.15	"Unless above himself he can Erect himself, how poor a thing is man!"] "Unless above himself he doth erect himself, How poor a thing is man!" R-AP *altered by Thoreau in pencil*
137.21	Captain] Capt. HM 13202 (p. 57)
137.31	"Vindictive"!] ᵛ ∼"!
138.34	Slavery] slavery HM 13202 (p. 60)

End-of-Line Hyphenation

THE compounds or possible compounds in list A, below, are hyphenated at the end of the line in the copy-texts (HM 13202, HM 13203, and R-AP) of "A Plea for Captain John Brown." The editor has resolved each to the form recorded in this list, in accord with the principles discussed in the General Introduction, page 246. List B records only those compounds hyphenated at the end of the line in this edition that should be transcribed with the hyphen in order to duplicate the copy-text forms.

LIST A

117.6	daylight	130.14	cannon-founder
123.36	kindredship	131.21	Railroad
128.32	underrate		

LIST B

115.16	pent-up	122.21	speech-makers
115.17	chimney-flue	126.4	State-House
121.8	new-fangled		

Martyrdom of John Brown

Textual Introduction

THIS fragment was Thoreau's introduction to an extended group of readings by himself and others presented at the "Exercises at the Town Hall, in Concord, on Friday, December 2, 1859, at 2 O'clock, P.M." as the event was referred to in the broadsides announcing it. Five such broadsides, covered with Thoreau's notes on the verso, are preserved with "Dispersion of Seeds and Related Matters," among 411 pages of holograph notes, unsigned and undated, in the Berg Collection of the New York Public Library, and one with MA 884 at the Morgan Library. The exercises commemorating the "Martyrdom of John Brown" were held concurrently with Brown's execution in Virginia, and over the protests of numerous members of the Concord community. Thoreau was one of a committee of four (which included Emerson, Simon Brown [Chairman of the Commemorative exercises], and John Keyes) "instructed by a meeting of citizens to ask liberty of the selectmen to have the bell of the first parish tolled at the time Capt Brown is being hung," but the request was refused. A "considerable part of Concord," Thoreau continued sardonically in his journal record (November 30, 1859), "are in the condition of Virginia today—afraid of their own shadow."

The idea for the commemorative service probably originated with Thoreau; at any rate, he had been thinking of it for some time. In his journal for November 18, he recorded that he was looking into the Church of England Liturgy for a service "applicable to the case of Capt. Brown." Bronson Alcott, in his

"Diary," left a record of his meetings with Thoreau
and Emerson prior to the service; and Alcott testified
that "Thoreau has taken a prominent part in the
movement and chiefly arranged for it."[1] Moreover,
MA 884 at the Morgan Library, containing all of the
papers used at the services, corroborates Alcott's statement; the different sections and the different readers
are designated by Thoreau in his own hand, though
others (including Emerson and his daughter Ellen)
did some of the copying. The service as Thoreau
planned it was far too long for the time available, and
so some of the material printed by Redpath as a part
of the service was not in fact read. Thoreau recorded
on what is now sheet 84r of MA 884 that "The following passages selected by A. B. Alcott, and original
poem, by a friend of Capt. Brown, were omitted for
want of time." Another complication arose in connection with Emerson's translation of a selection from
Tacitus, preserved in MA 884 on sheets 78 and 79,
r and v. Though the translation was read by Thoreau
at the commemoration, it was not the version later
printed by James Redpath in *Echoes of Harper's Ferry*.
Thoreau was apparently dissatisfied with Emerson's
rendering and retranslated the passage, giving instructions that his version be substituted for Emerson's in the Redpath printing. The two translations
are at many points so different as to be almost un-
recognizable as deriving from the same Latin text.
Sanborn explained the situation to Redpath in his
letter of transmittal on December 9, 1859 (sheet 24r
of MA 884 [typescript]): "The passage from Tacitus
read by Thoreau was so badly translated in Emerson's

[1] Several entries from Alcott's Diary that deal with the
memorial services were printed by Franklin B. Sanborn in
Recollections of Seventy Years (2 vols., Boston, 1909), I, 201-
02. The holograph manuscript of the diary is in the Houghton
Library.

copy, that Thoreau has made a new one, to take its place." Emerson's translation was preserved along with the remainder of the papers; Thoreau's holograph copy from which Redpath printed was somehow lost.[2]

There is no hard evidence that any of Thoreau's papers relating to the services were ever returned to him. After the commemorative exercises, Sanborn became the custodian of the papers, and it was he who sent them to Redpath in two installments to be printed in *Echoes of Harper's Ferry*. His letter of transmittal (cited above) begins: "I send you the rest of the Papers read at the meeting here a week ago. When you get proofs of them, please let me correct them." After Redpath had finished with the printer's copy, he returned the manuscript to Sanborn, who kept it until 1909 when he sold it to C. E. Goodspeed (sheet 24r of MA 884), who in turn sold it at once to Miss Belle Greene of the Morgan Library. At the time of the sale, Sanborn summarized for Goodspeed the printing history of the Thoreau material: "Thoreau's *Remarks* were printed in the volume 'Cape Cod and Miscellanies,' and before that in a volume edited by Sophia Thoreau in 1866, among 'Anti-Slavery and Reform Papers,'—in both taken from Redpath's volume of 1860."

But Sanborn's memory in 1909 was untrustworthy, as a check of the volume "edited by Sophia Thoreau in 1866" would have shown him. Sophia Thoreau did not reprint this selection from Redpath or from the manuscript; it did not appear in the *Yankee* at all. Horace Scudder in editing the Riverside Edition in 1893 was the first to collect this selection, basing his text upon the 1860 *Echoes*. The Walden and Manuscript editions were printed from the Riverside; so

[2] For a full account, see Wendell Glick, "Thoreau Rejects an Emerson Text," *Studies in Bibliography*, 25 (1972), 213-16.

those texts were not based directly upon that of the *Echoes* either. Sanborn was wrong on both counts.

The copy-text for the major portion of this selection is Thoreau's printer's copy (MA 884) in the Morgan Library. For Thoreau's translation from Tacitus, the copy-text is Redpath's *Echoes*, pages 444-45. Since Thoreau did not think of his contribution to the commemoration as a self-sufficient unit separate from the remainder of the service, several editorial problems arise: First, what part of this manuscript is to be printed as Thoreau's? The portion he read, made up largely of verse quotations? Or the portion he copied, a part of which was read by others? Or both? Second, which title has authority? Scudder, in editing the Riverside Edition, supplied the title by which the selection has since been known. No authority, however, attaches to it. In fact, "After the Death of John Brown" is a misnomer; the services were timed to take place simultaneously with the hanging in Virginia. Would not Thoreau have preferred that the title be drawn from the broadside he may have helped to prepare?

As a solution to the first problem, the editor has chosen to include only that matter Thoreau chose, copied, *and* read at the services, with the exception of the translation from Tacitus, which has been substituted for the Emerson version that Thoreau read at the meeting. As a solution to the problem of the title, the caption on the broadsheet announcing the entire service, "Martyrdom of John Brown," has been applied to Thoreau's remarks. Given Thoreau's close involvement with the planning, there is a good possibility that he may have chosen the heading himself.

Abbreviations used in the textual notes and tables for "Martyrdom of John Brown" are identified in section 6 of the General Introduction, "Symbols, Abbreviations, Collations," pages 253 to 260.

Textual Notes

139.title: Thoreau supplied no formal title for his portion of the service for Brown. The only caption in R-MJB is "Mr. Thoreau's Remarks." probably supplied by either Sanborn or Redpath. In MA 884, the only element set off from the text by Thoreau was "Henry D. Thoreau said—" which R-MJB expanded to "HENRY D. THOREAU then rose and said:". Since these are the exact words used by Sanborn in his minutes of the meeting (p. 27, MA 884), they are presumed to have originated with him. "Henry D. Thoreau said—" is deleted in PE. Thoreau's remarks followed immediately the opening prayer by Rev. E. H. Sears of Wayland and the opening hymn.

The title in PE is that of the broadside that announced the commemorative exercises.

139.18 "When the sword: From "Tom May's Death" (ca. 1650). In the final line of the extract, Thoreau has substituted "suff'ring" for Marvell's "wretched."

139.29 "All heads: Thoreau adapted this quatrain from James Shirley's "Contention of Ajax and Ulysses" (1659).

140.9 "The garments: The source of the poem is unknown.

140.17-18 "Hear them.: Sanborn asserted (p. 22r of MA 884) that he had in his possession in 1909 "the printed slip, cut from the Albany *Evening Journal* of 1843, which was before Thoreau as he copied the Raleigh poem, with certain omissions and alterations noted in ink on the margin."

141.35 When hate is cold.: Following this poem, R-MJB reads, "Mr. Thoreau also read these passages, selected for the occasion by another citizen of Concord," and prints the texts of poems from Collins, Schiller (2), Wordsworth, Tennyson, Chapman, and Wotton.

141.footnote *The selectmen: R-MJB has "*The selectmen of the town, not knowing but they had authority, refused to allow the bell to be tolled on this occasion." Thoreau identified the selectmen in pencil in the margin of his copy as "Geo. M Brooks, Barcillas Hudson, & Julius Smith."

142.1 You, Agricola: R-MJB is copy-text for this and the following paragraph translated by Thoreau from

Tacitus (*De Vita Ivli Agricolae*). The heading, "Tacitus.*" and the footnote "*Translated by Mr. Thoreau."
have been deleted. No holograph draft of this version is
included with MA 884. Emerson's original translation,
read by Thoreau at the services, comprises pp. 78 rv
and 79 rv of the MS.

Alterations in the Manuscript Copy-Text

139.1-2	transcendent moral] *blotted letters* MA 884
139.2	with] *followed by* such *cancelled in ink* MA 884
139.12	now] *blotted letter* MA 884
139.28	held] *written in ink over false start* MA 884
141.28	no] *preceded by false start*

Table of Textual Variants

THE following table records every variant affecting meaning, whether accidental or substantive,
between holograph printer's copy for "Martyrdom of
John Brown" (MA 884) and the first printing in
James Redpath's *Echoes of Harper's Ferry*. Thoreau's
translation from Tacitus (142.1 to 143.5), since it
did not appear in MA 884, is excluded. An asterisk
(*) indicates a textual note.

* 139.title	Martyrdom of John Brown] *no title* MA 884; Mr. Thoreau's Remarks. R-MJB
139.1	So universal] Henry D. Thoreau said— ~ ~ MA 884; Henry D. Thoreau then rose and said: R-MJB
139.2	so] MA 884; and ~ R-MJB
139.12	discerned] MA 884; discovered R-MJB
139.23	axel] MA 884; axle R-MJB

139.25	suff'ring] MA 884; suffering R-MJB
140.6	in the prison] MA 884; in prison R-MJB
140.8	What are] *no* ❡ MA 884; ❡ R-MJB
* 140.17-18	Hear them.] *Followed in R-MJB by title* "THE SOUL'S ERRAND."
140.30	Then give them both the lie.] MA 884; Give church and court the lie. R-MJB
140.32	others'] MA 884; other's R-MJB
141.6	Then give them all the lie.] MA 884; Spare not to give the lie. R-MJB
* 141 footnote	town refused] MA 884; ∼ not knowing but they had authority, ∼ R-MJB

Emendations of the Copy-Text

* 139.title	*supplied by editor*
139.1	So universal] *Preceded in MA 884 by* Henry D. Thoreau said—*deleted.*
139.7	Captain] Capt. MA 884
140.3	sabres and] ∼ & MA 884
140.13	Errand,"] ∼ ", MA 884
141.10	flesh,] ∼ ; MA 884
141.22	delay;] ∼ : MA 884
141.33	tolled—*] ∼ *— MA 884
* 142.1	You, Agricola,] *Preceded by* TACITUS* *deleted. A footnote,* *Translated by Mr. Thoreau. *is also deleted.*

End-of-Line Hyphenation

No compounds or possible compounds are hyphenated at line ends in the copy-texts (MA 884 and R-MJB) of "Martyrdom of John Brown." The only compound hyphenated at the end of the line in this edition that should be transcribed with the hyphen in order to duplicate the copy-text form is the following:

142.22	short-lived

The Last Days of John Brown

Textual Introduction

THOREAU prepared the text of this selection for delivery at the John Brown "celebration" on July 4, 1860, at North Elba, New York, where Brown was buried and where his wife was still living on the farm her husband had owned and used for marshalling his company for his foray into Kansas. Thoreau did not travel to North Elba for the celebration, but delivered his manuscript in person at Concord to R. J. Hinton, secretary of the meeting, who read Thoreau's paper as the last of the communications from absent persons, among whom were James Redpath, Thomas W. Higginson, Franklin B. Sanborn, and Frederick Douglass. Most apologized for not attending, citing prior commitments. Thoreau did not. Hinton prefaced his reading of Thoreau's paper (*The Liberator*, 30, no. 30 [July 27, 1860]) with an account of Thoreau's delivery of the manuscript to him:

> In conclusion, Mr. President, I desire to read the manuscript I hold. It was handed to me at Concord, with a note, while on my way here, by one whom all must honor who know him—Henry D. Thoreau. Of a fearless, truthful soul, living near to Nature, with ear attuned to catch her simplest and most subtle thought, and heart willing to interpret them to his eager brain, he often speaks undisguised, in most nervous Saxon, the judgment upon great events which others, either timid or powerless of speech, so long to hear expressed. So it was last fall. Mr. Thoreau's voice was the first which broke the disgraceful silence or hushed the senseless babble with which the grandest deed of our time was met. Herein, Mr. Thoreau gives us some recollections of that eventful period: —

The contents of Thoreau's note are unknown; it was not published in *The Liberator*, and both note and the holograph text of "The Last Days of John Brown" have disappeared. Hinton delivered the manuscript of Thoreau's address to Garrison, along with the other papers of the meeting, and Garrison probably discarded it.

The text of this essay Thoreau drew almost wholly from his journal for November and December 1859. Only eleven scattered sentences lack journal forms. The entries are distributed over a period from November 15 to December 9, and exclude passages Thoreau had already incorporated into "A Plea for Captain John Brown" and "Martyrdom of John Brown." Thoreau altered the journal entries to accord with the change in six months of his own estimate of the significance of the John Brown affair. He changed the tenses of some of the entries written before December 2, the date of Brown's execution; he revised some of his journal predictions (e.g., that a new sect of "Brownites" would spring up); and he modified his assessment of Brown's impact upon the North (e.g., "there was a revival of old religion" in the manuscript journal for December 6, 1859, becomes "and there was a slight revival of old religion" [PE 147.16-17]).

Thoreau apparently affixed no title to the essay he handed to Hinton, and none is mentioned in the *Liberator* copy-text. The present title appeared in the first book printing, *A Yankee in Canada, with Anti-Slavery and Reform Papers* (Boston, 1866), and may have had Thoreau's sanction. The title is not wholly appropriate, however, since the essay has little to do with Brown's last days. Instead, Thoreau turned it into a writ of censure upon all who failed to see in Brown a new "Cato or Tell or Winkelried"—the church, the press, the Massachusetts legislature, and the majority of Thoreau's neighbors. Collation reveals that the early printings of "The Last Days of John Brown" are sequential, each being based upon the version immediately preceding with few changes in substantives. Thus the 1866 *Yankee* printing is based upon the 1860 *Liberator* version, the 1883 printing (in the Riverside Edition) upon the 1866 version, and the 1906 printing (in the Walden and Manuscript editions) upon the 1883 version. The only substantive changes of the 1860 printing in 1866 are the correction of three misspelled words and the printer's misreading (presumably) of "even" as "ever" (PE 148.35). The changes in accidentals between versions, however, particularly in 1866, are extensive.

Abbreviations used in the textual notes and tables for "The Last Days of John Brown" are identified in section 6 of the General Introduction, "Symbols, Abbreviations, Collations," pages 253 to 260.

Textual Notes

145. title: The title is from Y; L-LD supplies none. Y keys the title with an asterisk to a footnote "Read at North Elba, July 4, 1860."

145.3-4   I . . . history.:   So in L-LD and Y. Thoreau had written in MJ (December 5, 1859): "I know of nothing more miraculous in all history."

145.28-29   contrast him, for he, then and there: MJ (December 6, 1859) reads "compare him, for he was above them all [.]"

148.9   Democrat: Word divided at end of the line in L-LD, with "c" missing. The "c" is supplied, on the grounds that Thoreau in this context would not have been punning.

148.35   even: Emended from "ever" in L-LD, judged a printer's misreading.

149.34   end: So in L-LD and Y. MJ (November 18, 1859) has "beginning."

150.17   history of the world: Thus in L-LD and MJ (December 6, 1859). Y has "History of the World," probably the result of editorial intervention, since in "Sir Walter Raleigh" Thoreau often did not italicize or capitalize this title.

150.32   editors ∧ :   So in L-LD and MJ (December 6, 1859). Y supplies a comma, which alters the appositive, creating a series. It seems probable that Thoreau intended to include editors and critics satirically among the class of "literary gentlemen."

152.7   Sharps':   Both L-LD and Y print "Sharpe's." See textual note to "A Plea for Captain John Brown" at 127.21.

152.12   "He nothing: In MJ (December 6, 1859) Thoreau signaled an elision between lines 2 and 3. No sign of deletion appears in the text of L-LD or of Y, though in fact Thoreau omitted

> But with his keener eye
> The axe's edge did try;

from "An Horatian Ode Upon Cromwell's Return from Ireland" (1650) by Andrew Marvell.

Table of Textual Variants

THE following table records all variant readings affecting meaning in the copy-text, L-LD, and the first book printing, Y. It records also significant variants between the copy-text and MJ. The asterisk (*) indicates a textual note.

* 145.title	THE LAST DAYS OF JOHN BROWN] Y; *title and footnote omitted in* L-LD
* 145.3	so miraculous] L-LD Y; more ~ MJ (December 5, 1859)
* 145.4	our history] L-LD Y; all ~ MJ (December 5, 1859)
145.19	this bird] L-LD Y; ~ grebe MJ (November 17, 1859)
145.3	appeared] L-LD Y; was MJ (December 6, 1859)
* 148.9	Democrat] Y; Demorat L-LD
* 148.35	even] Y; ever L-LD
* 149.34	end] L-LD Y; beginning MJ (November 18, 1859)
* 150.17	history of the world,] L-LD MJ (December 6, 1859); History of the World Y
* 150.32	editors ∧ and critics,] L-LD MJ (December 6, 1859); ~ , ~ ~ , Y
152.28	that account] L-LD Y; his ~ MJ (December 5, 1859)

Emendations of the Copy-Text

* 148.9	Democrat] Demorat L-LD
* 148.35	even] ever L-LD
* 152.7	Sharps'] Sharpe's L-LD

End-of-Line Hyphenation

ONLY one possible compound was hyphenated at the end of the line in L-LD, copy-text for "The Last Days of John Brown." It was resolved as indicated below. All words hyphenated at the end of the line in this edition should be transcribed as one word forms in order to duplicate the copy-text.

149.29 statesman

Life without Principle

Textual Introduction

"LIFE without Principle" was first published in *The Atlantic Monthly* for October 1863, seventeen months after its author's death. Under a succession of titles, it was Thoreau's most frequently delivered lecture.[1] It was first presented at New Bedford, Massachusetts, on December 26, 1854, under the title "Getting a Living"; and was repeated in Nantucket on December 28. It was delivered shortly after in Worcester on January 4, 1855, under the cumbersome title, "The Connection Between Man's Employment and His Higher Life"; and in Concord on February 14, 1855, as "What Shall It Profit?" At some time between October 24, 1856, and November 1 of the same year, Thoreau delivered the lecture at Perth Amboy, New Jersey. On October 9, 1859, under the new title "Life Misspent," he gave the lecture in Boston. On September 9, 1860, in Lowell, Massachusetts, he delivered it for the last time.

Though no reading draft of the lecture has been found, the surviving manuscript fragments, now widely scattered, suggest that Thoreau worked on his text throughout the six-year life of the lecture, all the while searching for a satisfactory title. The theme of "Getting a Living" engrossed him; *Walden* in a broad sense can be read as a treatment of it. But distilling a broad diversity of ethical commentary into a short space apparently caused problems. The series of lectures did not provide the spark that would

[1] According to Walter Harding. See the "Checklist of Thoreau's Lectures," *Bulletin of the New York Public Library*, 52 (February 1948), 78-87 *passim*.

fuse the material into a satisfactory unity so it could be moved into print.

The publisher, James T. Fields, apparently took the initiative that led to the first printing. On February 11, 1862, less than three months before his death, Thoreau wrote to the editors of *The Atlantic*:

> Only extreme illness has prevented my answering your note earlier. I have no objection to having the papers you refer to printed in your monthly—if my feeble health will permit me to prepare them for the printer (*Correspondence*, page 635).

His health was so feeble at the time that his sister Sophia had to copy this letter from his pencilled draft; he was too weak even to write in ink. The printer's copy for "Life without Principle" must have been in Sophia's hand, unless there existed sheets from lecture drafts which Thoreau found usable. By February 28, however, a short seventeen days later, Thoreau had a manuscript ready for dispatch to Ticknor and Fields (*Correspondence*, page 638): "I send you with this [Sophia wrote for him] a paper called The Higher Law, it being much shorter & easier to prepare than that on Walking." On March 4, acknowledging "the receipt of your check for one hundred dollars on account of manuscript sent to you," he authorized a change in the title of the selection:

> As for another title for the Higher Law article, I can think of nothing better than, Life without Principle. The paper on Walking will be ready ere long (*Correspondence*, page 639).

Since Thoreau was busy with his "paper on Walking" and the proofs of "Autumnal Tints," and since he was to die on May 6, he all but surely never saw the proofs of "Life without Principle." The assumption of the editor of the present volume is that his accommodation to Fields in changing his title was free and uncoerced.

The copy-text for this selection must be drawn from the first printing in *The Atlantic Monthly*, the only printing over which Thoreau exercised any measure of control. Printer's copy has not been found. The chances that Thoreau was responsible for authorizing any of the changes in the second printing in *A Yankee* in 1866 are extremely remote. Moreover, only one substantive variant exists, a shift from the article "the" at 157.33 to "a." Fifteen commas are deleted or added in the 1866 text, five hyphenations altered, four dashes removed, and four capitalizations changed. For such matters Thoreau had little concern even when he was healthy.

Since Thoreau's health was feeble when he prepared his printer's copy for this selection with the aid of his sister, all preliminary holograph material that could be gathered through collective effort has been examined in the preparation of the present text. The material represents many stages of composition. Notes and drafts of sentences and paragraphs turn up on at least eight different types of paper used by Thoreau in the late 1840s, the 1850s, and the early 1860s, both blue and white, lined and unlined, wove and laid. For some of the printed passages there are as many as four preliminary forms. Some begin with hardly more than echoes of what they were later to become. A genetic reconstruction of this text would be very revealing, if enough matter could be discovered to make a charting of its development possible.

The several classes of working forms consulted by the present editor may be briefly summarized as follows, by location:

1. folder 1, Houghton Library: three holograph forms, early and late, in both pencil and ink, on both blue and white paper.

2. folder 20, Houghton Library: forms of more than twenty passages from "Life without Principle," of varying lengths, and from different stages in composition. These drafts contain material not yet separated from material later rejected by Thoreau. One passage worked into "Resistance to Civil Government" indicates that some of the material pre-dates 1849; and the diversity of the paper, both blue and white, wove and laid, bearing diverse stationer's marks (H & Z Goodwin, Lawrence, Goodwin-Hartford, and others different but indistinguishable) attests to Thoreau's long effort to combine this matter into an organic whole.

3. recovered manuscripts bearing drafts of passages from "Life without Principle" that were bound into copies of the Manuscript Edition in 1906. There are many of these, some of which approach fair copy, others heavily revised and containing matter later expunged from the final draft. It seems unlikely that any of this matter was from the printer's copy used by Ticknor and Fields in 1863. Eighteen such sheets, usually filled on both recto and verso, have been located and identified, some still bound into copies of the Manuscript Edition, others detached and now in the possession of libraries and private collectors. The editor has had access to photographic reproductions (or authoritative transcriptions) of the texts of sixteen of the eighteen; in two instances he was not able to secure permission to photograph or examine.

4. twenty-six pre-copy-text forms in the manuscript

journal in the Morgan Library, some of which were apparently copied into the journal after having been written out in earlier versions.

Abbreviations used in the textual notes and tables for "Life without Principle" are identified in section 6 of the General Introduction, "Symbols, Abbreviations, Collations," pages 253 to 260.

Textual Notes

155.title: Thoreau submitted this essay to James T. Fields under the title, "The Higher Law." To Fields' request that he reconsider the title, Thoreau suggested "Life without Principle." When the essay was published in October, 1863, it bore the latter title. A period following the title in the copy-text is deleted.

156.25 in the outskirts: The strange idiom is the probable result of Thoreau's revision from MJ (September 7, 1851) where the passage read "in the N part of the town."

157.19 one of my neighbors: Identified in MJ (July 24, 1852) as Hayden.

160.35 synonymes: W accepts Thoreau's spelling.

161.15-17 "Greatness: Thoreau's source for this quotation has not been found.

164.29 Sulky Gully: Thoreau drew this place-name and the two others in the sentence from William Howitt, *Land, Labor and Gold, or, Two Years in Victoria* (2 vols., Boston: Ticknor and Fields, 1855), 1 *passim*. AM and Y have "sulky-gully." MJ (October 18, 1855) uses the Howitt form, here restored.

165.24 "He soon: The quotation from Howitt (see note on 164.29) is from volume 1, p. 21. Two commas in AM and Y are deleted on authority of Howitt and MJ (October 19, 1855). Following "wretch" (165.28) Howitt had written "—that was his phrase—" which Thoreau deleted.

165.36 "Murderer's Bar,": Howitt has "Murderer's Flat" (volume 2, p. 40). Thoreau makes the same change at 166.3. In MJ (October 19, 1855), Thoreau transcribed correctly, but may deliberately have altered the name because of its proximity to "Jackass Flat."

166.11 "In the dry season: A search of the *Tribune* for the decade of the 1850s did not disclose the source of this quotation.

171.7 "I look: Thoreau apparently copied this quotation from p. 96 of his commonplace book in the Berg Collection. He gives as his source "Ossian's Grecian Remains 'Literally translated by Macgregor.' "

175.26-27   "the first: The quotation is from volume
1, p. ii of Decker's *The Honest Whore* (1604), written in
collaboration with Thomas Middleton.

175.30   praetor: Emended from AM's "prætor" to accord with Thoreau's usage in a working draft in folder 20.

176.35   Lieutenant Herndon: The quotation appears
verbatim in the public document, *Exploration of the
Valley of the Amazon, made under the direction of the
Navy Department*, by William Lewis Herndon and Lard-
ner Gibbon (Washington: Robert Armstrong, Public
Printer, 1854), Part 1, p. 251. Thoreau's copy of this volume, inscribed "Henry D. Thoreau from Horace Mann,"
was sold as item 1066 at the Wakeman sale on April 29,
1924.

Table of Textual Variants

THE following table lists all variants affecting meaning, whether accidental or substantive, between the copy-text of "Life without Principle" (AM) and the second printing in Y. It records also a few significant variants between the first two printings and pre-copy-text holograph forms. An asterisk (*) signifies a textual note.

* 156.25	in the outskirts] ~ ~ N Part of the town MJ (September 7, 1851)
157.33-34	the window] AM; a ~ Y
162.27	immorality] morality MJ (February 1, 1852)
* 164.29	Sulky Gully] MJ (October 18, 1855); sulky-gully AM Y
* 165.36	"Murderer's Bar,"] AM Y; "Murderer's Flat" MJ (October 19, 1855). *Also at* 166.3
168.20	It made] AM Y; I confess that it made MA 2556 (Morgan)
168.24	forms,] *followed by* like crabs in cockle-shells rushing to the door to see who is there MA 2556
168.25	rest.] *followed by* The very lights of the world are frequently such hard cases with a crabbed inhabitant—and you must bore them in order to get at them. MA 2556
168.31	subtilest] AM Y; subtlest MJ (May 13, 1852)
168.33	meet,] ~ . We MA 2556
172.30	mountain-brooks] AM Y; mountain springs MJ (July 7, 1851)

Emendations of the Copy-Text

* 155.title	*Period following title deleted*	
* 164.29	Sulky Gully] sulky-gully AM	
* 165.25	horse ₍ₐ₎] horse, AM	
* 165.26	and ₍ₐ₎] and, AM	
166.11	*Tribune*] "Tribune" AM	
175.30	praetor] prætor AM	

End-of-Line Hyphenation

THE compounds or possible compounds in List A, below, are hyphenated at the end of the line in the copy-text (AM) of "Life without Principle." The editor has resolved each to the form recorded in this list, in accord with the principles discussed in the General Introduction, page 246. List B records only those compounds hyphenated at the end of the line in this edition that should be transcribed with the hyphen in order to duplicate the copy-text forms.

LIST A

155.23	anywhere		165.23	twenty-eight
156.24	money-making		169.20	newspaper
156.32	hard-working		170.9	twenty-five
157.2	praiseworthy		170.10	sidewalk
160.23	self-supporting		172.13	windmills
160.33	government-pension		176.25	sea-brine
			176.32	molasses-hogshead
162.16	make-shifts		178.28	half-consciousness

LIST B

156.32	hard-working		175.14	small-clothes
160.27	ninety-seven		175.35	heaven-born
160.33	government-pension		178.28	half-consciousness

Reform and the Reformers

Textual Introduction

PRESERVED among the twenty-one folders of Thoreau manuscripts in the Houghton Library under the general number bMS AM 278.5 are several collections of largely unpublished matter. The internal consistency and coherence of the material suggests that Thoreau intended to develop it into lectures, and perhaps subsequently into publishable essays, prior to the publication of *Walden*. The folders are designated, respectively, 14, 18, and 20. From the matter of folder 14 on the general subject of "Society and Government" Thoreau extracted six excerpts of varying lengths which he incorporated into "Resistance to Civil Government"; this folder, therefore, is noted in the textual introduction to that essay (page 316). Folder 20, containing holograph scraps on the general subject of "Getting a Living," includes working forms for twenty-one passages from "Life without Principle," and is discussed in the textual introduction of that essay (page 372). The matter of folder 18 is contained in two sub-folders, designated respectively 18A and 18B; and the matter in 18B, though not fair copy, is sufficiently close to a coherent essay on reform and reformers—indeed, on the reform *of* reformers—to warrant publication.

Folder 18A is the reservoir from which 18B was distilled. It provides also an early form of a long two-page unpublished passage in folder 14F, as well as a preliminary form of a passage revised into folder 20 and never published. Marginal notation and interlineation in both pencil and ink are frequent throughout the folder, in some instances so dim or so compressed as to be irrecoverable. Clearly, 18A is far from fair copy.

The manuscript of 18A consists of folded leaves stitched together, paginated by Thoreau to 78. Two leaves are torn out between pages 28 and 33; and two are apparently missing following page 59 verso, though there is no hiatus in the pagination. Nine leaves and portions of leaves have been inserted, one of them a form approaching fair copy, intended for inclusion in the derivative 18B draft, and keyed to the latter draft by a pencilled entry of the first line.

That 18B postdates 18A is clear from the paper as well as from the respective texts. The whole of the 18A draft, exclusive of insertions, is written on the very thinly lined white wove paper used extensively by Thoreau in the 1839-1845 period and manufactured by D. and J. Ames of Springfield, Massachusetts, one of the great American papermakers from 1802 to 1840, when the firm collapsed as a result of the panic of 1837. Thoreau apparently had enough of the Ames paper on hand at the time of the collapse (or was able to secure it) to continue using it for portions of the drafts of *A Week*; but the Ames stationer's mark (an encircling of the name "Ames" with oak branches within an octagonal frame) is an almost certain indication of pre-1845 composition. The significance of this early dating of the 18A material becomes apparent when one considers that Thoreau used the Ames paper for early drafts of "The Service," and for most of the final draft (HM 943, Huntington Library) of "Sir Walter Raleigh." Thoreau's thinking on political and social concerns may have overlapped his early, rather vapid, concern with soldiery and heroism; certainly the germs of *Walden*, "Resistance to Civil Government," and "Life without Principle" are clearly discernible here.

Thoreau's abortive winnowing from 18A of a lecture on reform and reformers—his composition of the draft now labeled 18B—was probably the work of the same period in which he was drafting the manuscript of *A Week*. In "Monday" of *A Week*, Thoreau interjected a "digression" on reformers; no part of the digression, however, was drawn from 18A or 18B. But the subject was on his mind. Moreover, the paper on which the draft of 18B was written, manufactured by two different makers, is that commonly used for drafts of *A Week*. Most of the 18B draft was written on a lightly lined white wove bearing the mark "Lawrence & Co." within an ellipse; the remainder of the essay was written on the familiar lined blue wove, distinguished by the stationer's mark of the circled rose and used also for some of the drafts of *A Week*. Thoreau's use of two different papers for the single manuscript suggests, of course, that he may have worked at least two different times on the 18B lecture; and internal evidence corroborates this hypothesis. The matter of 18B written on the blue sheets is distinct from that written on the white; no forms appear on one color of the 18B paper that are preliminary to later, revised versions on the other. Yet, though it is clear that at one time at least, before assembling the material for *Walden*, Thoreau intended to amalgamate the matter from the different colored units, he provided none of the familiar pencilled keys on the blue sheets to fix their position in the longer white text.

Difficult editorial problems arise in connection with the relationship between the blue and white matter. Affixed with a pin to page 58 recto of the 18A draft is a sheet of white paper with the Ames mark on which Thoreau has written a near fair-copy revision of a passage on the verso of blue sheet number 2 of 18B, as the sheets are now ordered in the Houghton folder. (The first words on the sheet are "his joy.") On white 13 recto (again according to the present Houghton ordering, beginning with the words "Now, if anything") of 18B, Thoreau has keyed the second paragraph of this 18A insertion into his 18B text by entering in pencil the first seven words of the paragraph, "There is no reformer on the globe." When Thoreau terminated his work on the 18B draft, he was apparently still working back and forth between the 18A and 18B drafts, and was perhaps one or two drafts away from fair copy.

There is an additional unique editorial problem. Before successfully welding 18B into a unity, Thoreau went to work on the final draft of *Walden* and found passages of the foetal 18B germane to his purposes there. In revised form, therefore, a portion of the 18A insertion found its way into the section on philanthropy in the final pages of "Economy," along with a considerable number of other passages from 18B. Thoreau's use of the 18B matter in both the first and last chapters of *Walden* may explain his neglect in bringing 18B to final form and to publication. Particularly in the second half of the present edited text the overtones of *Walden* are very strong. The therapy he had prescribed for reformers he discovered to be appropriate for all manner of men as well.

The decision to include in this printing of the lecture the matter transferred into *Walden* was made on the grounds that the autonomy of the lecture would suffer without it. Thoreau wrote much of this material with the intention of using it as the concluding section of this lecture, not of *Walden*; and his later adaptation of it for inclusion in the first and last chapters of that book does not alter the fact that it is an essential part of this text as well. To delete it would leave the terminal outline of the essay unformed.

The different colors of the paper in 18B divide the text of the manuscript into two very distinct sections, and it is the task of the editor to bring them into congruity. Other physical characteristics of the manuscript emphasize the division. There are differences in the ink both between the blue and white groupings and within each color section. There are differences in the patterns of pin perforations. Though the blue sheets are not contiguous in the Houghton folder, the matching pattern of pin perforations in the center left margin of the sheets indicates that at one time they were together. The perforation pattern in the left margin of the white sheets, however, though resembling that of the blue sheets, does not coincide with it. And there is a difference in the relationship between the parent manuscript, 18A, and the white and blue groupings, respectively. For approximately 75 percent of the matter on the white sheets of 18B there exists a preliminary version—often several preliminary versions—in the 18A reservoir. But for only one of the blue sheets is there antecedent matter in 18A. This sheet, curiously, seems to lack any firm link with the matter of the other blue sheets. It is a single sheet, written on recto and verso (beginning on recto: "If the philanthropist"), whereas the other blue matter consists of two four-page units, each a large leaf folded once into two sheets size $7\frac{7}{8}$" x $9\frac{7}{8}$". Nor is the matter on the single sheet itself internally consistent. What Thoreau seems to have done on this single blue sheet was to revise six scattered passages from folder 18A without fitting them into any sequence, and perhaps without even knowing at the time of revision where he would use them. Some of the material from the sheet finally came to rest in *Walden*; all of the material, with cancellations and transpositions, is relegated to the textual notes in this volume.

The editorial difficulties of establishing a text for an essay Thoreau did not complete are immense. What the editor has attempted here, however, is to follow scrupulously Thoreau's tracks, paying meticulous attention to all his pointers governing transposition, cancellation, and insertion of sections, and fitting the jumbled sheets into a sequence that eliminates, as far as possible, hiatuses in the train of thought. That a few hiatuses remain will be obvious to the reader. The placement of sections is at times debatable. Thoreau did not paginate the 18B manuscript; and his well-known practice of putting together sections of essays and books like pieces of mosaic renders it all but impossible to position sections by any known process of deduction. The positioning of the blue matter in relation to the white is particularly moot. The "drift" of the 18B matter, however, can be readily discerned: it is a movement from diagnosis to prognosis, as it were—from an appraisal of the disease afflicting those who are driven to reform institutions and other people (and the figure of speech is Thoreau's), to a strong humanistic statement reminiscent of, and even duplicating passages from, the "Conclusion" of *Walden*: "Direct your eye sight inward," and "be expert in home-cosmographie."

Though much closer to fair copy than the 18A matter, the manuscript of 18B was far enough removed from printer's copy that the problem of recapturing exactly what Thoreau wrote is a very real one. Thoreau apparently revised in ink as he composed, later revising in pencil. Interlineations and marginal accretions in both ink and pencil are difficult, and oc-

casionally impossible, to decipher, particularly when
there are revisions of revisions. Specific difficulties
are mentioned in the notes. Use marks are sometimes
difficult to differentiate from cancellations, since Thoreau's practice is not consistent. In some instances
he had apparently made no final decision about passages that did not please him completely, but that he
did not wish to throw out. The policy followed in this
volume, which obtains for the entire Thoreau Edition,
is to consider vertical lines—whether single, double,
or triple—as use marks, and heavy waved horizontal
lines as cancellations. Multiple slashing on the bias of
sections, often encircled, is construed as an intent to
cancel. All cases where editorial judgment is involved
are recorded in the notes.

The provenience of 18B (and, indeed, the matter of
all 21 folders comprising bMS AM 278.5 at the Houghton Library) is not fully clear. A note in the first
folder (unnumbered), dated November 21, 1955,
alleges: "These MSS were presented to Harvard in
1919 by William Augustus White (class of 1863).
White's source is not recorded, but he is known to
have had them as early as 1904." If White in fact
acquired the 18B manuscript as early as 1904, or earlier, it was probably a part of the cache of manuscripts, including the journal, that passed to E. Har-
low Russell upon the death of Harrison Gray Otis
Blake on April 18, 1898. In September 1904 Russell
sold all his manuscripts, except the journal, to George
S. Hellman, a New York autograph dealer, who in
turn immediately sold a large consignment to White.
White's early acquisition of the sheets may have
prevented their dispersal, a fate suffered by so many
of Thoreau's loose manuscripts at the time of the publication of the Manuscript Edition in 1906. Though
the stitched 18A is dog-eared, the loose sheets of

folder 18B, after passing through the hands of many scholars, retain generally smooth margins and full, sharp corners, a testimonial to the scholars who have used them and the librarians who have preserved them.

The present sequence of sheets in folder 18B, since they are unpaginated, offers no reliable index to Thoreau's original positioning of them. Even assuming that they came to the Houghton Library in the order Thoreau intended, their use for more than fifty years by scholars would result undoubtedly in some violations of the original ordering. The table below, therefore, which summarizes the positioning of the matter of 18B (and in a few cases of 18A) in the present text, identifies each sheet by:

1. Arabic numeral designating the order of the placement of the material of the sheet in this text
2. side of sheet (recto or verso)
3. beginning words on the sheet
4. color
5. stationer's mark, followed by present order in folder 18B.

Using this table, the interested scholar may easily check the present editor's ordering of the sheets comprising this essay, regardless of what has happened in the past or may happen in the future to the sequence of the sheets. Recto and verso of the same sheet are paired. Inserts and transpositions directed by Thoreau occasionally obtrude between sheets.

1. recto	"The Reformers are"	white	Lawrence	(4)
verso	"say *We* and *Our*,"	white	Lawrence	
2. recto	"unimaginable epoch"	white	Lawrence	(5)
verso	"put it into"	white	Lawrence	
3. recto	"In the midst"	white	Lawrence	(16)
verso	"poorhouse,"			

4. recto	"Now, if anything"	white	Lawrence	(18)
verso	[blank]			
5. recto	"There is no" [Second paragraph of sheet pinned between pp. 57, 58 of Folder 18A]	white	Ames	
verso	[blank]			
3. verso	"The Reformer who" [Final paragraph]	white	Lawrence	(16)
6. recto	"I ask of all"	white	Lawrence	(19)
verso	"He exhibits only"			
7. recto	"that the lecturer"	white	Lawrence	(20)
verso	"state of things"			
8. recto	"come to me"	white	Lawrence	(6)
verso	"rather than the"			
9. recto	"-dition of that"	white	Lawrence	(7)
verso	"private and intimate"	white		
10. recto	"rays penetrated"	white	Lawrence	(8)
verso	"From the side"			
11. recto	"Be sure your fate"	white	Lawrence	(9)
verso	[blank]			
12. recto	"When a zealous"	blue	[rose]	(10)
verso	"sincerity [,] love"			
13. recto	"A man must"	blue	[rose]	(2)
verso	"his joy" [early form of 5 recto deleted]			
14. recto	"take up a"	blue	[rose]	(3)
verso	"What! to be"			
15. recto	"So long"	blue	[rose]	(11)
verso	"drains flow"			
16. recto	"How infinitely"	white	Lawrence	(14)
verso	"see a man"			
17. recto	"can delight"	white	Lawrence	(15)
verso	"deserters go"			
18. recto	"To the sick"	white	Lawrence	(12)
verso	"and olives"	white		
19. recto	"greener and"	white	Lawrence	(13)
verso	[blank]			

The matter of what is now the first sheet in folder 18B (blue sheet, rose mark, recto "If the philanthropist" verso "Our great playmate") is relegated to the notes. A scrap containing a preliminary form of a portion of 4 recto in the above table, the last item in the folder, is not used in constituting the text.

In the following textual notes and tables to "Reform and the Reformers," "18B" refers to the copy-text (supplemented by folder 18A as directed by Thoreau) in bMS AM 278.5 at the Houghton Library. Since Thoreau supplied no pagination in 18B, each sheet is identified by the order number of its inclusion in the present text (PE). Recto and verso are distinguished with lower case abbreviations (2r, 3v, etc.). Included in these notes and tables are: (1) all emendations made in the copy-text by the editor; (2) all cancellations by Thoreau affecting the meaning to any substantial degree; (3) all interlineations and marginal additions; (4) all notations by Thoreau affecting the positioning of sections; (5) all use marks; (6) all exclusions from the present text including unrecovered matter; and finally, (7) defenses of moot editorial judgments.

Textual Notes

181.1   The Reformers are: External evidence proves this to have been the beginning of the text on the outside sheet of a manuscript originally held together by thread passed through perforations. The sheet is torn where the thread wore through (folder 18B, 1r).

182.22-23   Men now: Thoreau had apparently made no final decision as to how he desired this and the following sentence to read.

183.4   The disease: The first half of this paragraph (folder 18B, 3r), is marked with a single use mark, the latter with double use marks.

183.19   Now, if anything: This paragraph is a preliminary draft of a portion of a paragraph in "Economy," the first chapter of *Walden*. Thoreau did not include it in the essay originally, but keyed it in at this point by pencilling in "If anything ail –vs" after the paragraph preceding it here.

183.20-22   especially . . . left;:   Thoreau's pencilled parenthesis around this phrase may indicate that he thought at one time of cancelling it.

183.34   There is no: This paragraph, the second on the recto of an unpaginated sheet affixed by a pin between pp. 57 and 58 of folder 18A, is keyed to the text of 18B at this point by a pencilled entry, "There is no Reformer on the globe." The sheet, included under folder 18B, 5r, in the table above (see Textual Introduction, page 387), bears the Ames paper mark. The entire page is slashed by one vertical pencilled use mark.

185.20   There are: In light pencil, Thoreau interlined the whole of this paragraph and the next with light script, most of which is unrecovered, some of which was subsequently cancelled. In the left margin are numerals directing that certain sections be transposed. The original ink version is not cancelled but slashed vertically with one pencilled use line. PE prints the original version written in ink.

185.28-30   We . . . effective: Thoreau first positioned this passage on 6v of folder 18B (following "cupola." at 184.36), where he cancelled it. In its new location it carries over from 7r to 7v.

188.7   All that: This sentence (folder 18B, 9v), inter-lined in ink, is smudged by a horizontal pencilled line. Thoreau may have considered deleting it.

188.28   issues.:   Following this paragraph Thoreau ink-cancelled another in folder 18B, 10v, an early form of a passage in *Walden* that he transferred to a point immediately following the poem on 11r (189.15).

189.1   Be sure your fate: A portion of "Independ-ence," this poem is printed in variant form in *The Col-lected Poems of Henry Thoreau*, Carl Bode, ed. (Balti-more, 1964), pp. 132-33.

189.26   though it be hard;:   Folder 18B, 12r. A prob-able reading. Also possible is "bad" for "hard." The semi-colon is not clear in the manuscript, but the sentence is incoherent without it.

190.14   society.:   At the end of this paragraph (folder 18B, 12v) Thoreau interjects a pencilled key to the fol-lowing section ("A man must serve") and strikes a heavy vertical line through the following paragraph, which he introduces later in revised form on 15v (193.10).

191.13   I would say: Preceding this paragraph in folder 18B, 13v, is a prior version of material from folder 18A keyed by Thoreau with the words "There is no Re-former" into the text of the essay at 183.34 to 184.8. Since a revised version is already part of the essay, positioned where Thoreau instructed that it be placed, the repeated passage at this point is deleted.

194.3   Most whom I meet: In folder 18B, 16v, this paragraph followed the paragraph it precedes in PE. Thoreau clearly marked the two paragraphs for transposi-tion.

194.34-35   Erret: These lines (folder 18B, 17r) were apparently copied by Thoreau from his journal entry for May 10, 1841. They are interlined in ink on 17r. Thoreau identifies the source as "the last verses of Claudian's 'Old Man of Verona' " (MJ, May 10, 1841). His translation here differs from that in the "Conclusion" of *Walden*.

195.20   "Direct: Thoreau used these four lines of poetry also in the second paragraph of his "Conclusion" in *Walden*, where "eye sight" (line 1) is often rendered "eye right" as the result of a printer's misreading. The lines, quoted from "To my honoured friend *Sir* Ed. P. *Knight*," by William Habington, are rendered as follows by Kenneth Allott (*The Poems of William Habington* [London: Hodder and Stoughton, Ltd., 1948], p. 93):

> Direct your eye-sight inward, and you'le find
> A thousand regions in your mind
> Yet undiscover'd. Travell them, and be
> Expert in home Cosmographie.

195.24 Most revolutions: This paragraph (folder 18B, 17v) is stricken with a single ink use mark. Beginning with "Some events," the remainder of the paragraph is written in fine ink script in the left margin of the sheet and at the bottom. Spacing is so haphazard that it is not possible to determine whether Thoreau intended to begin a new paragraph at "Revolutions are." The questionable syntax and diction of the quotation in Middle English suggests that Thoreau may have been recalling it from memory.

195.32 In the year: folder 18B, 17v. In his journal for December 27, 1837, Thoreau wrote: "In 449 three Saxon cyules arrived on the British coast,—'Three scipen gode comen mid than flode, three hundred cnihten.'" In a letter to Mrs. Lucy Brown dated September 8, [1841], Thoreau identified the quotation only as an "old rhyme" that Margaret Fuller might "have occasion to remember" (*Correspondence*, p. 47).

197.16 But what: folder 18B, 19r. This concluding passage Thoreau wrote in light pencil on the lower half of the final page. All but the final sentence is stricken with a single use mark. The final sentence exists in two forms; and the initial form, not fully decipherable beneath a single cancellation line, is circled in pencil.

197.27 earth down too.: The following matter is transcribed from a single stray blue sheet in folder 18B which defies positioning in the text of this essay. It is made up almost wholly of revisions of paragraphs from folder 18A. No record is included in this transcription of use marks, transposition symbols, or cancellations:

RECTO

If the philanthropist were not so poor and inconsolable himself, he would not send his meat and raiment first, and lastly go himself to the poor. Sympathy should heal something of its own force. Can a man carry something with him better than himself?

Suppose you should read on a poor man's grave stone, if a poor man had any, Bread failed, and he died.—would you not say that it was not bread that failed, but men?

But if you give money to the poor, see at least that you build up your own credit meanwhile in the courts of love and justice by your deeds, that your gift may be current.

The most generous man has sympathy, I speak not now of pity, with the well and not with the ill. The great soul is said to sympathize with distress, because it finds a nobleness of soul in its subject, which cannot be distressed, and does not want sympathy, still at leisure to sport with its mate.

VERSO

Our great playmate and coeval, Nature, born with us and grown up by our side, taking her years on years without increase of age or sign of decay, why look thus sadly in her countenance, and withhold our sympathy?

The globe is yet fresh and unexplored. Even Britain is not all subject to parliamentary corn laws, but other laws and institutions, as well for parliaments, as for corn, do really govern the land and its inhabitants. Go into our city brick yards and you will find that we have hardly fathomed the beaver and musquash holes, which in the ages passed have riddled the ground. Our little light lasts but twelve hours, and then the interesting fertile night shuts down; and around the stateliest and most modern churches and exchanges the owls are ready to hoot as soon as it is dark. In the country, the cawing of the crow is heard farther than the voice of the husbandman, and the thrum of the mosquito drowns the hum of human industry. All man's works are but a feature of the landscape; the winds of heaven blow over them and the morning mist conceals them from my view.

Table of Alterations
in Manuscript Copy-Text

183.14   From] *altered from* from *preceded by* It
          would not be amiss to ask ourselves
          seriously and searchingly *circled in pencil*
          18B (3v)

* 183.19   Now,] *inserted in pencil above cancelled*
          At any rate *followed by* If any thing ail—VS
          18B (4r)

* 183.20   especially . . . left] *parenthesized, with use
          marks in pencil* 18B (4r)

183.24   partially] *interlined with a caret in pencil*
          18B (4r)

183.24   repents] *followed by* that is, having done it,
          is now pretty well aware that he has done
          it,—*cancelled in pencil* 18B (4r)

183.24   He sets] *altered in pencil from* Why he sets
          18B (4r)

183.27   reformed] *preceded by* changed *cancelled in
          pencil* 18B (4r)

* 183.34- There is no . . . explanation!] *use mark in
  184.8   pencil* 18B (5r)

184.9   The] *altered from* the *preceded by* At any
          rate *cancelled in pencil* 18B (3v)

184.12-14 but . . . man.] *circled, use marks in pencil*
          18B (3v)

184.15   I ask] *preceded by* Moreover *cancelled in
          pencil* 18B (6r)

184.26   society.] *followed by* that I may know what
          his large promises mean. *cancelled in pencil*
          18B (6r)

184.27-30 I cannot bear . . . beginnings.] *use marks
          in pencil* 18B (6r)

185.1   Men] *preceded by* But *cancelled in pencil*
          18B (6v)

185.1   well] *followed by* instinctively *cancelled in
          pencil* 18B (6v)

185.1   barren] *preceded by* men *cancelled in
          pencil* 18B (6v)

185.4   and resolution] *interlined in pencil with a
          caret* 18B (6v)

185.5   which . . . doors] *interlined above* away
          back by the doors *cancelled in pencil*
          18B (6v)

185.5   know] *followed by* very well *cancelled in pencil* 18B (6v)

185.8   to-night] *interlined above* immediately, *cancelled in pencil* 18B (6v)

185.8   but that] *interlined above* because *cancelled in pencil* 18B (6v)

185.10   audience,] *followed by* and so far from being excited to violence, they go night after night for entertainment and a pleasurable excitement merely. *cancelled in pencil* 18B (6v)

185.10   may chance to] *interlined above* perchance *cancelled in pencil* 18B (6v)

185.10   know] *followed by* some such unlucky fact as *cancelled in pencil* 18B (6v, 7r)

185.11   against . . . money] *interlined above* on property *cancelled in pencil* 18B (7r)

185.12   which] *interlined with a caret in pencil* 18B (7r)

185.14   him] *interlined above* the speaker *cancelled in pencil* 18B (7r)

185.15-19   After all . . . arguments.] *use marks in pencil* 18B (7r)

* 185.20   There] *altered from* there *preceded by* Thus *cancelled in pencil* 18B (7r)

185.22-3   The modern . . . Italians.] *circled, use marks in pencil* 18B (7r)

185.26   posterity] *preceded by* still *cancelled in pencil* 18B (7r)

* 185.28-30 We . . . effective] *cancelled in ink* 18B (6v)

185.30   rather] *interlined with a caret in ink* 18B (7v)

185.34   energies!] *preceded by* strength *cancelled in ink* 18B (7v)

186.11   does not] *followed by* simply *cancelled in pencil* 18B (7v)

186.22-26   The great . . . Arkwright.] *use mark in pencil* 18B (8r)

186.27-28   or communities] *interlined with a caret in pencil* 18B (8r)

186.29   rather than] *interlined above* and not *cancelled in pencil* 18B (8v)

186.30   inspiration] *interlined above* love or indignation *cancelled in pencil* 18B (8v)

186.30   high] *interlined above* strong *cancelled in pencil* 18B (8v)

186.31   necessarily] *interlined above* indeed *cancelled in pencil* 18B (8v)

186.32   sympathy or] *interlined with a caret in pencil* 18B (8v)

186.36   he may] *interlined above* then let him *cancelled in pencil* 18B (8v)

187.1   he may] *interlined above* let him *cancelled in pencil* 18B (8v)

187.1-2   There have been] *interlined above* I have heard of *cancelled in pencil* 18B (8v)

187.2   meetings] *followed by* before now *cancelled in pencil* 18B (8v)

187.3   men] *interlined above* some *cancelled in pencil* 18B (8v)

187.5   offered?] *followed by* I should like to know. *cancelled in pencil* 18B (8v)

187.6   or was] *interlined in pencil with a caret* 18B (8v)

187.7-9   did . . . imparted . . . had] *altered in pencil from* does . . . imparts . . . has 18 B (8v)

187.11   soul] *preceded by* animating *cancelled in pencil* 18B (9r)

187.11   members] *interlined above* hands *cancelled in pencil* 18B (9r)

187.15   as] *interlined above* if *cancelled in pencil* 18B (9r)

187.15   prize] *preceded by* indeed *cancelled in pencil* 18B (9r)

187.17   also] *added in pencil* 18B (9r)

187.18-30   Consider . . . counted!] *use marks in pencil* 18B (9rv)

188.1-4   The information . . . them.] *interlined in ink* 18B (9v)

188.1   give] *interlined with a caret in pencil* 18B (9v)

* 188.7-8   All that . . . within.] *interlined in ink, possibly cancelled in pencil* 18B (9v)

188.15   corrupt?] *followed by* Shall the genius
              whom the ages have prophesied born at
              length among the New Hampshire hills,
              come down to be come a spindle in the
              factory of society—(*altered from* ?) Shall
              (*cancelled*) to tend the flocks of Admetus,
              and devote his divine gifts to some "Great
              Cause"? 'Great Causes! it is only they who
              are engaged in a petty cause, having
              neglected (*interlined above* diverted
              cancelled) a great one, that talk about
              these things." *cancelled in pencil* 18B (10r)
188.16   we have] *interlined above* he has *cancelled*
              in pencil 18B (10r)
188.16   our] *interlined above* his *cancelled in*
              pencil 18B (10r)
188.17   offer.] *followed by* (Choose your calling!)
              cancelled in ink 18B (10r)
188.22-4   Thy . . . it."] *added in pencil* 18B (10r)
* 188.28   issues.] *followed by* One generation
              abandons the enterprises of another. How
              many an institution which was thought to
              be an essential part of the order of society
              has, in the true order of events been left
              like a stranded vessel on the sand.
              cancelled in ink 18B (10v)
188.29   would have] *interlined below* ask for
              cancelled in pencil 18B (10v)
188.30   some pure labor] *interlined with a caret in*
              pencil 18B (10v)
188.32-36   Show . . . arts.] *use marks in pencil*
              18B (10v)
189.15   How . . . virtue?] *interlined in pencil*
              18B (11r)
189.16   Many] *altered in pencil from* How many
              18B (11r)
189.20-   When . . . root.—] *use mark in pencil*
  190.9   18B (12rv)
189.35-6   equanimity, and] *followed by* in return,
              cancelled in ink 18B (12r)
190.10   verbosity] *interlined in pencil above*
              uncancelled wordiness 18B (12v)

190.12   which . . . antiquity,] *interlined in ink*
            18B (12v)

* 190.14   society.] *followed by* A man must serve
            in pencil and It is hard to make those who
            have talked much, especially preachers and
            lecturers, deepen their speech, and give it
            fresh sincerity and significance. It will be
            a long time before they understand what
            you mean. They will wonder if you don't
            value fluency. (◖) But the drains flow.
            (*interlined*) Turn your back (*interlined
            below* But wait *cancelled*) till you hear
            their words ring solid, and they will have
            cause to thank you. *cancelled by use mark
            in pencil* 18B (12v)

190.24   Though . . . not] *interlined in ink followed
            by* I don't want merely your wit nor your
            grit, your independence nor your freedom.
            I want not *cancelled in pencil* 18B (13r)

190.27   we] *altered from* I *cancelled in pencil*
            18B (13r)

190.27   and fruit] *interlined with a caret in ink*
            18B (13r)

190.28   at least] *interlined with a caret in ink*
            18B (13r)

190.29-31   This is . . . sins.] *interlined in ink* 18B (13r)

190.31   Our companion] *preceded by* We demand of
            followed by some greenness, some flowering,
            some ripeness. He *cancelled in pencil*
            18B (13r)

190.32   to us] *interlined with a caret in ink
            followed by* or the bearer *cancelled in
            pencil* 18B (13r)

190.32-4   or . . . bearer] *interlined in ink* 18B (13r)

190.36   undimmed] *interlined above* unpaled
            cancelled in ink 18B (13r)

191.7-9   It is rare . . . sympathy.] *interlined in ink*
            18B (13v)

191.25   influences,] *followed by* and strike
            cancelled in ink 18B (14r)

191.27   earth,] *followed by* where are the fountains
            of life *cancelled in pencil* 18B (14r)

191.35-   What! . . . forever.] *use marks in pencil*

192.10	18B (14v)
191.35	about,] *followed by* the *cancelled in ink* 18B (14v)
192.8-10	The traveller . . . forever.] *interlined in ink followed by* No one has yet grown entire to man's estate, sound in limb & in spirit, undaunted equal to his hopes. *circled in pencil and marked in left margin* Omit 18B (14v)
192.11-192.19	The . . . God.] *use marks in pencil* 18B (14v)
192.20-193.17	So . . . you!] *use marks in pencil* (18B 15rv)
192.20	the] *altered from* these men *circled in pencil with* Reformers *interlined above* 18B (15r)
192.34	to] *interlined above* with *cancelled in ink* 18B (15r)
192.34-193.1	The . . . theory.] *interlined in ink* 18B (15r)
193.2-9	When . . . strangers] *keyed with* Vnp (*See next page*) *in pencil* 18B (15v)
193.3	we should] *interlined above* let us *cancelled in pencil* 18B (15v)
193.19	chart?] *followed by* Like Central Africa? Here is the centre of Central Africa. *cancelled in pencil and marked in margin for transposition* 18B (16r)
193.20	Inward . . . return] *interlined in pencil* 18B (16r)
193.22	Niger] *followed by* beyond the mountains of Abysinnia. The most enterprising have only got as far as the Mount Pisgah of that country. *cancelled in pencil* 18B (16r)
193.23	lord] *followed by* and governor *cancelled in pencil* 18B (16r)
193.23	realm] *followed by* how infinite in its resources, how unexplored in its length and breadth, *cancelled in pencil* 18B (16r)
193.24-33	with . . . would] *use marks in pencil* 18B (16r)
194.1	simple] *preceded by* a *cancelled in ink* 18B (16v)

* 194.3-11   Most . . . being.] *marked for placement* 18B (16v)

194.24   What] *followed by* after all *cancelled in pencil* 18B (17r)

194.28   inlet,] *preceded by* passage and *cancelled in pencil* 18B (17r)

194.28   yet] *interlined above* all *cancelled in pencil* 18B (17r)

* 194.34-35   Erret . . . viae.] *interlined in ink* 18B (17r)

195.5   Here] *preceded by* If you would be a soldier, here is *cancelled in pencil* 18B (17r)

195.14   and] *interlined as* & *in pencil* 18B (17v)

195.17   travellers.] *followed by* He seemed to be forever approaching me, to *cancelled in pencil* 18B (17v)

195.18   on] *altered from* upon *in pencil* 18B (17v)

195.18   these words only] *interlined with a caret in pencil* 18B (17v)

* 195.24   Most . . . flode.] *use mark in ink* 18B (17v)

195.27-30   Some . . . calculate] *written in ink in margin* 18B (17v)

196.4   or at any time] *interlined with a caret in pencil* 18B (18r)

196.5-11   By another . . . sea.] *use mark in pencil* 18B (18r)

196.13   Wisconsin] *preceded by* Red River *cancelled in pencil* 18B (18r)

196.14   or the Sacramento!] *interlined* 18B (18r)

196.17-34   Shall I be . . . compared!] *use mark in pencil* 18B (18rv)

197.1   should I] *interlined with a caret in pencil* 18B (18v)

197.14   cannot] *altered from* can't *in pencil* 18B (19r)

* 197.16-27   But what . . . too.] *use mark in pencil* 18B (19r)

Emendations of the Copy-Text

THE table below lists all certain and all probable emendations of the holograph copy-text of "Reform and the Reformers." The state of the manuscript is such that in a few instances what Thoreau intended is unclear.

181.title	*supplied by editor*
181.2	generation,] possibly ~ ; 18B
181.23	property,] ~ ∧ 18B
181.25	Sometimes] sometimes 18B
182.14	Tom-and-Jerry] Tom-& Jerry 18B
182.19	Make-a-Stir] Make– a Stir 18B
182.24	and] & 18B; *also at* 183.32, 185.4, 192.13, 192.30, 192.32, 193.12, 193.22, 193.32, 194.4, 194.7, 194.28, 194.31, 194.32 (2), 194.33, 195.1, 195.14 (2), 195.16, 195.33, 196.2, 196.19, 196.24, 197.2, 197.5, 197.10, 197.26.
183.3	own.] ~ ∧ 18B
183.11	there.] ~ ∧ 18B
* 183.19	Now,] *indentation supplied*
183.28	Change] *possibly* change 18B
* 183.34	There] *indentation supplied*
184.26	society.] ~ , 18B
184.32	He] he 18B
185.10	audience.] ~ ∧ 18B
* 185.20-27	*unrecovered pencilled interlineation*
186.30	one's] ones 18B
188.11	disciplines,] ~ ∧ 18B
188.12	walks] walk 18B
188.30	labor,] *possibly* ~ ∧ 18B
189.15	virtue?] *possibly* ~ , 18B
189.16	Many] many 18B
* 189.26	hard;] *possibly* ~ , 18B
189.30	tie.] ~ ∧ 18B
189.38	sincerity,] ~ ∧ 18B
190.10	vices] vice 18B
190.25	reasons,] ~ ∧ 18B
190.31	Our] our 18B

402   REFORM AND THE REFORMERS

190.33	á mercury] *two following acute accents illegible* 18B
191.1	mirth,] ~ ∧ 18B
191.17	soil,] ~ ∧ 18B
191.17	Apollo's] Appolos 18B
191.26	wider,] ~ ∧ 18B
191.27	earth,] ~ ∧ 18B
192.5	find.] *spacing disregarded*
192.11	brags] *illegible* 18B
192.25-26	companions.] ~ ∧ 18B
192.34	anything] any thing 18B
193.14	don't] *possibly* dont
193.30	far] *possibly* Far
193.35	New Englander] New-Englander 18B
194.4	are] *blotted*
194.11	being.] ~ ∧ 18B
194.28	an] a 18B
194.33	one's] ones 18B
195.5	Here] here 18B
195.18	He] he 18B
195.27	Some] some 18B
195.34	flode."] ~ ᵛ 18B
196.7	exile] *possibly* Exile 18B
196.13	Wisconsin] or Wisconsin. 18B
196.19	Guinea?] ~ . 18B
196.22	steppes] *possibly* Steppes 18B
196.22	Brobdingnag] Brobdinag 18B
196.24	days'] ~ ᵛ 18B
196.30	South Sea] *possibly* south sea 18B
197.5	Yellowstone?] ~ . 18B
197.15	Tierra] Terra 18B

End-of-Line Hyphenation

THE compounds or possible compounds below are hyphenated at the end of the line in the copy-text (from folders 18B and 18A) of "Reform and the Reformers." The editor has resolved each to the form recorded in this list, in accord with the principles discussed in the General Introduction, page 246. All words hyphenated at the end of the line in this edition should be transcribed without hyphenation in order to duplicate the copy-text forms.

187.16	tea-parties	195.10	travel-worn
193.36	New Englander	197.11	rail-fences